Japan

**A TRAVEL GUIDE
BY CREATIVE
EBONY BIŽYS**

Sapporo

Akita

Matsushima
Shiogama

Nagano

Gifu

TOKYO

Kyoto
Osaka
Nagoya
Atami

Hiroshima

Naoshima

Fukuoka

Beppu

Okinawa

ABOUT
THE AUTHOR

Ebony Biżys is an Australian-Lithuanian art director based in Tokyo. Before moving to Tokyo in 2010, Ebony worked at *Vogue Living* magazine for 11 years, most recently in the position of Deputy Art Director. Ebony has art directed various projects, designed websites, hosted pop-up stores, hosted art exhibitions, art directed window displays and self-published numerous zines. Her clients include ISETAN, Tokyu Hands, LoFT, Kate Spade, Fujifilm, Ginza Magazine, Popeye Magazine, Qantas, Tourism Antwerp and mt masking tape. Ebony's work has appeared in many books and magazines, and has been featured on both NHK TV and J-wave radio station. Ebony has authored six books in various languages.

WEBSITE	www.hellosandwich.jp
INSTAGRAM	@HelloSandwich
CREATIVE	@HelloSandwichCreative
TWITTER	@HelloSandwich
FACEBOOK	@HelloSandwich

INTRODUCTION

Hello Sandwiches!

I am so happy you're holding this little book of Japan in your hands! This is a guide to some of my most treasured spots in this incredible country.

My love of Japan began when a Japanese street fashion book landed on my desk at *Vogue* magazine and I was amazed by the quirky and creative, playful style seen in Japanese culture and knew immediately that I needed to jump on a flight to Japan ASAP. After 9 trips to Japan I finally moved to Tokyo 'for a year' in 2010. Ten years later and I'm still here! Not a day passes where I don't find myself feeling so incredibly lucky to be able to call Tokyo home.

Hello Sandwich started as a blog in 2009 where I recorded snippets of Japan that inspired me. Often more on the quirky side of things,

I've always been particularly interested in the unique aspects of Japan and its culture. This is reflected in the contents of this book, where I lead you to my favourite spots, such as a kissaten that has been running for over sixty years and is still using the same retro manual cash register, or to a small town in Kyushu area which is dotted with a collection of 16 fruit-shaped bus stops. Oh, Japan!

As you use this book as a guide to visit some of my favourite locations, I hope it will also serve as a starting point for your own unique and special journey in this magical country. I encourage you to always take the back streets because, like most of the best parts of Japan, that's often where the best treasures are hidden.

Love you Japan!

Have a wonderful adventure!

TOKYO

SUCH A
FUN AND VIBRANT
CAPITAL CITY

35.677° N
139.765° E

01

東京

Call me biased, but when I meet people who come to Japan on holiday and choose to spend their entire two weeks or month in Tokyo, I'm always super impressed and have the utmost respect for these types of travellers. They know just how much Tokyo has to offer, and they realise that by spending time in the smaller neighbourhoods outside of Tokyo's main hubs, they can enjoy so many enriching cultural experiences in one place.

You'll find shopping that can rival any city and some of the world's best food (at the time of publishing Tokyo had 226 restaurants with Michelin stars, more than any other city). You might find yourself experiencing spiritual moments in a temple, like Gotokuji (*see* p. 12) or stumbling across incredible architecture, art and fashion at the footstep of the world's busiest train station. You might view the modern city from the Tokyo Skytree (*see* p. 8) or sit in Coffee Shop Ace (*see* p. 33), a kissaten (retro coffee house) from the 1970s. You might relax in the tranquil Inokashira Park (*see* p. 6) and then join Tokyo's cool kids, shopping in Harajuku (*see* p. 19).

Tokyo is listed annually in many surveys as one of the top worldwide cities to live in, and it's no surprise.

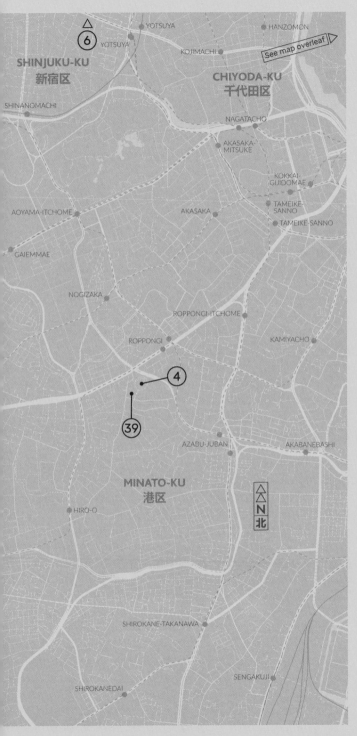

1 Shibuya | **ATTRACTION**

4 Mori Art Museum and Tokyo City View | **ATTRACTION/MUSEUM/VIEW**

5 Spiral | **ATTRACTION/CREATIVE SPACE/ GALLERY/SHOP**

9 Bathhaus | **ATTRACTION/SENTO/BAR**

10 LoFT | **SHOP/DEPARTMENT STORE**

11 Tokyu Hands | **SHOP/DEPARTMENT STORE/CAFE**

13 Harajuku | **SHOP/CAFE**

14 Utrecht Bookstore | **SHOP/BOOKSHOP/ART**

15 Daikanyama Tsutaya T-Site | **SHOP/ BOOKSHOP/MUSIC/CAFE**

18 Shibuya Publishing & Booksellers | **SHOP/ BOOKSHOP/GALLERY**

19 Tower Records | **SHOP/MUSIC/BOOKSHOP**

23 Newport Records and Bar | **CAFE/BAR/MUSIC**

24 Sidewalk Stand | **CAFE/KISSATEN**

26 Fuglen | **CAFE/BAR**

27 Alaska Zwei | **CAFE/VEGAN/SHOP**

29 Suezen | **RESTAURANT/TEISHOKU**

30 Commune | **RESTAURANT/FOOD COURT**

31 Golden Brown | **RESTAURANT/BURGERS**

32 d47 Shokudo | **RESTAURANT/TEISHOKU/SAKE**

33 Izakaya Shirube | **RESTAURANT/IZAKAYA**

34 City Country City | **RESTAURANT/BAR/MUSIC**

35 Brown Rice Canteen | **RESTAURANT/ TEISHOKU/VEGAN**

36 Spring Valley Brewery | **BAR/BREWERY**

39 Grand Hyatt Tokyo | **STAY/HOTEL/ RESTAURANT**

OFF THE MAP

2 Inokashira Park | **ATTRACTION/PARK** | 16km (10mi) W of Shibuya Station

6 Yayoi Kusama Museum | **ATTRACTION/ MUSEUM** | 6km (4mi) NE of Shibuya Station

7 Gotokuji Temple | **ATTRACTION/TEMPLE** | 6.5km (4mi) W of Shibuya Station

17 Nakano Broadway | **SHOP/MALL/ RESTAURANT/ IZAKAYA** | 9km (5.5mi) NW of Shibuya Station

21 Avril | **SHOP/CRAFT** | 17km (10.5mi) NW of Shibuya Station

28 Hattifnatt | **CAFÉ** | 11km (7mi) NW of Shibuya Station

37 Harmonica Yokocho | **BARS/NIGHTLIFE** | 17km (10.5mi) NW of Shibuya Station

38 Green Cabin (My Home in Tokyo) | **STAY** | Location provided on booking

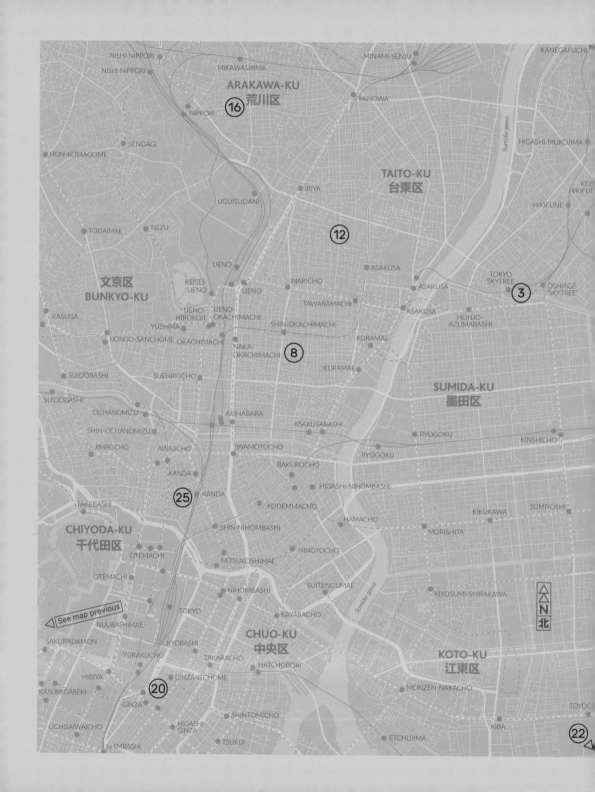

1 SHIBUYA
渋谷

S   Shibuya
W   shibuya-scramble-square.com/sky
A   1-2 Dogenzaka, Shibuya-ku, 150-0043

ATTRACTION/NEIGHBOURHOOD | Shibuya is an iconic and unique Tokyo experience that you shouldn't miss. Like Times Square in New York, only much larger and crazier! Bright neon lights, a million different sounds, multiple giant videos displayed on buildings and hundreds of people crossing the gigantic five-way Shibuya (also called Hachiko) Scramble Crossing. The volume of shops, restaurants, karaoke bars and live music venues makes it incredibly appealing for foreigners and Japanese alike.

The first thing I always did when I came to Tokyo on holidays before moving here, was stand at the Hachiko crossing and soak up the amazing buzz. When you're exiting the train station, be sure to take the Hachiko exit, which will land you right at the crossing. Surprisingly, in the ten years that I've lived in Tokyo, this crossing never gets old. I still love taking videos and photos of it.

If you head to d47 Shokudo (*see* p. 43) inside the Hikarie building for a teishoku (meal set), you'll have an amazing view of the crossing while you dine. Or you could even just view the crossing from the joining walkway at Shibuya station between the Ginza line and the Inokashira line and take some divine time-lapse photos. The new Shibuya Sky, which opened in 2019, has incredible 360-degree views over Shibuya crossing. Shibuya is extra photogenic when it's raining and the scramble crossing is covered with vibrant coloured umbrellas that stand out against the black-and-white lines of the crossing.

When the sun sets, if you fancy a drink head to Shibuya Drinking Alley. Located right beside the train tracks in Shibuya, this cute little alley of tiny six-seater bars should be on everyone's Tokyo must-see list.

2 INOKASHIRA PARK
井の頭公園

S   Kichijoji
A   1-18-31 Gotenyama, Musashino-ku, 181-0001

ATTRACTION/PARK | Inokashira-koen (park) is one of Tokyo's most famous parks and especially known for its sakura (cherry blossoms) and the cute swan boats that visitors are able to rent and paddle in. A note about the swan boats, though, rumour has it that couples who go on the swan boats together break up. So for long-lasting love, paddle alongside your pal instead!

The park is huge and features approximately 20,000 trees. The maple trees are particularly beautiful in autumn. In late hanami (cherry blossom viewing) season, the petals of the cherry blossom trees fall into the large lake and form the most divine sakura-covered lake that looks almost like an ice-skating rink along the edges.

If I haven't already sold you on this lovely park, can I mention that the park also has its own zoo! It's a small zoo that's perfect for little ones, with animals such as leopards, goats, penguins, wild boars and cranes, and there is even a wild bird forest and a Japanese bird house. Zoo entry costs just ¥400 for adults and children under 12 years are free.

Located in the Kichijoji area, just 20 minutes away from Shibuya station on the Inokashira train line, it's accessible by a 1-minute walk from Inokashira-koen station, or a 5–10 minute walk from Kichijoji station. I personally like to take the express train from Shibuya to Kichijoji to save time and then walk through the shops and local area of Kichijoji to the park. That way you can also pick up some snacks for a picnic, too.

1

1

2

3 TOKYO SKYTREE
東京スカイツリー

S   Oshiage (Skytree)
A   1-1-2 Oshiage, Sumida-ku, 131-8634

ATTRACTION/VIEW/RESTAURANT |
The Tokyo Skytree is an excellent way to
catch 360-degree views over Tokyo from
the eastern-Tokyo suburb of Sumida. With
construction starting in 2008, and opening
in May 2012, it is now the tallest tower in the
world at 634 metres (2080 feet) high. And it's
the second tallest structure in the world after
Burj Khalifa.

There are two observation decks, one at
350 metres (1,148 feet) and one at 450 metres
(1,476 feet). You can also find the Skytree
shop, Skytree cafe and Sky Restaurant 634 on
the same floor as the first observation deck.
Sky Restaurant 634 is 345 metres (1,131 feet)
above ground and has spectacular views.
The lunch course options range from ¥6,292
to ¥8,712 and the dinner course ranges from
¥1,592 to ¥19,602. The Muyabi dinner course,
for instance, includes French dishes such as
deep-fried langoustine with white asparagus,
an entrée of foie gras, a choice of various
mains, such as lamb or Nagasaki beef sirloin,
and a dessert of matcha mousse. It also serves
a teppan (iron griddle) course with delicious
iron griddle dishes, although you will be
seated around the teppan hot plate and not
right up against the divine views.

Tokyo Skytree is easily accessed by
Tokyo Skytree station, or by Oshiage station,
depending on which train line you're
travelling along. Regular tickets to the Tokyo
Skytree on weekdays are ¥3,100 and ¥3,400
on weekends. If you happen to visit on a
day when the weather isn't all blue skies,
fear not; the Skytree offers a virtual reality
experience for when viewing isn't optimal.

My pro tip is to visit in the afternoon
before sunset, so you can see both daylight
and night-time views over Tokyo. Last
admission is at 8pm.

4 MORI ART MUSEUM & TOKYO CITY VIEW
森美術館

S   Roppongi
W   mori.art.museum/en;
    tcv.roppongihills.com/en
A   Mori Tower, 6-10-1 Roppongi, Minato-ku,
    106-6150
T   03-5777-8600

ATTRACTION/MUSEUM/VIEW | Don't
miss Mori Art Museum and Tokyo City View
for an inspiring afternoon of both art and
urban architecture. The view from both of
these venues gives you a grasp of just how
large this incredible city is. I am always in
awe when I look out over the buildings and
think to myself, 'Oh my gosh I can't believe
I live in this incredible city!'

Both venues are located in the Roppongi
Hills area on the 52nd and 53rd floors of Mori
Tower. The tower is located just a 3-minute
walk from exit 1C of Roppongi station on the
Tokyo Metro Hibuya line.

The Mori Museum showcases various
contemporary art exhibitions and I definitely
recommend visiting. Be sure to check
the website to find out what exhibition is
showing. Entry costs ¥2,000 and the ticket
counter is on the 3rd floor of Mori Tower, or
you can buy tickets online. Please enter from
the 'Museum Cone'.

Above the museum is Tokyo City View,
which features an indoor observation
deck 250 metres (820 feet) above sea level
and a Sky Deck outdoor observation deck
270 metres (885 feet) above sea level. This is
one of the best views over Tokyo, and entry
tickets are ¥1,800. The rooftop Sky Deck is
such a beautiful experience, walking around
the helipad area, and if you visit at sunset you
can see beautiful stars in the middle of one of
the world's biggest cities!

You could easily spend a day exploring not
only the museum and observation decks, but
also wandering around the many restaurants
and cafes in the Roppongi Hills area.

3

4

5 SPIRAL
スパイラル

S   Omotesando
W   spiral.co.jp/en
A   5-6-23 Minami-Aoyama, Minato-ku,
    107-0062
T   03-3498-1171

**ATTRACTION/CREATIVE SPACE/
GALLERY/ SHOP/RESTAURANT/
BAR** | Spiral is an arts complex that
was created in 1985 with the concept of
connecting culture, lifestyle and art. It's
a one-stop exhibition space and shop for
those who are interested in the arts. Super
conveniently located right in front of
exit B1 of Omotesando station, the Spiral
complex contains a fantastic gallery,
restaurants, a cafe, a multipurpose hall, a
bar, a pop-up gallery and shop space, and
a homewares store.

    The shop sells so many locally made
goods – stationery, ceramics, homewares,
cards, vessels and apparel – and it's often
frequented by local and international stylists.

    It's also an incredible spot to view a wide
range of various types of arts and crafts.
Over the years, I've seen a paper exhibition
hosted by one of Japan's most famous
paper production companies, a divine tile
exhibition, various fashion exhibitions and,
back in the day, the Tokyo Designers Week
used to host exhibits here.

    There is usually no cost to enter the
exhibitions, and there is often more than
one exhibition taking place. On the ground
floor with the pop-up gallery and shop,
you can view some smaller collections, and
then you can either take the lift or walk up
the spiral ramp through the gallery space to
Spiral Market, located on the 2nd floor.

    The name of the complex stems from
the building's design, featuring an ascending
spiral, designed by architect Fumihiko
Maki. Spiral is a wonderful place to spend
an afternoon.

6 YAYOI KUSAMA MUSEUM
草間彌生美術館

S   Waseda
W   yayoikusamamuseum.jp/en
A   107 Bentencho Shinjuku-ku, 162-0851

ATTRACTION/MUSEUM | Yayoi Kusama
Museum was founded by well-known
Japanese artist Yayoi Kusama and opened
in 2017 in Shinjuku. One of the floors is
dedicated entirely to one of Kusama's infinity
room installations titled *Pumpkins Screaming
About Love Beyond Infinity*. Each year the
collection of Yayoi Kusama Foundation's
works are showcased in two exhibitions.
Although Kusama is now well known around
the world, with her work being shown in
major museums, biennales and triennales
internationally, the museum aims to present
a display of her new work in addition to her
earlier works.

    The museum is a five-floor building
and was designed by Japanese architectural
firm Kume Sekkei. The building features
curved edges and is illuminated beautifully
in the evening from inside light that shines
through large windows.

    Entry is ¥1,100 for adults and ¥600 for
children aged between 6 and 18. However,
tickets aren't available at the door, so be sure
to purchase them in advance (for a specific
timeslot) through the museum's online
booking system. To access the museum, it's
best to take the Tokyo Metro Tozai line to
Waseda station and take exit 1, and from
there it's a short 10-minute walk to the
museum. This is not to be missed for Yayoi
Kusama fans.

7 GOTOKUJI TEMPLE
豪徳寺

S Gotokuji
A 2-24-7 Gotokuji, Setagaya-ku, 154-0021
T 03-3426-1437

ATTRACTION/TEMPLE | Hidden in a lovely little residential area, and easily accessible via the Odakyu train line, you will find Gotokuji Temple, the adorably cute cat-lovers temple. In fact, as soon as you exit the ticket turnstiles at Gotokuji station, you will see a maneki neko (cat statue) and you'll know you're on the right track.

The temple is a 15-minute walk from the station and is beautiful in itself, but if you walk to the left of the main building you will find an enormous collection of cat figurines. You can also purchase a cat and leave it at the temple for good luck, with the idea that the cats are returned to the shelf when the wishes are granted.

Gotokuji is beautiful all year round, especially in autumn when the maple tree leaves turn red and crunch under your steps. If you happen to be in Japan for New Year's Day, you can visit the temple for hatsumode (the first temple visit for the year) and make a wish and drink amazake (hot sweet rice wine).

The small Setagaya tram line has some of its trams painted with a cat face at the front of the tram as a homage to the temple. If you're lucky you might catch a glimpse of this cat tram.

8 ALMOST PERFECT GALLERY AND RESIDENCE
オールモスト パーフェクト

S Kurumae
W almostperfect.jp
A 2-3-2 Kojima, Taito-ku, 111-0056
T 70-1313-3328

ATTRACTION/CREATIVE SPACE/ GALLERY | Run by a creative husband-and-wife team, Luis and Yuka, Almost Perfect is a gallery and creative residency located in Kurumae. The beginnings of Almost Perfect make for a sweet story. Luis would often go to the area to have sketchbooks made at Kakimori store, and one day he bumped into a friend there who mentioned that a pretty old rice shop was vacant. And before long Luis and Yaka renovated this incredible space and turned it into a gallery and residency space where creatives can live, work and show their work, making it much more than just a gallery.

Almost Perfect hosts cinematographers, musicians, sculptors, photographers, writers, illustrators, designers and painters. Resident creatives can expect a nice old traditional house with modern commodities and help to meet peers, make connections and get to know Tokyo quickly. The shortest residency is 2 weeks and the longest is 1.5 months. The gallery space showcases regular exhibitions, too, so be sure to pop by and check it out. It's a one-stop shop for any creatives!

Almost Perfect have also made a map of the neighbourhood for visitors. It's a lovely paper map that is free and features some of their favourite neighbourhood hangs.

9 BATHHAUS
バスハウス

s   Yoyogi-Hachiman & Yoyogi-uehara
w   tokyosento.com/bathhaus
A   1-50-8 Nishihara, Shibuya-ku, 151-0066

ATTRACTION/SENTO/BAR |
Bathhaus in Nishihara was reopened in February 2020 and is a sento (public bath) and bar rolled into one. Take one peek at its website or Instagram and you will get a sense of how design-focused this new sento is. The Bathhaus bar features a bright-green, corrugated curved bar, and the walls are painted in a bright pop of canary yellow paint.

Entry to the little public bath is ¥700, and you can rent a towel for ¥150. Shampoo, conditioner, body wash and lotion are available free of charge. The bath is modern and minimal, and I love the little canary yellow bath seats contrasting against the soft fluorescent low lighting.

After your bath, enjoy chilling out at the bar with a domestic craft beer, highball or soft drink, or try one of their small snacks like sandwiches. They do seasonal drinks, too. For instance, in summer they serve the cutest soda floats in their Bathhaus-branded glassware. You can also purchase Bathhaus T-shirts as a lovely memory of your time at this cute sento. Definitely recommended!

If you fancy an inner-city sento, this is the place for you. It's located just 10-minutes' walk from Yoyogi Hachiman station on the Odakyu Odawara line, or Yoyogi-koen station on the Chiyoda line. Pop in here for a sento followed by a cool-down beer. It's the perfect place to relax.

10 LOFT
ロフト

s   Shibuya
w   loft.co.jp
A   21-1 Udagawacho, Shibuya-ku, 150-0042
T   3-3462-3807

SHOP/DEPARTMENT STORE | I once met up with my friend's daughter from Australia, and when I asked her what she wanted to do when she was grown up she replied: 'Work at LoFT Shibuya'. It was so cute, and it makes you realise just how iconic this department store is. It's indeed one of Japan's best department stores.

LoFT has branches all over Tokyo, but here at the Shibuya branch you can buy anything from homewares to furniture. An entire floor (B1F) is dedicated to stationery, which I suspect might be just why my friend's daughter wanted to work here. You can't imagine the stickers, mt tape, photo albums, photo album accessories, pencil cases, post-it notes and endless amounts of every other kind of stationery your mind can dream up.

Another floor (2F) is dedicated to health and beauty. Think anything from quirky throat and chin massage products or character face masks, to decorative nail stickers and patterned toothbrushes.

The kitchen and homewares floor (3F) is a lot of fun. You can stock up on all of the bento box essentials and onigiri moulds, or small presses that put a love-heart shape in your sandwich.

If you can imagine it, there's a good chance that you can find it at LoFT!

11 TOKYU HANDS
東急ハンズ

S   Shibuya
W   tokyu-hands.co.jp/en/list/shibuya
A   12-18 Udagawacho, Shibuya-ku, 150-0042

SHOP/DEPARTMENT STORE/CAFE |
Tokyu Hands is perhaps Japan's best and
most well-known department store, and I
can highly recommend spending an hour or
more here. Its motto is 'creative life store',
and you can find anything and everything,
such as camping gear, luggage, homewares,
bedding, furniture, stationery, art supplies,
kitchenware, travel accessories, wrapping
materials ... basically anything that you can
use to improve your daily life.

The Shibuya store also has a DIY section
on the basement level where you can buy
timber and other home renovation materials.
There is even a workshop where you can
have your timber cut to size. I realise that you
most likely won't be needing any timber cut
if you're in Tokyo on a holiday, but this just
serves as an example to describe to you how
dedicated this store is to elevating lifestyles.

As you walk around this large store
(it's so large that they even write the calories
you've burned by walking up each stair, but
of course there is an elevator, too), you might
stumble across products that you didn't
even realise you needed in your life, such as
a plastic mould to shape your boiled eggs
into star shapes. Everything in this store is
so enticing!

If it all gets too much, a cafe is located
on the top floor, serving snacks such as
pulled pork sandwiches and drinks, so you
can have a mini retreat mid-shopping. I've
spent many a Christmas shopping break in
this cafe surrounded by shopping bags!

12 KAPPABASHI KITCHEN STREET
合羽橋 かっぱ橋道具街

S   Tawaramachi
W   kappabashi.or.jp/en
A   3-18-2 Matsugaya, Taito-ku, 110-0036

SHOP/KITCHENWARE | Do you love
kitchenware? Japanese ceramics? Japanese
knives? Chopsticks? Unique sake glasses?
Bamboo baskets? How about plastic food
displays? Yes? Okay, then imagine all
of those for a cheap and cheerful price,
all located on the one street in Tokyo.
Amazing, no?

Kappabashi is a street filled with every
kind of kitchen item you could imagine.
The area, which now features 170 stores,
started in 1912. In addition to items that are
easy for travellers to pop into their suitcases,
you can also find items for restaurants, like
baking ingredients, stoves, tables, chairs and
lanterns. Even if you're not in the market for
kitchen items, it's still fun to walk around the
shops to give you a sense of dining and foods
in Japan.

I recommend picking up a special timber
or stainless steel bento box that you can
use when you're back home, so you can
remember Japan in your lunch breaks at
work, or a famous Japanese knife. You might
even like to have your knife engraved.

To access Kappabashi street, you can take
the Ginza line on the Tokyo Metro, and it's
just a short walk from Tawaramachi train
station. Keep in mind though that a lot of
shops are closed on Sunday, so be sure to
head here on any other day of the week.

Enjoy exploring this fun kitchen street
and pack a spare bag to carry all of your new
goodies home in.

11

12

12

14

13

13 HARAJUKU
原宿

S   Harajuku & Omotesando
A   1 Jingumae, Shibuya-ku, 150-0001

SHOPS/CAFES | Harajuku area is one of Tokyo's fashion centrals for youth culture. It's packed with fashion outlets ranging from Beams and Forever 21 to H&M and so, so many vintage clothing stores. If you are after fashion, Harajuku has it all.

Large shopping complexes, such as La Foret and Tokyu Plaza are here, located opposite each other at the Omotesando station crossing. Tokyu Plaza opened a few years ago and features a mirrored entrance that is quite popular on Instagram as a hot photo spot. It features a rooftop open garden terrace, coffee shops and a Tokyu Hands with unique handmade craft items.

There are also many great smaller shops on the backstreets behind Tokyu Plaza. Keep an eye out for my favourite vintage clothing store, Punk Cake. You won't miss it with its colourful multicoloured striped façade. Here you can find vintage Chanel, assorted tees, lots of accessories and '80s dresses. Punk Cake is so beautifully curated that the price reflects this high level, so if you're looking for something cheaper and don't mind a rummage, Kinji (located on the basement level just next door to Tokyu Plaza) is the spot for you.

Takeshita street (located just off Harajuku train station) is well known for being touristy, and by all means take a peek, but in my opinion it's just a very busy street dotted with shops selling cheap costumes and accessories and not very enjoyable. However, if you're after the famous rainbow coloured cotton candy that you might have seen all over Instagram, this is where you'll find it. Make a quick dash up to Totti Totti and then escape the street as soon as you can with your cotton candy. You will also find Santa Monica Crepes at the end of Takeshita street furthest from Harajuku station.

I recommend strolling along Cat street, a cute street that leads to Shibuya that is filled with apparel shops and cafes. If you're in the mood for coffee, pop into Chop Coffee (just off Cat Street) for a caffeine hit mid shopping.

14 UTRECHT BOOKSTORE
ユトレヒト

S   Omotesando
W   utrecht.jp
A   5-36-6 Jingumae, Shibuya-ku, 150-0001

SHOP/BOOKSHOP/ART | Utrecht is definitely Tokyo's coolest bookstore, selling an impeccably curated collection of art books and zines created by both Japanese and international artists, such as Cy Twombly. Like many good things in Tokyo, it's almost impossible to find, hidden on a backstreet behind a parking lot, but it's well worth the Google Maps detective work, I promise you. Located on the 2nd floor in a warehouse-like building, Utrecht is quiet and cosy and filled with light.

Look out for the work by HIMAA and Ken Kagami, two of Tokyo's quirkiest artists and zine makers. You'll be able to find them on Instagram, too, if you'd like to take a sneak peek of their work so you'll know what to look out for when you're in the store.

On my last visit to Utrecht, I found a zine of an artist who dined at various cafes and restaurants and asked the waiter to take his photo. The zine was a collection of these portraits. It was so fascinating to see how each waiter captured the moment. This kind of quirky unique thinking is plentiful here at Utrecht.

Utrecht also host a range of events and exhibitions, so check the website for details before your visit.

15 DAIKANYAMA TSUTAYA T-SITE
代官山 T-SITE

S   Daikanyama
W store.tsite.jp/daikanyama/english
A   17-5 Sarugakucho, Shibuya-ku, 150-0033
T   03-3770-2525

SHOP/BOOKSHOP/MUSIC/CAFE |
Daikanyama Tsutaya T-site is so incredible
that it might be quicker to list what it doesn't
include! The space is a bookshop, magazine
shop, stationery shop, DVD shop, DVD and
CD rental shop, lounge-style cafe, Starbucks,
Family Mart convenience store, cute camera
shop and electronic bike shop all joined
together in one peaceful and hip location,
It's such a lovely place to spend an afternoon.

Obviously the books and magazines are
the true stars here, but in the music section you
can listen to any rental CD before borrowing.
You can also bring your Starbucks coffee from
the cafe downstairs up to the listening docks,
and enjoy relaxing with some delightful views
whilst listening to some new music.

On the 2nd floor, there is a fancy lounge
(coffee is ¥900!) where customers can read
books and enjoy a sandwich and a glass of wine.
Naturally, on a Sunday this place gets packed
with a long queue to get a seat. On the plus
side, while you wait in line you can browse the
menu on iPads that are given to you to order.

Continuing on the iPad theme, in the
DVD rental section you can search for a DVD
on the many iPads that are located amongst
the shelves. Once you type in your DVD
of choice, you are taken to a screen which
precisely locates the exact spot of the DVD.
Very convenient and very Japanese.

The outside space that connects the two
main bookstore buildings is a peaceful place
to relax and read your new books, or simply
take a short break. You can find the popular
Ivy restaurant located in the same complex,
which features Western-style breakfasts
served early (unusual in Japan) for those who
want to fuel up for a day of Tokyo travel.

16 NIPPORI FABRIC TOWN
日暮里繊維街

S   Nippori
W nippori-senigai.com/en
A   Saito Shoten, 4–33–3 Higashi-Nippori,
    Arakawa-ku, 116-0014

SHOP/FABRIC/CRAFT | Nippori Fabric
Town is a famous shopping strip filled with
over 60 fabric shops, perfect for sewing
and crafting lovers alike. From the Taisho
era (1912–26) to the end of the Showa era
(1926–89), the area was a dedicated wholesale
town but over time it has welcomed
retail shoppers.

There are so many shops on the ground
level, or 1F as we say in Japan, but be sure to
look above to 2F and beyond, as many gems
of shops can be found up there, too.

Alongside fabric, you will also find a
range of items for sewing and handicrafts,
such as buttons, threads, sewing patterns,
wool, cotton, silk, lace, ribbons, sewing
machines, fashion accessories, costumes,
and even kimono.

Tomato is perhaps the most famous and
largest of all the stores in Nippori, with a
few stores on the same street. At the main
Tomato store (6-44-6 Higashi-Nippori), you
can find fabrics for ¥100 per metre! As we all
know, fabric can get quite heavy, so if you
happen to buy a lot you can also pay for a
courier (very reasonably priced) to deliver it
to your Tokyo accommodation.

Just take the Yamanote train line from
Shibuya to Nippori for a 12-minute journey.
The shopping area spans the area from
Nippori station to Nippori Chuo street.

17 NAKANO BROADWAY
中野ブロードウェイ

S   Nakano
A   5-52 Nakano, Nakano-ku, 164-0001

**SHOP/MALL/RESTAURANTS/
IZAKAYA** | Attention all lovers of
anime and gaming! Nakano Broadway
is an indoor shopping mall filled with
otaku (geek) gadgets, games and gaming
arcades. It opened in 1966 when Japan had
reached a high level of growth on export-
led goods and the country was rapidly
becoming Americanised.

Pop up to the 2nd and 3rd floors to find
anime and idol item shops, such as for
figurines, game consoles, video games, idol
key chains, manga and an abundance of
collectors' items. Although this retro-style
shopping centre is well known for its wide
range of anime-related items, you can also
find fashion shops, second-hand items
and even a fresh food market. This makes
it the perfect place for gamers and general
shoppers alike to enjoy time inside a mall,
especially on a rainy or hot day when trying
to escape the weather.

If you're in the mood for dinner or a
drink after your fun shopping experience,
head to the side streets near Nakano Sunmall
on your way back to the station and you will
find many izakaya (small bars) where you can
have an ice-cold beer and say otsukaresama
(roughly translates as 'job well done') as you
kanpai (cheers) your beer and hard work
shopping for treasures.

To access Nakano Broadway, simply
take the JR Chuo line from Shinjuku for
a 5-minute ride and from there it's just a
short walk from Nakano station. You can
walk along Nakano Sunmall from Nakano
station to Nakano Broadway, which is a cute
shotengai (undercover shopping street) filled
with everyday necessities stores, such as
cafes, pharmacies and bookstores.

18 SHIBUYA PUBLISHING & BOOKSELLERS

S   Shibuya
W   shibuyabooks.co.jp
A   Kamiyama Terrace, 1F, 17-3 Kamiyama-
    cho, Shibuya-ku, 150-0047
T   03-5465-0588

SHOP/BOOKSHOP/GALLERY |
Shibuya Publishing & Booksellers is one
of my favourite bookstores in Tokyo. Here
you can expect to find a wide range of both
zines and creative books, covering art,
architecture, photography, lifestyle and
design, and also select magazines. It offers
one of Tokyo's most impressive selections of
books and zines. You'll also find a tiny gallery
space inside the store where you can discover
the work of local Japanese artists.

With the rebuilding of Shibuya, it has
also opened up a small store in the Shibuya
Scramble Square. In addition to books and
zines, this branch also sells gifts. They have
selected over 1,000 gifts that fall under their
concept of 'pleasant to choose and happy
to receive', which just sounds so divine and
sweet. These include stationery, accessories,
fragrances and home items.

You can also find another branch of the
store in the Toranomon area, but I personally
love the original store in oku-Shibuya.
With its location a little out of the bustle of
Shibuya, but only a short walk away towards
Yoyogi Hachiman, it's a lovely quiet area with
lots of my favourite cafes, and the Monocle
store is nearby, so it makes for a very pleasant
afternoon stroll.

20

19 TOWER RECORDS
タワーレコード

S   Shibuya
W   tower.jp
A   1-22-14 Jinnan, Shibuya-ku, 150-0041
T   03-3496-3661

SHOP/MUSIC/BOOKSHOP | Tower Records is one of Shibuya's largest record stores where you can stock up on Japanese music not available in your home country. With store branches all over Japan, the Shibuya branch is unique in that it also has a fantastic bookstore on the 7th floor, with many Japanese-themed books and magazines in English that are perfect to soak up more info about Tokyo and Japan.

Tower Records in Shibuya is a must for anyone on the search for some sweet Japanese tunes. It always has a great selection of new releases and recommended CDs available to listen to at the listening docks. One visit here is a fantastic way to find out about cool new J-pop! I also love the clear glass lift to enjoy the view of Shibuya as you make your way to 7F.

It's extremely easy to access Tower Records Shibuya. Just take the Hachiko exit of JR Shibuya station, cross the intersection and walk towards Marui JAM. You can't miss it with its vibrant yellow and red signage, and it's only a 5-minute walk from Shibuya station. Enjoy the cute Japanese tunes!

20 MUJI & MUJI CAFE
無印良品

S   Shibuya & Ginza
A   21-1 Udagawa-cho, Shibuya-ku, 150-0042
     (Shibuya store)
     3-3-5 Ginza, Cho-ku, 104-0061
     (Ginza store)
T   03-3770-1637

SHOP/CAFE | Muji lifestyle store and cafe is a Japanese brand that has gone global. This recently renovated Shibuya store is popular with both travellers and Japanese visitors alike.

The store is a great place if you're in the market for anything from stationery or luggage to clothes or beauty items, or even furniture or kitchenware. It also sells simple calico tote bags that, once purchased, can be decorated and customised at the unique Muji stamping station located instore. I also recommend buying some of the Muji essential oils, which can be used to keep your home smelling beautiful.

On the 2nd floor you will also find Muji cafe, where you can enjoy a cup of tea, a cake or even a set meal from the deli choices and relax during your busy shopping and sightseeing day. Somewhat cafeteria in style, you order first, enjoy your meal and then take your receipt to the counter near the downwards escalator to settle the bill after dining. Solo diners will enjoy the large windows along the counter as a lovely place to watch Shibuya pass by.

The Shibuya store is just a 3-minute walk from the Hachiko exit at Shibuya station. For diehard Muji fans, the Ginza flagship store, which was recently relocated, also includes the Muji hotel, and is a must visit.

21 AVRIL
アヴリル

S   Kichijoji
A   2-34-10 Kichijoji Hon-cho, Musashino-ku, 180-0004
T   04-2222-7752

SHOP/CRAFT | Originating from Kyoto, Avril is Japan's most beautiful yarn shop. Only available in Japan, the US, Korea and Malaysia, these beautiful and unique yarns are unlike any threads anywhere else in the world.

The Tokyo branch is located in Kichijoji. It's not a large shop, but the amount of threads displayed on spools covering the walls are so incredibly beautiful that as soon as you walk in you'll smile with delight and want to start making all sorts of things out of yarn. They have so many different variations of yarn, my favourites are the ones with speckles of glitter running through the yarn. The yarn can be used not only for crochet and knitting but also for various crafts, gift wrapping and making accessories.

The shop also sells tools and tutorials (some are in English). If you just want to dip your toe into the Avril yarn world, buy one of the small mixed cards, which have a few different yarns mixed like a little sample. The way they mix the various yarns is always so inspiring. Otherwise, you can buy by weight from the spool. You simply put the large spool into a basket and tell them how many grams you would like. Depending on what type of yarn you select, a small ball that sits in the palm of your hand will cost about ¥500. Enjoy and happy creating!

22 MORERU MIGNON
モレルミニョン

S   Urayasu (Chiba)
W   ikspiari.com/shop/shops/1746
A   1-4 Maihama, Urayasu-ku, Chiba, 279-8529
T   04-7305-5802

SHOP/CRAFT | This is absolutely Tokyo's cutest purikura (sticker print store)! Although it's a little far from Tokyo, located near Disneyland in Urayasu in Chiba, it's absolutely a must see for anyone who loves all things kawaii (cute) and/or all things pink.

The shop is top-to-bottom pink with retro elements and pink phone booths, pink neon lights and even a pink *Alice in Wonderland* play-on-scale room with a giant book that my friends designed!

If you need to touch up your make-up or hair before you have your photo taken (¥500) in one of the booths, there is a beauty prep room complete with stools and mirrors where you can re-apply. If you happen to forget your make-up case, fear not, you can always add those details in 'post' when you decorate your photo stickers in the booths. They also have curling irons and straightening irons available for rent if your hair is out of place. Oh Japan, what don't you think of?!

This is absolutely one of my must-sees in Tokyo for all lovers of kawaii. The photo stickers will make such a fantastic Tokyo memory!

PINK G

PINK GENIC
BOOK
STORE

22

23 NEWPORT RECORDS AND BAR
ニュウポート

s Yoyogi-Hachiman
w nwpt.jp
A 1-6-8 Tomigaya, Shibuya-ku, 151-0063
T 03-5738-5564

CAFE/BAR/MUSIC | Cafe by day, wine bar by night, and Newport also doubles as a record bar! It's the perfect spot to relax and chill during your Tokyo day.

Newport is a great place to pop in for a drink or to feast on a healthy colourful lunch dish. It serves seasonal vegetable dishes and a wide range of selected natural wines. I recommend the falafel plate or one of the seasonal salad plates. The owner is so lovely and speaks English, and will help you select a glass of organic wine to pair with your meal. You can, of course, just pop in here for a coffee, tea or cake.

You'll note the record station at the front of the cafe when you walk in, and it also hosts music event nights from time to time, so be sure to check its Instagram or website for upcoming event details.

It's conveniently located just a few minutes' walk from Yoyogi Hachiman station on the Odakyu train line. The area itself is lovely to wander around too, and is dotted with a few gems of shops.

24 SIDEWALK STAND
サイドウォーク スタンド

s Nakameguro
w sidewalk.jp
A 1-23-14 Aobadai, Meguro-ku, 153-0042
T 03-6712-2590

CAFE/COFFEE/SANDWICHES | Sidewalk Stand is one of Nakameguro's hippest coffee and sandwich stands. Located on a sunny corner, a short 10-minute stroll along the canal from Nakameguro station, you'll find this original branch of the popular coffee hotspot.

Sidewalk Stand's coffee beans are roasted in-house daily, and each cup of coffee is carefully brewed one by one. You can also find artisanal bread and bagels, and craft beer delivered directly from the brewery. I also recommend ordering a famous hot sandwich. My favourite is the Ruben sandwich with a generous serving of pastrami. Other sandwiches include the DTC, which is full of dried tomatoes and chicken, and vegetarians might enjoy the smoked cheese & mushroom sandwich. For those craving something different, try the 'cava' sandwich, which features marinated mackerel, gouda cheese, homemade chilli salsa and fresh coriander.

This quiet side street of Nakameguro alongside the canal has some street benches, so you can enjoy your sandwich and coffee overlooking the canal. It's especially gorgeous during hanami (cherry blossom viewing) season when the sakura (cherry blossom) trees are in bloom. You will really enjoy relaxing in this quiet and fashionable pocket of Tokyo.

You can also find branches of Sidewalk Stand near Inokashira Park (see p. 6) and in the lovely neighbourhood of Yutenji.

24

23

25

25

25 COFFEE SHOP ACE
珈琲専門店エース

S   Kanda
A   3-10-6 Uchikanda, Chiyoda-ku, 101-0047

CAFE/KISSATEN | I love the simplicity and uniqueness of Coffee Shop Ace in Kanda. Originally opened in the early '70s, this kissaten (retro coffee house) serves over 40 types of coffee and several types of sandwiches. With its red-and-white striped awning, tiny potted garden and extensive menu on a timber board outside the store, you get a sense of how retro Coffee Shop Ace is before you even enter.

My recommendation here is to try the nori (seaweed) toast, which is perhaps Coffee Shop Ace's most famous menu item and, unbelievably, it's only ¥140! It's made with slightly sweet, white Japanese bread, buttered, with a dash of soy sauce and a slice of nori lightly grilled on the top of a gas stove, and is served best with drip coffee.

Sit at the red trim counter on '60s-style red leather stools with tiny black bases. The rest of the burnt-orange leather seating, a staple of Showa-era (1926–89) kissaten, features curved dividers between each table.

I once photographed this kissaten for a story for a Japanese magazine, and the team of brothers who run the place were so kind they let me go behind the counter and try and make some nori toast myself. Their smiles are so utterly heartwarming.

Although it's a little far away from the other listings in this guide, if you are a nostalgia fan and love a kissaten, you won't want to miss Coffee Shop Ace! It is bound to be one of the most memorable parts of your Tokyo trip. The journey from Shibuya to Kanda takes approximately 25 minutes by train.

26

27

26 FUGLEN

フグレン

S   Yoyogi-koen
W   fuglen.no
A   1-16-11 Tomigaya, Shibuya-ku, 151-0063
    (Shibuya branch)
    2-6-15 Asakusa, Taito-ku 111-0032
    (Asakusa branch)

CAFE/COFFEE/BAR | Originating in
Oslo, Fuglen is a coffee lovers' haven by
day, and in the evening it turns into a bar
serving Norwegian and Japanese craft beers,
as well as an eclectic selection of cocktails. A
vintage decor and outdoor seating makes this
a great spot for a morning caffeine hit or an
evening cocktail.

Travellers and locals alike seem to love
this coffee shop. With Tokyo's cafes often not
opening until late morning, Fuglen stands
out with its 8am weekday opening time.
Patrons can sit either inside and be cosy or
on bench seats in one of the many outdoor
seating areas.

Fuglen Tokyo also offer a roastery in
Nobolito that is open from 9am until 6pm
daily. The roastery is also a cafe, so you
can pop in for a coffee and baked goodie
whilst enjoying the divine smell of freshly
roasted coffee.

You can also find another Tokyo branch
of Fuglen in Asakusa that is open from 7am!
So wherever you are in Tokyo, there might be
a Fuglen coffee shop near you.

27 ALASKA ZWEI

アラスカ ツヴァイ

S   Nakameguro
W   alaskazwei.theshop.jp
A   2-5-7 Higashiyama, Meguro-ku, 153-0043

CAFE/VEGAN/SHOP | Alaska Zwei
is a cute little completely vegan cafe. The
interior is cosy with a warm timber vibe
mixed with an industrial-like feel, such as
cement and large warehouse-style doors.
The low hanging grey industrial lights and
almost elementary school-chair seating gives
a relaxed atmosphere. You'll notice it from
the street with its little bench seat and cute
collection of plants out the front.

Dishes include curry or tofu katsu-don,
but I recommend the soy 'meat' cooked
karaage-style (fried) set with green salad, a
seaweed side dish and rice. The vegan taco
rice is also an excellent option. The bread is
also delicious, so be sure to try a bagel! They
even have miso–cream bagels! And if you
have a sweet tooth, you might like to have a
muffin or cookie to take away to enjoy later.

Alaska Zwei also has a small shop selling
ceramics, olive oils, condiments, coffee beans
and even a vegan cupcake mix that comes in
a jar, so that all you need to do is add some
simple ingredients and you can create your
own slice of Tokyo at home!

The cafe is approximately a 10-minute
walk from Nakameguro station.

KAWAII & QUIRKY JAPAN

When you think of Japan, you might think of Tokyo's bustling Shibuya Scramble Crossing (*see* p. 6), traditional tea ceremonies or the fine art of ikebana (flower arranging). But Japan is also obsessed with kawaii (cute) culture and quirky cartoon-like graphics.

You might find yourself on a train and notice that the warning to not put your hand in the closing doors is represented by a cute smiling bear. Or perhaps you walk past a construction site and the road blocks are in the shape of Hello Kitty. And speaking of construction sites, you will often find a cartoon-like character bowing to apologise for the inconvenience of a site being under construction. Often, popular nature scenes are printed on temporary walls on the outside of construction sites, but I recently saw a construction site that had actual pot plants around the outside of it, but instead of real plants there was a laminated photograph of flowers attached to each pot. The attention to detail and customer service in Japan never ceases to blow my mind, even after 10 years of living here.

Let's not forget the buses and trams that are shaped in animal motifs, such as cats, Pokémon, Doraemon and even Snoopy. Head to Tokyo's Gotokuji Temple (*see* p. 12) – the cat-lovers temple – and catch a Setagaya line tram painted with cat faces as a nod to the temple. If you spend some of your time in Tokyo's Shibuya and Harajuku areas, you are likely to find the community dog-shaped bus that runs between the two nearby suburbs. It costs only ¥100 per journey (just pop your ¥100 coin into the slot at the front door entrance of the bus).

But one of my all-time favourite quirky Japan treats are the fruit-shaped bus stops in Nagasaki in Kyushu. In the sleepy Nagasaki town of Konagi, you will discover 16 such bus stops (there are five variations: a melon, strawberry, mikan (like a sweeter, smaller mandarin), tomato and watermelon). They were originally designed and built for the 1990 expo in Osaka but were relocated and maintained as functional bus stops in Konagi. I took a 2.5-hour local train from Fukuoka to Konagi just to visit these cute bus stops, and I highly recommend this experience for those who love all things kawaii!

28 HATTIFNATT
ハティフナット

S Koenji
W hattifnatt.jp
A 2-18-10 North Koenji, Suginami-ku, 166-0002
T 03-6762-8122

CAFE | Duck as you enter through the teeny-tiny kid-size door into this treehouse-themed cafe in Koenji. Hattifnatt is sure to bring out your inner child with its handpainted forest wall murals and loft-style treehouse dining area. Adorable too are the hand-crocheted stool covers, made by the owner's family, and the blanket-stitched fabric menu covers. No detail is left untouched here.

Just a 3-minute walk from the north exit of Koenji station, this cute cafe with a concept of 'childlike playfulness' is a charming way to spend an afternoon tea or lunch.

On the menu, you'll find items such as a cute matcha latte with an adorable face motif in the latte foam that is sure to bring a smile to your face. I won't spoil anything for you, but let me just say that the dessert cakes are ridiculously cute, too. Savoury dishes, such as taco rice and omuraisu (omelette rice), are also on the menu.

Be sure to check out the connecting store next door, which features cute handmade accessories displayed in tiny timber boxes. It's a real treasure trove and your inner child's dream come true.

Step back in time in this cute Hattifnatt cafe. There is also a branch in Kichijoji.

29 SUEZEN
末ぜん

S Daikanyama
A 20-8 Sarugakucho, Shibuya-ku, 150-0033
T 03-3461-8234

RESTAURANT/TEISHOKU | Suezen is a cheap and cheerful Japanese teishoku (meal sets) restaurant located in the fashionable and hip area of Daikanyama. It's quite unique to find a restaurant with such a cosy feeling and with such reasonable prices located in a oshare (fashionable) area.

You'll notice the entry of Suezen with the noren (traditional Japanese fabric dividing curtains) in the doorway. Once you enter, you can select from table seating or traditional low Japanese tables in the tatami floor area. The tatami area has light neutral tones and textural finishes that create a cosy feeling, as does the scattering of everyone's shoes at the entrance to this area. It's almost like an invisible wall where relaxation begins as you step out of your shoes! And, a little side note: it's polite to cover your feet with socks, so be sure to wear them or pack some in your bag to pop on before entering the tatami area.

The set meals here range from ¥1,000 to ¥2,000. Meal options are seasonal but come with a main dish, such as grilled fish or pork cutlets, along with miso soup, rice, a salad and pickles. Can't read the Japanese menu? Don't worry! The friendly staff will bring out a collection of laminated photos complete with English explanations.

It isn't, by any means, a large restaurant, but rather a small and cosy casual establishment located just three minutes walk from Daikanyama station. Do yourself a favour and make it here!

29

29

28

30 COMMUNE

S   Omotesando & Shibuya
A   3-13 Minami-Aoyama, Minato-ku,
      107-0062

RESTAURANT/FOOD COURT |
Commune is an open-air food court where
creatives, both foreigners and locals, gather
around the various food trucks and food
booths. Pop in here for a Heartland beer, a
coffee, some Brooklyn fries or a burger, and
listen to some DJ sets.

Commune started many years ago after
Tokyo Designers Week in an unused space of
land on a popular street nearby fashionable
Omotesando station. At the time, the space
was only to be used until the land was sold
and developed, and back in the day there
was a countdown clock when you visited
the Commune website. By some luck of
fortune, the lease was renewed. The concept
remains the same, and patrons are able to
purchase their drinks or food from any of
the vendors and then sit freely anywhere they
like in the open-air setting. In winter, the
space is covered with a giant tent, making
it slightly warmer than being outside and a
lovely place for a cosy drink.

At the back of the space you will find
a small gallery, a tiny bookstore, and even a
shared working space called Midori.so. It's
undeniable that this place has a somewhat
Western feel, but with a Japanese twist. It
might be just what you're searching for in
the middle of your Tokyo trip!

Commune has also recently opened up a
rooftop bar in PARCO in Shibuya. If you visit
on a Wednesday night it has a free live jazz
band playing!

31 GOLDEN BROWN
ゴールデンブラウン

S   Nakameguro & Omotesando
W   goldenbrown.info
A   2-3-1 Higashiyama Meguro-ku, 153-0043
      Omotesando Hills shopping complex,
      4-12-10 Jingumae, Shibuya-ku 150-0001
T   03-6661-8560

RESTAURANT/BURGERS | Golden
Brown is, in my opinion, one of Tokyo's best
burger shops. It is yet another example that
Japan not only does Japanese food incredibly
well but does most things incredibly well,
and burgers are no exception! I recommend
the avocado cheese burger.

Golden Brown was founded three years
ago by Nobuya Hisatomi in a small corner
shop a short walk from Nakameguro station.
The interior is rustic with timber tables and
gold details, and is almost log cabin in vibe.
The cute signage was handpainted by an
artist who works under the name of NUTS,
and the staff who work here are always
super cute.

A second branch can be found in the
Omotesando Hills shopping complex and
maintains the brand's cosy feel, despite
being located inside a very different
feeling building.

It is said that between the two stores,
Golden Brown makes over 2,500 burgers a
week! It is quite the popular hotspot so if you
don't fancy lining up, be sure to get there for
an early lunch. The burgers come inside a
little triangle paper bag, making it easy to eat
your burger discretely. Oh Japan, you think
of everything, don't you!

33

32

32 D47 SHOKUDO
d47食堂

S   Shibuya
W   hikarie8.com/d47shokudo
A   8F, 2-21-1 Shibuya, Shibuya-ku, 150-8510
T   03-6427-2303

RESTAURANT/TEISHOKU/SAKE | Located in Shibuya's Hikarie building, d47 Shokudo is a stunning Japanese restaurant set on the 8th floor with window seating that allows for a beautiful view over the bustling Shibuya Scramble Crossing (*see* p. 6). Although it's located in the centre of Shibuya, dining at d47 Shokudo is a moment of peace and tranquillity, and you definitely don't get the feeling you're in the middle of a shopping complex. It serves regional Japanese teishoku (meal sets) and is a great way to explore the taste of different regions in Japan if you aren't able to travel to each and every region.

For instance, the Miyazaki set includes chicken nanban, a karaage-like (fried chicken) dish served with a sweet tartar sauce that is famous to the Miyazaki region. Other regional teishoku include Nagasaki fried mackerel and the Tokushima region set with miso somen noodles with sudachi citrus fruit. Certain meals are seasonal and some are only served on the weekends. The teishoku are served on beautiful round timber trays and each dish is served in gorgeous dishes and unique bowls.

d47 Shokudo also offers a wide range of Japanese sake and local craft beers. I recommend the sake tasting flight. You can also try a range of desserts, such as soy milk ice-cream, fruit sandwiches and handmade yoghurt.

This restaurant is popular with locals and tourists alike. Expect to queue during the lunch service. Reservations can only be made over the phone for dinner.

33 IZAKAYA SHIRUBE
汁べゑ 下北沢店

S   Shimokitazawa
A   2-18-2 Kitazawa, Setagaya-ku, 155-0031
T   03-3413-3785

RESTAURANT/IZAKAYA | Izakaya Shirube is one of Shimokitazawa's most well-known izakaya (small bars). The fun and vibrant atmosphere, open kitchen, course menu and delicious food make it the kind of place you'll leave smiling and want to come back to on your next trip to Tokyo.

Tucked on a side street just near Mister Donuts, the name on the noren (traditional Japanese fabric dividing curtains) outside actually says 'izakaya ism' but don't be confused, it is Izakaya Shirube. Once you go through the sliding doors, the staff will greet you and you can take your shoes off and store them in a shoe locker.

The seating is 'hole in the floor' Japanese dining, so you have the experience of sitting low but it's comfortable, thanks to the clever hole cut out in the floor. The delicious food includes sashimi, karaage (fried chicken), spicy edamame, oden and 'dragon' sushi rolls. An English menu is available, and you can order items individually. If you're hungry and happy to go along with the staff suggestions, I recommend the course menu, which also includes all-you-can drink. This is priced at around ¥4,000 per person.

One of the best dishes here is the mackerel, which is lightly blow-torched at your table, and you are asked to participate in the fun by squeezing a slice of lemon over the fish when the staff give you the cue. The entire staff sometimes chime in and say 'nice lemon' and clap after you've completed your fun cooking duties!

34 CITY COUNTRY CITY
シティー カントリー シティ

S　Shimokitazawa
W　city-country-city.com
A　Hosawa bldg, 4F, 2-12-13 Kitazawa,
　　Setagaya-ku, 155-0031
T　03-3410-6080

RESTAURANT/BAR/VINYL | City
Country City is not to be missed when you're
in Shimokitazawa. Pop in here for vinyl, tunes,
pasta, coffee or a cocktail. Opened in 2006,
and just a 1-minute walk from the south exit
of Shimokitazawa station, this place has it all.

You'll spot the sandwich signboard out the
front of the building, and you can head up the
stairs at the entrance or take the elevator in
the back to the 4th floor. There's a charming,
casual vibe here – timber floorboards, timber
record boxes, mismatched timber tables
and chairs, lightbulbs hanging down from
red ropes, and windows on two sides of the
restaurant give it lovely light and atmosphere.

Take a seat at the counter and chat
with the friendly staff or at one of the tables,
order some food or a drink and browse the
records while you wait. All of the records
in this cosy space can be test played before
purchase, so feel free to use the in-store
turntable to see if it's your vibe or not.

City Country City specialises in
pasta and offers a set that includes pasta,
drink and salad, and you are also welcome
to order the pasta on its own. You'll find one
of the popular Japanese-style pastas here,
which has a cream cheese and tomato cod roe
sauce, or you can stick to the regular options,
such as neapolitan, carbonara or a seasonal
vegetable sauce. A range of international and
Japanese bottled beers are available, as well
as Heartland (my favourite) draft beer on tap.

If you fancy something sweet, the cakes
here are all housemade and include banana
chiffon cake, gato chocolate with vanilla
ice-cream, and apple cheesecake. The cake
set menu with a drink included is ¥800, but
the cakes can also be ordered separately for
¥500 each. The cafe menu includes coffee,
chai and even hot milk with a dash of rum.

35 BROWN RICE CANTEEN
ブラウンライス

S　Omotesando
W　nealsyard.co.jp/brownrice/welcome
A　5-1-8 jingumae, Shibuya-ku, 150-0001
T　03-5778-5416

RESTAURANT/TEISHOKU/VEGAN |
Brown Rice Canteen's slogan is 'Deliciously
Vegan', and, while I'm not vegan, I can attest
to it being absolutely delicious. Showcasing
just how much care is put into ensuring all
of the food is vegan, and that allergies are
catered for, on my last visit the staff even
asked if it's okay if food has been prepared in
the same room as certain other ingredients.

You can find the cafe down a tiny alley in
the backstreets, and the view is of lovely little
trees, allowing you to forget that you're in the
middle of Aoyama. The interior is modern
with a warmth that comes from the timber
tables. All of the dishes are served on plates
made by local potters and artisans.

Although the menu changes seasonally,
I recommend the bamboo basket steamed
vegetable teishoku (meal set), which comes
with over 20 different and colourful
vegetables, including renkon (lotus root)
and shiitake mushroom, brown rice, organic
miso soup, homemade dipping sauces and
Japanese pickles.

The incredibly beautiful and colourful
Japanese food here is prepared without
additives, preservatives, chemicals or any
mass-produced condiments. Rather, Brown
Rice Canteen use condiments from local
artisanal suppliers.

36 SPRING VALLEY BREWERY
スプリングバレーブルワリー

S   Daikanyama
A   13-1 Daikanyamacho, Shibuya-ku, 150-0034
T   03-6416-4960

BAR/BREWERY | Craft beer lovers will adore Spring Valley's beers that are brewed onsite. The brewery has an outdoor deck terrace that's perfect for cooler afternoons and evenings and a large modern indoor dining area. Adding to the atmosphere, or perhaps creating the atmosphere, the brewery is situated on the recently opened Log Road, which is not dissimilar to New York's The High Line.

In addition to beers, the range of dishes use fresh ingredients direct from farms and producers in the spirit of farm-to-table. Every dish – from appetisers to desserts – is created with the aim of pairing it with a Spring Valley beer. For instance, the 496 brings out the umami of the T-bone steak, its signature dish, and a salad made of kale pairs beautifully with the Jazzberry beer. If you would like to try a range of beers with some snacks, I recommend the craft beer pairing flight.

If you don't fancy a craft beer, you can select from a range of cocktails and non-alcoholic drinks, too. The brewery is such a lovely place to spend a casual and relaxing afternoon on the weekend.

It is located just a 3-minute walk from Daikanyama train station.

37 HARMONICA YOKOCHO
ハモニカ横丁

S   Kichijoji
A   1-2 Honcho Kichijoji, Musashino-ku, 180-0004

BARS/NIGHTLIFE | If you take the Inokashira train line from Shibuya to Kichijoji and take the north exit, you'll find yourself just a minute's walk from Harmonica Yokocho. This area is where Kichijoji's amazing nightlife shines with charming alleys filled with many izakaya (small bars) and restaurants in a shotengai (undercover shopping streets) grid maze. You'll find all types of cuisines, such as yakitori (grilled skewers), sushi and dumplings, and there is even a place serving cheese and olives.

If I'm just there for a quick and easy meal, especially at lunchtime, you'll often find me at Minmin, a no-frills gyoza restaurant that is popular with the locals. I recommend the Minimin gyoza rice set, which comes with rice, five gyoza, pickles and a side soup.

If it's evening time and you're in the mood for a drink and izakaya snacks, it's just so fun walking around and getting a feeling for whichever place takes your fancy, because each izakaya has its own unique charm and the charisma is infectious! Many of the bars are in tiny locations, so it's easy to strike up a conversation with other diners and have a fun and memorable evening!

You might be interested to know that this area began after World Word II as a flea market.

36

37

36

38 GREEN CABIN (MY HOME IN TOKYO)

s   Shibuya/Ebisu/Daikanyama
w   myhomeintokyo.com/services
A   Address given on booking
T   03-4333-1234

STAY | Although My Home In Tokyo features a range of homes to stay in, I recommend staying in the most recent addition to the portfolio, Green Cabin, which is on design point.

The building is located in a prime position between Shibuya, Ebisu and Daikanyama, so you have the best of three incredible locations nearby. Spend an afternoon at the Tokyo Photographic Art Museum in Ebisu, followed by some drinks and dinner at one of the many izakaya (small bars) in the area, and then walk home to your Green Cabin. Daikanyama is also walking distance so getting to T-site (*see* p. 20) will be a breeze. And of course, it's an easy walk to Shibuya where the activities are endless.

I absolutely adore the design of the Green Cabin, with its traditional Japanese timber high ceilings contrasting against the modern and simple features, such as a 20th century-style table, simple industrial kitchen bench, paper lantern hanging lighting and plywood wall details. The Green Cabin also features plants, which definitely adds to the 'I live in Tokyo now' vibe of staying here.

The Green Cabin features a large and comfortable double-sized bed and a Japanese unit bathroom, where the toilet and shower are combined into one room. Body soap, shampoo and conditioner are provided. And then there's the cute little kitchen, equipped with all the essentials to feel like you 'live' in Tokyo.

Rates start at ¥12,000 per night.

39 GRAND HYATT TOKYO
グランドハイアット東京

s   Roppongi
w   hyatt.com/en-US/hotel/japan/grand-
    hyatt-tokyo/tyogh
A   6-10-3 Roppongi, Minato-ku, 106-0032
T   03-4333-1234

STAY/HOTEL/RESTAURANT | The Grand Hyatt Tokyo is a fantastic hotel for families, couples and solo travellers. The luxurious rooms are spacious with everything that you would expect from the Hyatt group. Divine fluffy beds and pillows, electronic window shades, bluetooth speakers, Apple TV connectivity, room service and delightful views. I recommend requesting a room with the Tokyo Tower view for the full Tokyo experience. There's not many things more 'Tokyo' than pushing that window shade opener and spotting the Tokyo Tower first thing in the morning before you head down to the buffet breakfast.

Another excellent point is that it is literally located in the Roppongi Hills complex, so galleries, Mori Art Museum (*see* p. 8), shops and restaurants are right on your doorstep.

The hotel has ten unique restaurants to select from, but I must truly recommend booking a lunch at Shunbou Japanese restaurant. Pretty please try the Shinsai lunchbox, which costs ¥5,600 but is a three-tiered box containing sashimi and appertisers in the upper box, charcoal grilled items in the middle box and a simmered dish and deep-fried fish in the lower box. Of course, the lunchbox comes with steamed rice, miso soup, pickled vegetables and dessert. It's a little treat that was one of the prettiest bento boxes I've ever had in my life.

39

39

38

THEMED RES—TAURANTS

THE LOCK-UP

w lock-up.jp
A Shirobasha Bldg 1-4-12
    Doyamacho, Kita-ku,
    Osaka, 530-0027

CINNAMOROLL CAFE

w cinnamorollcafe.com/food
A Uraderacho, Nakagyo-
    ku, Kyoto-shi, Kyoto-fu,
    Kawaramachi OPA 3F,
    604-8026

KAWAII MONSTER CAFE

w kawaiimonster.jp
A YM Square 4F, 4-31-10,
    Jinjumae, Shibuya-ku,
    Tokyo, 150-0001

**HEDGEHOG CAFE &
PET STORE HARRY
HARAJUKU**

w harinezumi-cafe.com
A Harajuku Bldg, No.2 4F,
    1–13–21 Jingumae,
    Shibuya-ku, Tokyo,
    Champsère, 150-0001

ROBOT RESTAURANT

w shinjuku-robot.com/pc
A Shinjuku Robot bldg,
    B2F, 1-7-7 Kabukicho,
    Shinjuku-ku, Tokyo,
    160-0021

CAFE RON RON

w cafe-ronron.com
A 6-7-15 Jingumae, Shibuya-
    ku, Tokyo, 150-0001

KYUSHOKU TOBAN

w kyusyokutoban.jp
A 1-4-4 Motoasakusa,
    Taito-ku, Tokyo, 111-0041

Japan is well known for its delicious food, but it also has a variety of themed restaurants and cafes – from pets and robots to monsters – where the focus is often on the fun atmosphere, rather than the food. This entry is mostly about themed cafes in Tokyo but there are many more around Japan, like the prison restaurant called The lock-up in Osaka and the Cinnamoroll Sanrio character cafes in both Kyoto and Tokyo.

One themed cafe that I recommend if you're travelling with kids in Tokyo is the Kawaii Monster Cafe, which is quite a popular new-ish kid on the block. You enter the restaurant through the 'mouth' of a bright kawaii (cute) monster and can order quirky food such as an artist's palette of pasta or a cocktail (for the grown-ups) that comes in a beaker that you 'mix' yourself, much like a science experiment. While you're eating your playful food, you are treated to a monster show on an extravagant, colourful and crazy moving set in the middle of the restaurant.

For those who love sipping on their coffee or tea with a four-legged friend, you might like to try one of the many cat, dog or hedgehog cafes. At Harajuku's Hedgehog Cafe you are assigned a hedgehog each, and the staff will help you with gloves and teach you how to feed the hedgehogs while you enjoy your drink! At most of the dog and cat cafes, you are welcome to sit on low seating amongst the animals and pat them as they freely pass by you.

The Robot restaurant in Shinjuku puts on an extravagant, light-filled, robot-packed dancing show that is unforgettable. What is even more impressive, however, is the hologram-lined wall bar that you are ushered to after the performance. The interior also has giant gold snail chairs! It's a feast for the eyes.

Cafe Ron Ron in Shibuya, which opened in 2018, has a 35-metre (115 foot) long conveyor belt of sweets, like cakes and pancakes served on pretty pastel pink plates, as well as burgers and sandwiches. The concept is like sushi conveyor belts but with delicious desserts.

Another one of my recommendations is Kyushoku Toban, which serves kyushoku (Japanese school lunches). In Japan you don't bring your own lunches to school, instead they are provided and everyone sits and eats together. Even the teacher! The lunches often consist of rice, a main dish such as stew or fish, a salad, a small carton of milk and a piece of fruit like a frozen mikan (similar to a sweeter, smaller mandarin). The food at this themed cafe is served in a room that has a blackboard and school desks to experience the full school-lunch vibe!

TOKYO DAY –TRIPS

1 HAKONE
箱根

s   Shinjuku
w   odakyu.jp/english/romancecar
     (Romance Car)
     hakone-retreat.com/hotel/en
     (Hakone Retreat före)
     hakone-oam.or.jp/en (Open Air Museum)
     hakoneropeway.co.jp/foreign/en
     (Hakone ropeway)

Hakone is the perfect daytrip, or overnight trip, from Tokyo. In only 1.5 hours from the city, you can find yourself surrounded by beautiful nature. There is a train by the sweetest name, the Romance Car, running along the Odakyu train line that departs from Tokyo's Shinjuku station. Or you could rent a car and drive, giving you a lot of freedom once you arrive in Hakone.

Hakone is delightful all year round, but is at its most picturesque in autumn and is a famous place to see the colours of the changing leaves.

If you have the time, I recommend spending a night here, especially at Hakone Retreat före, which is so utterly divine. I can still hear the soft birdsong from our room in my memory. Hakone is famous for onsen (hot springs) and the open-air onsen inside Hakone Retreat före is so beautiful.

I also recommend visiting the Hakone Open Air Museum and exploring the outdoor sculpture garden and Picasso gallery inside. It's the perfect way to see both the natural setting and art at the same time. Oh, and to breathe in that mountain air!

Definitely don't miss Lake Ashi, where you can see (or ride) swan boats, and also walk around the lake to Hakone-en, the famous red torii (gate) that is immersed in the lake. On a clear weather day, you can catch a beautiful view of Mt Fuji from Lake Ashi, too.

I also suggest taking the Hakone ropeway, which travels between Sounzan station and Togendai station (where Lake Ashi is located), and reaches a peak of 1,044 metres (3,425 feet) right near Mt Fuji, giving you a beautiful 'shutter chance' of the famous mountain. A return trip is ¥2,600.

1

1

1

2 MT TAKAO
高尾山

s   Shinjuku
w   takao599museum.jp (Takao 599 Museum)
    takaosan-onsen.jp (Keio Takaosan Onsen
    Gokurakuyu)

Mt Takao is a truly lovely way to escape into nature and is less than an hour by train from Tokyo. It's divine all year round but is most popular in autumn when the leaves change colour, and also equally as beautiful in spring when the sakura (cherry blossoms) are in season. These usually bloom a little later than the trees in Tokyo, so if you happen to miss the hanami (cherry blossom viewing) season while you're in the city, this might be a great daytrip for you! On a clear day, you are able to view Mt Fuji from the peak of Mt Takao.

You can access the mountain via the Keio train line, which takes 50 minutes from Tokyo's Shinjuku station and costs just ¥390 for a one-way ticket (takaotozan.co.jp). Once you arrive at Takaosanguchi station you can either climb the mountain on one of the tracks of varying difficulty levels or take the chairlift up (¥490 one-way; it runs from 9am to 4.30pm, or 4pm in winter). I recommend walking on trail number 1, which is a paved road track and the most popular route. It's a good workout that takes about 90 minutes, but you'll enjoy walking through nature on your hike up. If you take this path you will notice the monkey park along the way, and further up the mountain you will find Yakuoin Temple, a rather unique temple with its vibrant red facade adorned with blue, green and gold decorative motifs.

You can take the chairlift back down to the base of the mountain, and there you will find Takao 599 museum, worth a look to learn about the nature surrounding Mt Takao. There is also the beautiful onsen, Keio Takaosan Onsen Gokurakuyu, at the base of the mountain, which is the perfect way to relax after your hike!

3 ENOSHIMA
江ノ島

s   Shinjuku
w   odakyu.jp/english/romancecar
    (Romance Car)

Enoshima is one of the closest beaches to the centre of Tokyo and a popular spot to enjoy summer fun. Seeing this beach is a unique experience, especially through my Australian eyes. It has little pop-up summer beach huts serving as restaurants during the summer period, and some even have tatami flooring! There are also hair dryers set up for after your swim!

Enoshima also produces its own beer with a cute turtle logo, so if you happen to see this for sale, be sure to try it. You might even like to collect the bottle as a take-home treasure to be used as a cute vase. The perfect summer treat, however, is kakigori (shaved-ice dessert). I recommend ordering this if you have a chance. When I last visited there was a dance stage set up on the beach for evening parties, too!

At the edge of Enoshima beach, there is a bridge that connects you to Enoshima Island, which has a little town that feels something like Kyoto. It is so lovely walking through the historic streets up to the shrine, keeping cool under the giant trees and taking a rest at the lookout. There is even a giant escalator if the walk up is too much for you. I highly recommend ending your day in Enoshima with a trip to this lovely island.

There are a number of train lines that head to Enoshima from Tokyo, including the Odakyu train line and the JR Shonan train line. Or for a slightly more comfortable ride, you can take the Romance car on the Odakyu train line between Shinjuku and Katase Enoshima stations, which is only slightly more expensive.

If you happen to find that Enoshima beach is a little too crowded, you can take the number 12 bus to Zushi, where you will find a less crowded beach.

2

3

HELLO SANDWICH JAPAN

ATAMI

**THE PERFECT
OVERNIGHT
SEASIDE RETREAT**

35.095° N
139.073° E

02

熱海

Atami is a lovely seaside town perfect for an overnight trip from Tokyo. It's set just near the volcanic hills near Mt Fuji and Hakone (*see* p. 52) so it's quite hilly. It's full of beautiful onsen (hot springs), and there's a little manmade beach on Sagami Bay, too.

I recommend staying at '80s-style Hotel New Akao (*see* p. 62) where most of the rooms have futons and tatami mats. Hatoya Hotel (*see* p. 61) has retro decor and traditional furnishings like tatami and futons too, and there is an onsite sento (public bath). You almost won't want to leave your accommodation, but if you do want to explore a little, I also recommend that you head to Pine Tree (*see* p. 61), a kissaten (retro coffee house), for a fruit parfait or to Restaurant Furuya (*see* p. 58) for an ice-cream float and omurice (omelette rice).

Atami is just a 2-hour drive or 1-hour shinkansen (bullet train) ride from Tokyo.

1 RESTAURANT FURUYA
レストランフルヤ

A   8-9 Tawarahon-cho, Atami, Shizuoka,
     413-0011
T   0557-82-4048

CAFE/KISSATEN | If you're travelling to Atami via train, this kissaten (retro coffee house) should definitely be your first stop, as it's just a one-minute walk from Atami station. The decor is Showa-era (1926–89) retro. If you sit in the very far corner, to your right when you enter, you will see a quirky musical box positioned above you on the wall. All through the year this plays Christmas carols and Happy Birthday songs and if you stay long enough you get them on repeat. It's these little quirks that make me love kissaten so very much. There is a spiral staircase that leads to upstairs seating.

I ordered the mixed sandwich which was so delicious, but I had some serious FOMO when I later saw the images of omurice (omelette rice) on Instagram and Tabelog. So, if I were you, I'd order the ice-cream float and omurice, which is quite a classic dish here in Japan. It's rice that's often mixed with chicken and some ketchup and then topped with the most perfect fluffy omelette. To get some inspiration, you might like to watch *Lunch Queen*, a Japanese drama where the lead character works at an omurice shop. I used to watch this in Sydney before I moved to Tokyo, and I'd often end up in nostalgic tears and craving the comfort and simplicity of the perfect omurice.

And here's a pro-tip for you: when you drink your ice-cream float, be sure *not* to push the ice-cream in before taking a few sips. I learnt this the hard way, but it did make the toilet paper on the table make more sense! Seriously, there is pink toilet paper rolls in little fabric covers on each table in place of napkins. Yet another Japanese kissaten quirk.

2 BONNET
ボンネット

A   8-14 Ginza-cho, Atami, Shizuoka,
     413-0013
T   0557-81-4960

CAFE/KISSATEN | Bonnet is a super adorable kissaten (retro coffee house) located in the middle of Atami city that is just not to be missed for those who love a good retro Showa-era (1926–89) kissaten. I adore the orange perspex and glass case display cabinets that double as dividers in the middle of the cafe, the faded cream couch seating, the period retro light fittings and the curved service counter.

The speciality to order here is the cheeseburger. (They are so delicious that we were tempted to order another!) The staff will bring out the burgers in little baskets, with the onion to the side of the dish, and politely explain that it's best to enjoy it with the onion. The burger here was one of the best burgers of my life! Such a homestyle cooking taste! I recommend pairing your burger with a soda float (a drink with soda that is served topped with ice-cream) to complete your retro Japanese experience. And for those of you who really want a step back in time (and I will say no more), you should definitely pop into the bathroom located at the back right of the kissaten.

I also absolutely adore the font and logo on the receipt from this kissaten. The design and kerning is absolutely genius!

1

1

2

3

3

4

3 PINE TREE
パインツリー

A   7-7 Ginza-cho, Atami City, Shizuoka,
    413-0013
T   0557-81-6032

CAFE/KISSATEN | This kissaten (retro coffee house) features a sea of leaf-green leather couches and, if you're lucky, a table made from an arcade game. If you can get one of the gaming tables, you're one of the chosen ones! All of the details at Pine Tree are swoon worthy. The logo on the original glasses, the polka dot paper covers for the straws, not to mention the decor featuring stained-glass lampshades and retro magazine racks.

Be sure to order one of the many fruit parfaits here for a colourful and fun treat. I also recommend the ice-cream coffee float, which comes in a tall glass with an extremely tall spoon for a perfect and refreshing afternoon caffeine hit.

On our visit there was a summer parade along the street, and the owners kindly announced it to all of the patrons so we could pop outside and enjoy it. In true Japanese fashion, we all left our bags and belongings on our tables and chairs. Such an incredibly safe country where nothing ever gets stolen. The only exception to this rule, I guess, is umbrellas and bicycles. Be careful with those. Your laptop, purse or iPhone however, it seems, no problem!

4 HATOYA HOTEL
ハトヤホテル

W   hatoyagroup.jp
A   1391 Oka, Ito, Shizuoka, 414-0055
T   0557-37-4126

STAY/HOTEL | Hayota is an amazing retro hotel located on the top of a hill overlooking Sagami Bay and the Ito skyline where you can see the peaks of the Amagi mountains. But that is not the main reason why I suggest spending an evening at this retro hotel. Not only does Hatoya have beautiful typography signage and an overall retro Showa-era (1926–89) vibe, but there is an incredible floating corridor connecting the two buildings that is like something out of *Austin Powers*, with striped carpet and curved windows.

The hotel has a large public bath for you to enjoy a relaxing soak after dinner, and most of the rooms have tatami mats and a futon-style bed, so you are able to enjoy a truly Japanese experience. The large dining hall with tatami floor looks divine! The hotel also has plans to open Western-style rooms and you'll be able to choose whether or not to include breakfast, so you can enjoy flexibility when booking.

Hatoya Hotel is in a group of hotels, so if you have an interest to stay in this gem, please be sure not to make the mistake of staying at the sister hotel called Hatoya Sun Hotel, which I am sure is also incredible but might not be the particular retro style you have in mind. Take care also when directing your rental car or taxi to your hotel.

5   HOTEL NEW AKAO
ホテルニューアカオ

W   i-akao.com/en/newakao
A   1993-250 Atami Shizuoka, 413-8555
T   0557-82-5151

STAY/HOTEL | This hotel is an absolute must for anyone who is looking for an overnight trip from Tokyo. Think of it as an '80s bubble boom-style hotel with an excellent dinner and breakfast.

When we arrived, they invited us to 'welcome drinks' in the grand ballroom, complete with giant chandeliers and a stage. We sat on cream-coloured fabric chairs sipping our selection of teas, coffee and grapefruit juice while we overlooked the beautiful view of waves crashing against the rocks.

Every room has an ocean view so you can fall asleep listening to the sound of crashing waves. No white-noise podcast required! You can select from a Japanese tatami-style room, or Western-style rooms. This is one of those hotels that you could easily spend your entire stay in and never set foot outside the hotel. There's a gift shop, a photobooth service and even karaoke!

If you're staying at the hotel, you can pay an additional ¥1,000 for dinner and a show in the most amazing, grand dining hall. Not to drop any spoilers, but the show is a musical feast. As I was sitting there at dinner, looking around at the guests wearing the hotel-provided yukata (traditional Japanese robe), I thought to myself, what an amazing and peculiar country I live in. Imagine dinner at a resort hotel in Australia with all of the guests wearing pyjamas! The dinner at Hotel New Akao is a Japanese course meal with so many courses. An assorted pickles starting plate, sashimi and sushi dishes followed by a Western-style roast beef dish, a nabe hot pot with rice and then, dessert! When you go back to your room after dinner your futon will have been magically set up by hotel staff.

Start your Atami morning off with the buffet breakfast and try to get a table with a sea view. There are assorted Japanese breakfast essentials, such as miso soup, fish, rice and pickles. I selected a colourful mix of salads, breads, meats and fruits. They serve an incredible hot-pink jelly, which is such an artificial pink colour I just had to try it, but the taste was, well, questionable. For the brave, you might like to try natto, fermented soybean with a slimy texture and a strong smell similar to blue cheese.

The swimming pool area is painted with vibrant primary colours, which looks incredible set against the rocky side of the ocean. We visited just at the end of summer when the cliffs were covered in the most magical lush greenery, but it would be beautiful to see the colours change along with the seasons. Hotel New Akao is one of my most favourite hotels.

KYOTO

A DIVINE CITY
FULL OF MAGICAL
TRADITION

34.998° N
135.745° E

03

京都

Kyoto, once the capital of Japan, is a wonderland full of tradition, from the golden temple of Kinkakuji (*see* p. 73) and the thousands of red torii (gates) at Fushimi Inari Shrine (*see* p. 73) to enjoying kaiseki ryori (Japanese cuisine course restaurants) and spotting kimono-clad maiko (geisha in training) in Gion (*see* p. 68). In this city you can spend your afternoons in a macha green tea ceremony at Ippodo Tea (*see* p. 85) or take part in a highly recommended ikebana class at Kokinse (Kinse Inn Ikebana, *see* p. 68). Whatever you do in Kyoto, you'll undoubtedly slow down.

In the Kyoto Botanical Garden (*see* p. 70), you can visit a zen garden and bonsai collection, and there is a charming and cute children's library housed in purpose-built mushrooms. Only in Japan! If time permits, take a day out to Arashiyama (*see* p. 76) to immerse yourself in the bamboo forest or sit by Kyoto's Kamo River (*see* p. 74) and feel comforted by the surrounding mountains.

You might like to take advantage of Kyoto's relatively flat terrain and explore the city on rented bicycles. It's easy to navigate with its grid-like city planning, unlike the maze that is Tokyo.

UKYO-KU
右京区

UTANO

NARUTAKI

9

SAGA-
ARASHIYAM

TOKIWA

RANDEN-SAGA   ROKUOIN

UZUMASA

TOROKKO-
ARASHIYAMA

KURUMAZAKI-   ARISUGAWA
JINJYA

SATSUEISHO
UZUMAS
KORYU.

ARASHIYAMA

KATABIRANOTSUJI

KAIKONOYAS

ARASHIYAMA

N
北

MATSUO-TAISHA

KAMI-KATSURA

NISHIKYO-KU
西京区

KATSURA

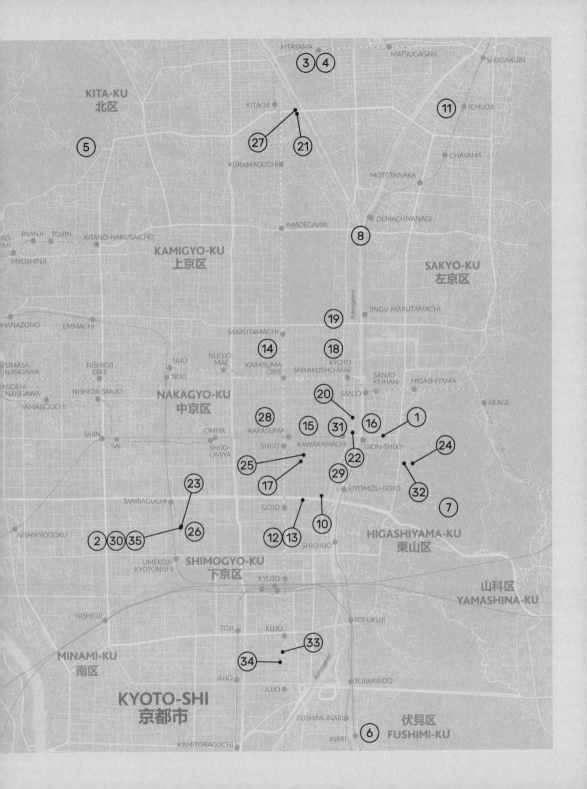

1 GION
祇園

ATTRACTION/NEIGHBOURHOOD |
The beautiful historic area of Gion is
Kyoto's most famous geisha district. The
area between Shijo avenue and Yasaka Shrine
marks the border of Gion, and here you can
find tiny bars, restaurants, tea houses and a
few small shops. You might also spot geisha
or maiko (geisha in training) clad in colourful
traditional kimono. Gion is well worth going
to but now extremely touristy, so please be
mindful of this. You can access the area by
walking from Gion bus station or Gion-Shijo
train station.

At the time that Gion was built, the
property taxes were based solely on the
size of the storefronts, so as you wander
through the machiya (traditional houses)
here you will notice small entrances, but in
fact the properties expand up to 20-metres
(65-feet) long!

Be sure to head to Hanami-koji street,
which is filled with many kaiseki ryori
(Japanese cuisine course restaurants). It's
definitely not cheap and cheerful, but this is
absolutely a memorable lifetime experience.
Gion is so lovely at dusk, when the sun is
setting and the lanterns and izakaya (small
bar) lights are being turned on. You might
feel the energy change, and if you're lucky,
your experience will be embellished with
the soundtrack of the click-clack of wooden
geta (traditional Japanese wooden thongs
worn with traditional dress). Don't miss
the wooden Tatsumi bridge and the vibrant
nightlife and atmosphere of Shirakawa
Canal, as the sake bars and izakaya come
alive when the sun sets. And if your budget
allows, enjoy a traditional dining experience
in a townhouse in the Gion district.

2 KINSE INN IKEBANA
きんせ生花

W kinseinn.com/ikebana
A 80 Tayucho, Nishishinyashiki,
   Shimogyo-ku, 600-8827
T 75-351-4781

ATTRACTION/WORKSHOP | I had
been interested in the art of Japanese floral
arrangements for a long time and was forever
on the lookout for an ikebana class that
wasn't over-the-top touristy. Nothing with
a teacher wearing a kimono, reinforcing
Japanese stereotypes. Then I discovered
Kokinse (Kinse Inn, *see* p. 104), run by
Seanacey who has over 10 years' experience
in the Sogetsu school of ikebana, which
focuses on a relaxed form of ikebana.

Kinse Inn's classes are offered in the hall
of Seanacey's family's 200-year-old ryokan
(traditional Japanese inn). It's the most divine
space that will put you in an ikebana mood
as soon as you take your first steps inside. But
the space also has a modern feel with a hip
bar and oshare (fashionable) clientele. During
the classes, students are able to complete
two arrangements in vases of their choice:
one traditional and one more contemporary.
During my class, we were whisked to a
narrow sunroom with two tressel tables
covered in vases inherited by Seanacey's
aunt-in-law. After the class, students are able
to take their arrangements home, or they can
leave them to adorn the beautiful ryokan hall.

This class is perfect for all skill levels. If
you feel like you want limited guidance and
wish to roam free, Seanacey's intuitive style
will just let you explore this beautiful art on
your own, but if you prefer to have one-on-
one guidance through the placement of each
stem, then Seanacey is right there to help you.

All materials and tools are provided and
participants are welcome to keep their flowers
after the workshop. The cost is ¥6,000 and
the workshop goes for 90 to 120 minutes.

There is also a cafe (*see* p. 99) where you
can relax after your workshop.

2

2

1

3 KYOTO BOTANICAL GARDEN
京都府立植物園

W pref.kyoto.jp/plant
A Shimogamo Hangicho, Sakyo-ku,
   606-0823
T 075-701-0141

ATTRACTION/GARDEN | A visit to the Kyoto Botanical Garden is a divine way for plant lovers, or for those who like to just absorb a little nature when in a city, to spend an afternoon. I am not generally one to search out botanical gardens, but after my last trip to Kyoto I will definitely be adding them to my list of must-see locations when I travel.

This unique garden houses an impressive 12,000 species of plants. It was founded in 1924 and is, as such, the oldest comprehensive public botanical garden in Japan. Look out for the zen garden, the bonsai collection and, depending on which season you visit during, you can spot some gorgeous camellia and hydrangea, and sakura (cherry blossoms). On my last visit I absolutely adored watching the afternoon sunlight flicker over the lotus garden.

Entrance to the gardens costs a mere ¥200, and tickets can be purchased from the vending machine to the left of the entrance. Your ticket is valid for multiple visits on the same day, so if you fancy popping out for lunch or a coffee break, or perhaps to pick up an extra camera memory card after taking so many gorgeous flower photos, feel free to. I recommend also picking up a refreshing Pokari Sweat (energy replacement) drink from the vending machine (swap that out for a hot can of coffee or tea in the cooler months), pop some Debussy in your headphones (my favourite is Clair de Lune) and soak up Japan's floral beauty from the relaxing benches found throughout the gardens.

The garden is located alongside the Kamo River (*see* p. 74), so you may also like to enhance your nature intake and refresh your mind at this gorgeous location. To get here, take Kyoto City subway and get off at Kitayama station (exit 3). This is honestly such a perfect way to take a moment to relax on your Kyoto trip. You definitely shouldn't miss the children's library here, too.

4 BOTANICAL GARDEN CHILDREN'S LIBRARY
きのこ文庫

ATTRACTION/GARDEN | Is this not the cutest library you've ever seen? A handful of these little mushrooms are dotted around Kyoto's botanical garden, each hiding a range of children's books available for loan. As you enter the gardens using the main entrance, head left past the vending machines (or you can pick up a drink en route), take a seat on one of the park's benches and you'll discover this enchanting only-in-Japan library.

While you'll need to be a resident and member to borrow books, you can still enjoy the fun of watching the joy on kids' faces as they open the mushroom doors and pull out books to read. This library is such a playful and fun way to get children inspired to read books. Having worked in the magazine industry for over a decade, I'm incredibly passionate about seeing places like this that inspire children to be outdoors and also read.

I've only visited these mushrooms in summertime, but I can imagine how adorable they must look in the snow!

6

6

5

5   KINKAKUJI
金閣寺

W   shokoku-ji.jp/kinkakuji
A   1 Kinkakujicho, Kita-ku, 603-8361
T   075-461-0013

ATTRACTION/TEMPLE | You won't find me at many touristy places when I travel, but Kinkakuji is one little exception. This beautiful zen temple is my absolute favourite temple in Kyoto, because anyone who knows me knows I love metallic – and this golden pavilion is just breathtaking! The grounds around the temple feature beautiful Japanese gardens, a large pond and a small stone garden.

Quite a walk from the main road, the walk itself gives you time to slow down, reflect and prepare yourself for the meditative moments you will experience here. There are always so many tourists viewing this temple, so be sure to prepare yourself for this, otherwise it can be quite overwhelming.

The temple is completely covered in gold leaf and overlooks a beautiful large pond. If you stand facing the pavilion, you can catch a startling reflection of the golden structure. Built as a retirement residence for the shogun Ashikaga Yoshimitsu, it then became a zen temple after his passing in 1408 – as per his request. Each level of the three-tiered structure is built representing a different architectural style. The first floor is built in the Shinden style from the Heian period, the second floor in the Bukke style from the Samurai residence style and the third is built in a style similar to a Chinese zen hall and is gilded in gold, both inside and out. Unfortunately the pavilion has been burned down numerous times during both wars and by arson, but the current structure was rebuilt in 1955 and has remained intact since then.

The entrance fee for adults is a mere ¥400. It's in the northern area of Kyoto and easily accessed by Kyoto station via the 101 or 205 bus (which take around 40 minutes) or a train and taxi combination might be more comfortable, as the bus can be quite crowded during peak times. Charge your cameras before you visit this beautiful temple. It's such a special place!

6   FUSHIMI INARI SHRINE
伏見稲荷大社

W   inari.jp
A   68 Fukakusa Yabunouchi-cho, Fushimi-ku, 612-0882
T   075-641-7331

ATTRACTION/SHRINE | Fushimi Inari Shrine is one of Kyoto's most famous places, due to the thousands of red torii (gates) that lead up to the main shrine. It was built in 711 in the Nara period, so it's over, 1300 years old! People who love to get their Fitbit steps in during their holidays will love the 233-metre (764-feet) high journey to the top. The torii are beautiful donations from companies and individuals, and if you look closely, you can find the donator's name inscribed on the back of each gate.

The shrine is located at the top of Mt Inari and features statues of foxes, that are believed to be the messengers of this famous sacred mountain. A return trip to the top of the mountain and back will take you about 2–3 hours, unless you stop for lots of photo opportunities. You will spot some beautiful views over Kyoto city as you walk up the path.

Fushimi Inari shrine can be accessed via JR Inari station, just a 5-minute train ride from Kyoto station. It's free to enter the shrine, and it is always open!

7 KIYOMIZU-DERA
清水寺

W   kiyomizudera.or.jp/en
A   294 Kiyozomizu, Higashiyama-ku,
     650-0862

ATTRACTION/TEMPLE | Located halfway up Mt Otowa is Kiyomizu-dera (temple). This beautiful Buddhist temple is part of the Historic Monuments of Ancient Kyoto UNESCO World Heritage Site. It opened in 777 and is one of the most gorgeous temples in the city.

With its location easily accessible from the centre of Kyoto, the surrounding area is also well worth a stroll around for a step back to ancient Kyoto times. The street leading to the temple is lined with souvenir stores and cafes, making for a lovely and inspiring journey. Head up the slow incline stone hill to the temple. Be sure to leave those kitten heels at home – you definitely don't want to get stuck in the uneven areas of the pathway here. As you slowly ascend towards the temple structure, take time to look back down over the city, and you might be lucky and catch a breathtaking sunset.

The main entrance of Kiyomizu-dera was burnt down during a civil war but reconstructed in the early 16th century. It now stands as a magnificent two-storey gate. Be sure to enter through the side of the gate as opposed to the centre – that space is reserved for the gods to enter. Don't miss the dramatic, dark main hall with ornate lanterns and the Okuno-in hall, which boasts a beautiful balcony area that overlooks the Kyoto cityscape and is quite the hotspot for 'shutter chance' photo ops. You might also like to visit the Otowa waterfall with 'healing' waters.

The temple grounds boast approximately 1,500 sakura (cherry blossom) trees, making it a popular hotspot in spring. It's also particularly beautiful in autumn when the leaves change colours. Take a stroll and have your camera ready at all times, as you never know when the light will bounce in just that perfect way.

8 KAMO RIVER
鴨川

A   Kyoto, Kyoto-fu

ATTRACTION/NATURE | An iconic Kyoto landmark, the Kamo River spans 31 kilometres (19 miles) from the Kyoto basin to the Yodo River. The breeze and atmosphere alongside the river is one of the many very special things about Kyoto. The riverside path is perfect to jog along, or bring a little picnic mat (pick up a cheap and cheerful version from the 100 yen shop) and spend time sitting and sketching the beautiful scenery or writing a postcard. You might hear people refer to this as 'Kamogawa', but 'kawa' (pronounced as 'gawa' here for ease of pronunciation) literally means 'river', so you can either say 'Kamo River' in English or 'Kamogawa' in Japanese.

Because of its long length, you'll find yourself passing the river often on one of its many bridges, dining beside it at riverside restaurants or strolling along one of its many pathways. It's a lovely landmark and way to keep your bearings in Kyoto. In the mornings, you'll see people walking their cute little puppy dogs, and in the evenings, you'll see the river lit up with lanterns and lights from izakaya (small bars) that cast beautiful light and reflections onto the water.

There are stepping stones across the river located near the Kamo bridge in Kawaramashi that you can actually use to cross the river. (Some of these stones are used in the glaze of the traditional raku pottery style.) However, the gaps are quite large so please be careful – especially if you're holding your fancy camera or phone.

One of the most popular viewing points on the river is the Pontocho area. Pontocho is the area between Sanjo and Shijo streets. From Kyoto station you can take buses 4, 5, 17 or 205 to the Shijo Kawaramachi stop to access this area.

9 ARASHIYAMA & SAGANO SCENIC RAILWAY
嵐山

A   Ukyo-ku, 616-0007
W   sagano-kanko.co.jp/en/

ATTRACTION/DAYTRIP/NATURE |
Undoubtedly the most famous daytrip from
Kyoto is a trip to Arashiyama 'bamboo
forest'. The train journey takes approximately
20 minutes, and although it's short, I really
enjoy this local train trip, listening to the
clink of the train tracks underneath before
I head off to the forest. To get to Arashiyama,
take the JR train from Kyoto station on the
JR Sagano/San-in line to Saga-Arashiyama
station. The forest is easily accessed by
a 10-minute walk from the main street
of Arashiyama.

Once you arrive at the forest, just follow
the one path through the forest that leads
you very slowly uphill to the middle of the
grove. This is a super touristy spot, so be
prepared to battle it out with the masses for
a wander through the forest, or a photo for
that matter. It's most beautiful and serene
in the morning before the tourists arrive,
but at any time of the day the sound of the
beautiful tall bamboo swaying in the wind is
unforgettable, and makes the trip well worth
it. Once you've walked along the bamboo
forest path, you might want to head to
%Arabica, a popular spot for a coffee.

For those looking for more adventures,
take the Sagano Scenic Railway that runs
along the Hozugawa River. The peaceful
flowing river gives off a lovely refreshing air
that is a divine contrast to the density and
tunnel-like atmosphere in the bamboo forest.
The super-cute retro trains with windows
that open up make it the perfect way to view
nature scenery. Perhaps the most picturesque
season to take this trip is during autumn,
when the scenery is dotted with mustard and
orange-toned leaves. This scenic railway is
closed during the winter months, so check
the information centres before planning
your trip. A one-way trip between Torokko
Saga and Torokko Kameoka stations will cost
adults ¥630 and the railway operates daily
between 9am and 4pm.

10 DAIGI BOOKSTORE
大喜書店

W   daigibookstore.com
A   563-3 Fuyacho-dori, Shimogyo-ku,
     600-8059
T   075-353-7169

SHOP/BOOKSHOP | You can tell from
the hip exterior that this tiny bookstore
knows its stuff. Slide the timber and glass
door open, and you will be rewarded with a
haven of design books. There is a real charm
to this store, with its dim lamp lighting and
peaceful music. It's the kind of place you'd be
happy getting stuck in during a rainstorm.

Though it has a Japanese vibe in scale,
with one small table of books and three walls
of bookshelves, the curated range of design
and architectural books sure pack a punch. If
you're interested in ikebana, Japanese garden
design or art, this is the place for you. Whilst
most of the books are in Japanese, some are
either bilingual or so beautifully designed
that you'll want to buy them for reference –
regardless of the language.

I even found a design book that I'd only
ever seen in a friend's house in Ghent – a
book on Japanese small space architecture
known as 'pet' architecture, where small
spaces are turned into beautiful and
functional white, minimal living spaces
in a way that only Japanese architects
could imagine.

Come here and be immersed in a
collection that showcases all the wonderful
design that you've been exploring during
your Japan trip.

12

12

11 KEIBUNSHA BOOKSTORE
恵文社一乗寺店

w   keibunsha-store.com/about/en
A   10 haraidono-cho, Ichijoji, Sakyo-ku,
     606-8184
T   075-711-5919

**SHOP/BOOKSHOP/HOMEWARES/
STATIONERY** | Keibunsha in Kyoto's
Ichijoji area is undeniably the city's best
bookstore. Actually, I would go so far as to
say it's one of Japan's best bookstores. It also
has a soft spot in my heart because I did my
first ever book signing here.

The range has been carefully selected
by knowing staff members. Just look at its
website and you really get a sense for their
deep love of books by the way they say
that you are able to 'peacefully and slowly
receive information with the analogue style
of books'. It's a great place to go on one of
your first days in Kyoto because the Kyoto
travel section here is fantastic, so you're
bound to pick up some books and mooks
(magazine/books) that will lead you to
discover special places.

Wooden shelves fill this eclectic
bookstore, and you can wander the cosy
space and discover treasures in each corner.
Keibunsha also stock a select range of
homewares and stationery items, such as
chopsticks, vases and accessories. There
is also a fantastic range of artist-made
zines, with a focus on illustration, poetry
or photography. My little Hello Sandwich
Tokyo Guide zine was stocked here before
all of the copies sold out. They have also
opened up a gallery annexe space at the
back area of the bookstore that they rent
to students or local artists.

Keibunsha is slightly away from the
main area of Kyoto but absolutely worth a
trip. I usually ride a bike to visit Keibunsha,
but it's also accessible via bus 5 and bus
206 from Kyoto station, followed by a 7- or
5-minute walk, respectively.

12 WORK & SHOP BY
BOX AND NEEDLE

w   boxandneedle.com
A   Jimukinoueda bldg, 3F-303, 21 Takakura-
     dori, Sakai-cho, Gojo-dori, Shimogyo-ku,
     600-8191
T   075-354-0351

SHOP/STATIONERY/WORKSHOP |
Stationery and paper lovers won't want to
miss this gorgeous store on the 3rd floor of
the Jimukinoueda building. Here you will
find boxes in all shapes and sizes made from
paper by a long-established Kyoto-based
paper maker, as well as beautiful papers from
all around the world, such as Italy, England,
France and Finland. On my last visit some
of my favourite papers were colourful and
geometric papers from India and Nepal.
Upon request, the staff will also show you
inside drawers filled with more papers!
Endless papers!

If the large sheets of papers prove a little
difficult for you to travel home with, you can
also find beautiful paper products, such as
the most delightful handmade notebooks.
These books would make gorgeous Japan
travel journals or gifts.

Box and Needle have also published
an eponymously named book, which is
published by BNN – the same publisher as
my first Japanese craft book. It's a delight
to look through with its colourful and pop
styling. If you can only pick up one thing
from this store, I recommend this book. It
will inspire you to be creative during your
trip in Japan.

There is also a workshop space in-store,
so be sure to check the schedule.

13 &PAPERS
アンドペーパーズ

w boxandneedle.com
A Jimukinoueda, bldg 1F, 21 Sakaicho,
Takakura-dori, Gojo-dori, Shimogyo-ku,
600-8191
T 075-354-0351

SHOP/STATIONERY | In the same
building as Box & Needle (*see* p. 79), you
will find &Papers. The space is part shop,
part museum and part factory. The colourful
shop, located on the ground floor, is fitted
out in primary colours and is eye-catching,
set just back from the street on a reasonably
main road.

On my visit, there was no trademark
Japanese irasshaimase (welcome) into the
store, so there was a split second when I was
unsure if I'd walked into an artist's studio
instead of a shop. But fear not, this is, indeed,
open for retail – and you can find almost
everything made from paper that your mind
can dream up.

Here you will find beautiful geometric
foldable boxes and vessels made out of
colourful paper. Not to mention all the
classics, such as postcards and notebooks.
Need to catch up on your correspondence?
Select unique handmade envelopes to match
unique sheets of screen-printed papers made
in store. You can even customise your own
notebook here – everything from the inside
papers right down to the elastic clasp can be
made to your tastes. Simply select the items
of your choice, and the helpful staff will
swiftly turn it into your very own unique
Kyoto notebook. How is that for a souvenir!

A Hello Sandwich recommended
item from this store is a beautiful paper
vase – they come in vibrant colours. Perfect
for displaying cute dried flowers on your
sideboard to remind you of your wonderful
time in Japan.

14 CREATIVE STUDIO & SPACE OOO

w creativeooo.com
A 740-1 Tatedaionji-cho, Nakagyo-ku,
604-0012
T 075-203-9259

SHOP/GALLERY/WORKSHOP SPACE
| If you love quirky Japanese architecture and
are looking to pick up some unique artworks,
Creative Studio & Space OOO is a must-visit
for you. Hidden in a reasonably residential
area of Kyoto, this quirky building, with a
façade in the shape of a face, is home to a
creative space: a shop, gallery and workshop.

Once you walk through the 'mouth'
entrance of the building, you can find
handmade goods from both local and
international artists. Think jewellery,
stationery, ceramics, handpainted glassware,
bags, paintings and pouches. You can also
find a selection of super-cute zines. The
stock is constantly changing, meaning you'll
discover new artists and new works on each
visit. Pick up woven bags from Thailand,
plastic two-way handbags designed in Kyoto,
bracelet pieces from Germany and zines from
Portland. The owner is really charming and
can converse with you in English and she has
a fine eye for selecting the finest handmade
goods, both locally and internationally.

For those wishing to take a shot of this
incredible architecture, you might want
to bring a special lens as the street is quite
narrow and you can only get a certain
distance back from the space (respect the
local residents of this area). Or, if you arrive
with your phone, just take a cute shot
from an angle. Perfect for your memory
and scrapbooking!

I can guarantee you'll leave here inspired
and most likely with a little bag full of
handmade creations. Please be sure to say
hello from Hello Sandwich.

13

14

14

15 NISHIKI MARKET
錦市場

W   kyoto-nishiki.or.jp; kyotofu.co.jp/shoplist/
     monjya
A   609 Nishidaimonji-cho, Nakagyo-ku,
     604-8054
T   075-211-3882

SHOP/MARKET | Nishiki Market is a lively food street that spans over five blocks in the centre of Kyoto. This famous market started with its first shop opening in 1310, and over the centuries it changed from a wholesale market to a retail market.

I adore the retro shotengai-style (undercover shopping street), with green, yellow and red lighting design illuminating the long market stretch. You'll enjoy a stroll to pick up some wagashi (Japanese sweets), pickles, seafood and seaweed, among other items. You can also find a range of yakitori (grilled skewers) here, and almost everything is locally produced.

It's quite a busy sightseeing location, so be sure to prepare for an onslaught of tourists. If you're after a more local-style market, I would suggest heading to one of the smaller markets in the residential neighbourhoods. This market makes up for its fame, however, with its buzzy atmosphere, and chirpy irasshaimase (welcomes) from shopkeepers and unique displays of traditional Japanese food.

Kyoto is known all over Japan for its Kyo-yasai (Kyoto vegetables), so keep an eye out for some beautiful looking vegetables. For those who have a sweet tooth, be sure to pick up some of the famous bite-size tofu donuts from Konna Monjya.

Eating outside the stalls or while walking is banned, so instead I recommend picking up some snacks and heading to Kamo River (*see* p. 74) to sit down and enjoy your delicacies at a slow and relaxing pace by the riverside.

Take a 5-minute walk from Kyoto, Karasuma or Kawaramachi station. The market runs parallel to Shijo avenue.

16 PASS THE BATON
パスザバトン

W   pass-the-baton.com/news/category/
     kyotogion
A   77-6 Sueyoshi-cho, Higashiyama-ku,
     605-0085
T   075-708-3668

SHOP/HOMEWARES/CAFE/BAR | Set beside a river, this beautiful store in the Gion area (*see* p. 68) can be accessed via a grand bridge over the river. Pass the Baton is a design and homewares concept store based on the idea of 'new recycle'. Almost an art gallery in style, the shop fit-out is made up of lots of cute small rooms with porcelain, kimono, accessories and small zakka (lifestyle) items.

Essentially, it sells not only second-hand luxury goods but also items from personal collections that have been found and loved, and that convey the personality of the person who previously used them. It's an impeccably well curated collection. It also sells new items from brands such as United Arrows and Rhodia, as well as some original merch like hand towels featuring the Pass the Baton logo.

The store also features a tea and sake space. It's such a beautiful minimal space to relax and enjoy a moment of quietness overlooking the river during your day in Kyoto. The tea and sake room, which goes by the name 'Tasuki', acts as a cafe by day and bar by night. I recommend ordering the Roasted Bancha Highball for ¥1,300. Many of the cocktails here are based on the concept and flavour of tea. Why not enjoy a 'night-time tea'? You are on holidays after all! There are also shops in Tokyo's Marunouchi and Omotesando areas.

17

17

18

17 D&DEPARTMENT

w   d-department.com
A   397 Shinkaicho, Takakura-dori Bukkoji,
    Shimogyo-ku, Kyoto-shi, 600-8084
T   075-343-3217; 075-343-3215 (cafe)

SHOP/CAFE | D&Department is one of my most favourite design stores in Japan. The Kyoto branch is set in the most beautiful temple buildings, and it's such a special experience and atmosphere entering through the temple gates (don't enter through the centre of the temple gates, as that space should be left for the gods to come and go).

The store prides itself on collecting the finest craft pieces made by artisans from all over Japan – and they've really done the work for you. Think the thinnest glassware, the most beautiful copper tea strainer and even a peppermint oil insect repellent so organic that you can even drink it. I particularly adore the tin coffee can with spoon from Kaikado, a long-established tea cylinder store in Kyoto founded in the Meiji era (1868–1912). You can also find a range of beautiful Takahashi craft timberware and especially beautiful is the Takahashi craft cara cup, just hold it in your hands and then try to walk out without buying it!

The company also release a partially bilingual design magazine featuring one of Japan's 47 prefectures per issue. You can find these magazines here, which might inspire you to explore Japan more deeply.

In the building next to the store is the cafe, where you can enjoy a tea, a glass of sake or a regional teishoku (meal set) lunch in a traditional setting. It's so beautiful sitting on tatami, enjoying your meal and looking out over the temple buildings. One of those pinch-yourself moments.

The Japanese love their stamps and love a good stamp rally. Visitors can collect a stamp at a range of train stations, stores and attractions. This design shop also participates in this tradition, so be sure to get your D&Department stamp.

18 IPPODO TEA
一保堂茶舗

w   ippodo-tea.co.jp/en/shop/kyoto.html
A   52 Tokiwagi-cho, Nakagyo-ku, 604-0915
T   075-211-4018

SHOP/CAFE | Ippodo is undoubtedly one of Kyoto's most famous green tea stores, and it also has a store in Tokyo's Marunouchi area and one in New York. The philosophy behind this brand is not only to provide beautiful green tea to customers, but in this special Kyoto store, they also run classes, tearooms and various activities to promote the allure and charm of traditional Japanese green tea. It has an atmospheric and traditional Japanese heavy, dark timbered interior.

During the tea classes, you will learn how to carefully prepare the perfect green tea with the correct temperature, stirring technique and serving etiquette, using a kyusu teapot. The classes cost ¥5,400 per person, but the information and experience is invaluable.

If you would prefer to just pop in for a tea made by the store's professionals, head to the Kaboku Tearoom and order from a range of matcha, gyokuro, sencha or bancha teas. Each tea is served with wagashi (Japanese sweets) and prices range from ¥660 to ¥2,090.

One of the most popular and premium teas on offer is the Ummon-no-mukashi matcha. Not only is this type of Japanese tea famous for its presence in the art of the Japanese tea ceremony, it's also popular for its health properties. It's made from cultivated leaves that have been finely ground on a stone mill to create a powder that contains all of the natural flavour and nutrients of the entire leaf. As you prepare the matcha tea, you will discover a most incredible green colour, rich aroma and full-bodied sweetness with each sip. This is the perfect Kyoto keepsake, and the packaging is design-focused, too.

19 UCHU WAGASHI
ウチュウワガシ

w   uchu-wagashi.jp
A   Ura Nobutomi-cho, Shintomicho,
    Teramachi-dori, Kamigyo-ku, 602-0875
    (Teramchi store)
T   075-754-8538

SHOP/CAFE | Uchu Wagashi is one of
Kyoto's most famous cute wagashi (Japanese
sweets) companies. The design and colourful
and playful packaging is so adorable – and
don't even get me started on the taste! These
sweets make the best take-home gift or even
a cute treat at your hotel at the end of the day
wandering in Kyoto.

The main store is in Teramachi, but
with three other stores in Kyoto, you are
quite likely to stumble across these sweets.
You can enjoy sweets and tea inside the
Teramachi store. The menu changes with
each season, but, as an example, when I
was there in spring, they served a cute plate
of bird-shaped sweets with a hot matcha.
Art on a plate. The store is so beautiful and
simply designed, with a peaceful zen garden
and a minimal timber-based shop fit-out,
leaving focus on the sweets, which are spot-
lit with low-hung lighting.

All of the sweet designs are ridiculously
cute, but my favourite has always been the
classic 'drawing' set. The box of colourful
candy can be turned into various 'drawings'
by rearranging the pieces. This particular set
contains 20 pieces of candy and is priced at
¥780, and almost too cute to eat. It includes
sweets in blue, pink, purple, white, yellow
and green – perfect for pastel lovers.

And if you're still looking for another
reason to stock up on these cute sweets, allow
me to mention that the expiry date is three
months after the manufacture date, so you
can be sure to enjoy these fresh when you're
back at home. Simply pull out a pack of Uchu
Wagashi and you will be instantly teleported
back to your gorgeous Kyoto trip.

20 TRAVELING COFFEE
トラベリング コーヒー

w   facebook.com/kyototravelingcoffee
A   310-2 Bizenjima-cho, Nakagyo-ku,
    604-8023
T   080-3853-2068

CAFE/COFFEE | For me, a well-designed
cafe logo is often an enticing sign that means
good things await, and Traveling Coffee is no
exception. Situated alongside a pretty little
river, this is a gorgeous bright and airy cafe
for a coffee pick-me-up during your travels.

You can sit outside overlooking the river,
and there are a few tables and chairs inside
with windows that look out over the river,
so even if it's a less than perfect day, you
can still gaze over the rippling water as you
get your caffeine hit. I recommend ordering
the iced hand-drip pour-over coffee in their
special original blend. But you can also pick
up a cosy hot coffee here, too.

The cafe is housed in an old elementary
school building that is now also home to a
library. The interior vibe is library-meets-
elementary-school with a collection of
baseball bats behind the counter. While you
wait for your coffee you can enjoy exploring
the unique travel-themed books, and you
can also pick up some free Kyoto tourism
flyers. The quirky character here gives you
the feeling that you've stumbled across a
hidden gem.

Conveniently located in the centre of
Gion's Shijo area, Traveling Coffee is such a
convenient place to relax and rest your tired
feet after wandering and exploring Kyoto.

20

19

21 WIFE & HUSBAND

W   wifeandhusband.jp/-shopinfo
A   106-6 Koyamashimouchikawara-cho,
    Kita-ku, 603-8132
T   075-201-7324

CAFE/PICNIC | Pop into Wife & Husband for a truly unique picnic experience. The vibe in this cosy ten-seater cafe is *Kinfolk-meets-rustic-Japanese*, with neutral colours, a timber fit-out and a lot of cane details. Although you can dine inside, you can also borrow all kinds of carefully curated picnic essentials and set off for Kamo River (*see* p. 74), just a 5-minute walk away, for a picnic.

For your picnic, the staff will pour you a wicker cane thermos full of hot or cold coffee and pack it into the most adorable rustic picnic basket filled with essentials, such as mugs, napkins and a linen table cloth. You can select your own stool, table and other picnic supplies – not to mention the cutest straw hats – from the arrangement hanging outside the store, which looks somewhat more like a prop shop than a cafe. You'll then receive a little ticket with the time you're due back, usually 90 minutes, so until then you can relax and enjoy the river breeze with your special coffee.

If you're a bit more than just peckish, you might want to pop into Hasegawa (*see* p. 96) across the road to pick up one of their amazing sandwich bento packs. I recommend the ham sandwich set, which might remind you of your childhood days of devon meat and tomato sauce sandwiches. Perhaps I'm giving away my age here?

When it's time to return your picnic basket, why not pick up some of Wife & Husband's original roasted coffee beans to enjoy during your trip or as a gorgeous take-home good. You can select from medium- to dark-roasted beans. Or pop back on another day, as it's easily located just a 4-minute walk from Kitaoji station.

22 SOIREE
喫茶 ソワレ

W   soiree-kyoto.com
A   95 Shin-cho, Nishikiyacho-dori,
    Shimogyo-ku, 600-8001
T   075-221-0351

CAFE/KISSATEN | Conveniently located near Gion Shijo station, Soiree is a cute little kissaten (retro coffee house) to rest those sore feet after a day of wandering beautiful Kyoto. Pop up to the 2nd floor, grab a window booth and order the jelly soda for a multicolour retro experience. The first thing you'll notice is the blue light that encompasses the room. The owners selected this style of lighting on advice from a friend who said blue light is flattering. Whether it is or not, this kissaten is beautiful and quiet. When I visited, there wasn't even a peep of music playing, instead patrons were enjoying an almost meditative, tranquil atmosphere.

Although there are a few cakes on the menu, along with some of the thickest toast you've ever seen, people mostly come to Soiree for the drinks. The real eye candy drink here is the jelly range. The colourful jelly squares inside drinks were added to the menu in 1978, and the recipe has not changed since its invention! My favourite is the jelly punch, but the jelly milk also looks amazing, with the colourful jelly floating around in its own little milk bath. If you're more of a neutrals kind of person, try the jelly coffee float.

Because you're on the 2nd floor, it's the perfect place to watch people pass by or to sit quietly reading a book with your jelly-filled drink. Don't leave without buying a two-tumbler glass set, a design keepsake that features the sweetest portrait illustration.

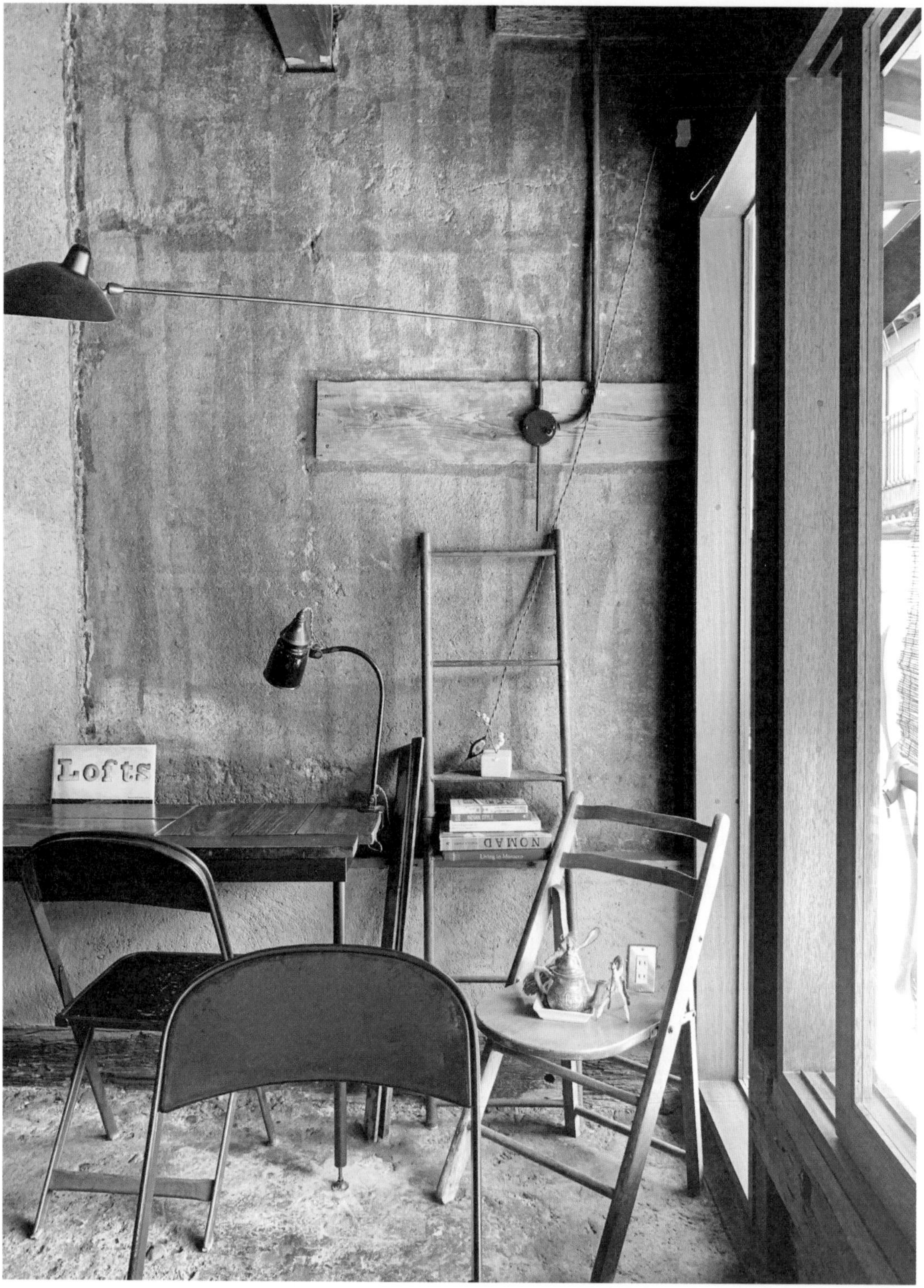
Lofts

23 HYGGE
ヒュッゲ

A   74 Nishishinyashiki Chudoji-cho,
Shimogyo-ku, 600-8816

T   075-708-7956

CAFE | Hygge is a family run cafe in a lovely residential area that will have you dreaming of moving to Kyoto while you sip your coffee. It's owned by a lovely husband-and-wife team, originally from Tokyo. They've really captured the cosiness implied by the Danish name. The decor is Kinfolk-meets-Japan-industrial and is dotted with gorgeous feature pieces, such as a matte black lamp from Japanese design store Idee. If you're feeling like being cosy, I suggest sitting in the back tatami room on the mats. Just don't forget to take off your shoes.

The owners live above the cafe, and I'm told this style is 'very Kyoto' by locals. The amount of times I heard 'renovated machiya' (traditional houses) during my most recent trip to Kyoto enforced this. On one visit at 7.30am, I was the only customer, and at the front table was the owner braiding her daughter's hair while she ate a small onigiri (rice ball). Moments later the two of them took off on their mamachari (mama-style bicycle). Does it get more divine than that?

The menu is simple and limited. My favourite dish is a nostalgic 'pizza toast', with house-made tomato sauce. Local drip-coffee is served in a beautiful ceramic cup on a fabric coaster and is best enjoyed black. I also hear good things about the chai.

I visited this cafe twice on my most recent trip to Kyoto, and on my second visit they asked me how the picnic was that I'd been planning on going on the day before. I absolutely adore this community style, and I wish this cafe was in Tokyo so I could make it my local.

24 KISSA ISHIBE
喫茶いし塀

A   463 Shimokawa-cho, Higashiyama-ku,
605-0825

CAFE/KISSATEN | I adore a kissaten (retro coffee house) but this one is just extra special. It's only a short walk from Kiyomizu-dera (temple), hidden on a backstreet and almost impossible to find if you were only sticking to the main streets, but it's worth a walk through these charming and paved narrow streets if you prefer a less commercial and touristy experience. If it weren't for the small sign and red noren (traditional Japanese fabric) flags, you might miss this cute place. And going by the 'no photos' signs in this area, it's a bit of a hidden-away treasure.

Upon entering, you will notice all of the beautiful ikebana arrangement on almost every table. Enjoy this absolutely peaceful space and floral arrangements as you sip on a coffee. If you take a seat along the retro Showa-era (1926–89) bench seating, you can look out over the beautiful Japanese garden through the large glass windows.

At the time of my visit, the kissaten was run by one obaachan (grandmother) who moved around fixing coffee and sandwich sets for customers with the ease only known to someone who has years of experience. In terms of what to order, I recommend getting the breakfast set. They are the sweetest things made of your childhood dreams with a nostalgic vibe, like if your grandmother or mum was Japanese and made it for you. My set had a little peeled half banana. And when I looked closely, I could just see the bacon under the toast. The set comes with chopsticks, which I just adore. But if you require a knife and fork I am certain they could accommodate this for you.

Oh, and be sure to visit the bathroom for those retro tiles!

SENTO

Sento (public baths) are a common part of everyday Japanese life. Many people plan trips around visiting particular sento or onsen (hot springs). The main difference between sento and onsen is that onsen is a natural hot springs bath, whereas sento use the burning of timber to create heated water. You will often see tall towers in Japan that let off the smoke from burning the timber, creating the unique sento smell that instantly places you in Japan. There's one near my apartment in Shimokitazawa, and if the breeze blows in the right way, I can smell the timber burning.

Japan has a strong bath culture, and many people take a bath before bed without showering again in the morning. It's common for a household to reuse the water of one bath per evening. They do this by following long-established rules of bathing, where people wash themselves thoroughly before entering the bath, thus keeping the water clean. Many home baths have an automatic temperature setting, where the bath water can retain its temperature until it's turned off by constantly replenishing the water to keep it hot. The tap water in Japan is usually set to a particular temperature, so there is no need to adjust the taps to try and get the perfect temperature. You simply set it once, and the hot water will always come out at this temperature. Oh, Japan, you really think of everything.

When bathing at a sento or onsen in Japan, first take your shoes off at the entrance and your clothes off in the locker room. Then you must wash your body and hair in the communal shower area, then enter the bath naked, and then finally shower again after your soak. It's polite to sit down on the small stools provided to shower, rather than stand up, and always rinse the seat and any soap from the area before entering the bath. You should take care not to let anything, such as your privacy towel, touch the water. Instead, place this folded neatly on the top of your head while you are in the bath. It's best to tie your hair up if it's long. Bathing is divided into men's and women's baths. Tattoos used to be generally banned at sento and onsen but these rules are gradually being relaxed, so best to double check before entering, just in case. Super sento and private ryokan (traditional Japanese inn) baths have different rules, such as some super sento like Spa LaQua in Tokyo allowing communal bathing in swimsuits.

Japan has a range of sento styles and many feature beautiful tile mosaics and murals to gaze at during your relaxing soak. Midori-yu in Tokyo has some divine mosaic tiles, and the bathroom features the main bath in the centre of the room, which also features a bubble bath, quite rare for Japan. The pastel shades in the bathroom are divine! Mitake-yu in Tokyo's Urawa in Saitama is a bright and colourful sento with a nostalgic retro feel, featuring a Mt Fuji mural painted by the painter Nakajima-san. And Taisei-yu in Tokyo's Shinjuku area features a bath with a Renoir-esque vibe in the women's bath and a seascape in the men's bath. For a more modern, renovated vibe, try Sakae-yu in Shinjuku, which was constructed in 1940 but renovated in 2017 by Japanese architect Imai Kentaro. You'll love the pops of colour and design at Tokyo's Bathhaus (*see* p. 14), and if you're on Naoshima Island you must go to I Love Yu (*see* p. 219) for its beautiful tiles and art.

Be sure to try a sento while you're in Japan. Such a beautiful and refreshing experience.

25 CAFE MARBLE BUKKOJI
カフェマーブル

W cafe-marble.com
A 378 Nishi-maemachi, Shimogyo-ku,
    600-8083
T 075-634-6033

CAFE | I visit this cafe every single time I visit Kyoto, and I'm sure you'll adore it too. Set inside a, you guessed it, 'renovated machiya' (traditional house), this cafe is so relaxing and peaceful, especially with its kawaii (cute) French bossa nova tunes and traditional Japanese garden. You will feel like you've walked into someone's home, only this home is so earthy and cute, and dotted with cosy accessories like books, hiking items and assorted cushions and throws.

Cafe Marble's speciality is quiche and it doesn't disappoint, served with beautiful salads. The menu also includes curries, sandwich plates and salads. I recall the menu is only in Japanese, so maybe pop onto its website (with an English menu) or Instagram to see what kind of dishes take your fancy. They also sell one of my favourite Japanese beers, Heartland Beer, and in summer it comes served in a chilled jug. Definitely recommended for a break after walking around Kyoto!

If you need to use the bathroom, it's a good excuse to admire the beautiful Japanese garden. The sound of the sliding door that opens out to the courtyard garden is quintessentially Japanese and so unique to Kyoto style. I wish I could bottle that sound!

The loyalty points card here is so cute, and I recommend getting one if you intend to pop back, or visit their other branch in Chiekoin. I won't give too many spoilers, but … if you go enough times, you'll see a little picture on your card!

Its website has a lovely 'location guide', pointing out cute things to do in the local area. You might even like to get a take-away tart and chai tea for while you explore the neighbourhood. Treat yourself, yo!

26 WATANABE
わたなべ

A 6 Ninintsukasa-cho, Shimogyo-ku,
    600-8824
T 075-361-1561

RESTAURANT/OKONOMIYAKI | This little 16-seater teppanyaki and okonomiyaki (Japanese savoury pancake) restaurant is chilled, casual and absolutely delicious. The perfect trifecta, right?

Hidden on a quiet little corner in a residential area, Watanabe is a hotspot for locals. Its no-fuss decor with counter seating and open timber doors makes it the perfect place to enjoy some famous Kansai region food.

While most okonomiyaki is made using cabbage as a base, Watanabe also offers a negi (shallot) base okonomiyaki. This could be fun to try if you've already tried regular okonomiyaki before. The name 'okonomiyaki' is, in itself, interesting: 'yaki' means to fry, and 'okonomi' roughly translates as 'as you like', so in this sense you could say that it roughly translates as 'whatever you like fried'. The options of toppings include items such as cheese, prawns, seafood mix, squid and pork. Or if you're unsure, the mixed option is always delicious!

Many okonomiyaki places pass you your ingredients in a bowl and then you cook the food yourself. But at Watanabe the chefs prepare your dishes for you, taking out a lot of the stress for first-timers, or for those who want to concentrate on chatting with their friends rather than cooking.

Watanabe also offers yakisoba (stir-fried noodles), where you can select the ingredients and toppings you would like to include. For two people, I suggest ordering one okonomiyaki and one yakisoba. Then your Kansai region food tour is off to a good start. Best enjoyed with a nama draft beer of course!

25

25

26

27 HASEGAWA

A 68 Koyamashimouchikawara-cho,
    Kita-ku, 603-8132
T 075-492-9921

RESTAURANT | Hasegawa is a perfect
example of Japanese–Western food, such
as hamburg (meat patties) with rice. It
may sound a little odd, but these types
of restaurants are extremely popular all
over Japan. It's worth eating here for its
comfortable and cosy family restaurant/
kissaten-style retro decor. There's always
something about this style of interior
that makes me feel so comfortable. The
leather seats, the dated decor, the quirky
ornaments … it's all so nostalgic. With
many windows and a slow-paced feel, you
can really relax here and escape from the
heat (or cold), depending on which season
you're travelling in.

The menu includes dishes such as pork
katsu, croquette, hamburg and omuraisu
(omelette rice) – a type of chicken rice with
a ketchup flavour wrapped in a soft omelette
and topped again with ketchup. It's quite
hard to select off this menu, as everything
looks delicious. The 'ebi fry' deep-fried
prawns are also delicious! And they do
Japanese pasta dishes. My recommendation
is that you order one of the 'hamburg' sets,
which come with a salad, miso, pasta and
your choice of rice or bread.

Hasegawa also has a large range of
take-away sandwich bento boxes, including
tempura prawn sandwiches or pork katsu
sandwiches. They even have a ham and
tomato sauce sandwich, taking a real
approach to Western-style food.

Outside the store is a display cabinet
with plastic models of the dishes, so if you're
a little worried about your Japanese language
skills, fear not and use the point and smile
technique here.

28 AWOMB
アウーム

W awomb.com
A 189 Ubaynagi-chou Nakagyo-ku, 604-8213
T 050-3134-3003

RESTAURANT/SUSHI/GALLERY |
Awomb is a Kyoto classic that has been
around for years, which is always a great
sign – especially in Japan where everything
is always rapidly changing. Awomb is an
exhibition space, shop and incredible sushi
restaurant. I first visited when I moved to
Japan and a friend had an exhibition here.
At the Karasuma branch, you can enjoy the
beautiful moss and tree arrangement and
stone garden view as you eat your sushi.
Their motto is that they would like to convey
'Deliciousness, fun and happiness' through
their food and service.

Awomb is famous for their teori sushi
plates. These plates are extremely colourful
and picturesque, and create a fun dining
experience. It's quite a popular hotspot with
queues forming from 11am, even though it
doesn't open until midday. Order one of the
beautiful deconstructed sushi plate set menus,
which contain all of your sushi ingredients
and spices on a platter with a side of rice and
suimono (clear soup), and you can make
your own rolls. It's a fun and contemporary
take on temaki (hand-rolled sushi) and the
staff will guide you in how to construct
them. The ingredients are seasonal but can
include eggplant, chicken, mackerel, cherry
blossoms, renkon (lotus root), pumpkin and
Japanese mustard spinach. The sushi sets cost
between ¥1,500 and ¥2,500, and there is also
an English menu available.

Drinks-wise, I recommend trying
the house-made ginger ale or soda made
from Kyoto sparkling water, or you can
try from a range of local Kyoto beers or sake.
I prefer sake that's reasonably dry – try the
Tamano hikari sake.

Awomb has a few branches but I
recommend the original Karasuma store, a
7-minute walk from Shijo train station.

27

28

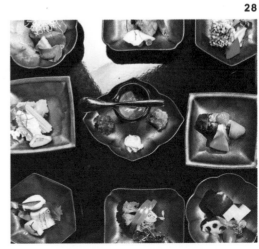

29 COFFEE & WINE VIOLIN
ワインバー コーヒー専門店 喫茶店

A   297-1 Shimizu-cho, Shimogyo-ku,
600-8025

BAR/CAFE | Who doesn't love a coffee and wine bar with a kitsch signature drink? In this case, it's an incredible blue soda float in the shape of a rose! The 'rose' is made of vanilla ice-cream and sits on top of a blue soda.

The decor here is dark timber meets blue velvet, with an almost church-like vibe created by gold metallic detailing, and the plush blue velvet counter seats will set you right in the mood for your blue soda float.

The cafe also boasts an extensive wine list by Japan's standards, so pop in for a glass of Margaux 2014 du Chateau Margaux or Mie Ikeno Chardonnay. And the opening hours reflect this focus on a little glass of wine, staying open until 1am. A small range of snack dishes, such as cheese, quiche, pâté, and pasta with meat sauce, are also served if you're a little peckish. Or you can enjoy chocolate cake or apple sherbet for dessert.

Conveniently located just beside the Kamo River (see p. 74), the closest access is via Kiyomizu Gojo station, drinks here will set you back anywhere between ¥1,000 and ¥2,000. Surprisingly, it's a non-smoking establishment, which is quite rare for this type of retro place.

30 KINSE INN CAFE
きんせ旅館

W   kinseinn.com
A   80 Tayu-cho, Nishishinyashiki, Shimogyo-ku, 600-8827
T   75-351-4781

BAR/CAFE | Set in Kokinse (Kinse Inn, *see* p. 104) a 200-year-old ryokan (traditional Japanese inn), Kinse Inn Cafe is the most divine place to get your caffeine fix or, come sunset, to enjoy a local Japanese gin. You will feel worlds away in this 2nd-floor space, and it's incredibly special that it still exists. We can thank husband-and-wife team Kojiro and Seanacey for preserving it.

You'll find books dotted throughout the cafe, beautiful antique tables and chairs, Taisho-style stained-glass windows and Taizan tiles. Be sure to check online about any upcoming events, as they often have musical events in the ryokan hall, featuring mostly Japanese music groups but also some international acts. The mix ranges from ambient electronica to jazz, hip hop and even piano. One of my favourite artists, Yeye, a sweet-sounding Japanese group, performed here and has also performed in Lithuania and Australia (both of my heritage).

One morning my iced-coffee was served in a beautiful cut-crystal glass fit for an old-fashioned cocktail, complete with a golden brass straw. It was one of the best iced-coffees I've ever had. One Sunday afternoon I went in for a tipple, and, in true Kyoto style, bumped into a friend who lives in the city. He had popped in for a drink alone and, while he was there, another of his friends also came in for a drink, and so the three of us drank local Japanese gin from Tatsumi Distillery and chatted away. It was the most beautiful local vibe.

I was introduced to Seanacey by my best friend David, who used to live around the corner from Kinse Inn Cafe. As he will attest, you'll always enjoy a friendly atmosphere at the cafe. If you go alone you'll be able to chat to the bar staff. Say hello from Hello Sandwich!

31 SOUR

w   sour.jp
A   607-19 Uradera-cho, Nakagyo-ku,
    604-8041
T   075-231-0778

BAR | You'll love hanging out at this little standing bar serving fruit cocktails (previously a vintage clothing store) hidden on a backstreet. Pop in for a twist on the usual sour (shochu-based Japanese cocktail) drink found in most izakaya (small bars). Here you will find specialities such as Okinawan tumeric and Korean carrot! And all of the sours (there are over 30 to select from!) are made from fresh fruits – not a premade syrup in sight!

Japan has really mastered the art of standing bars, and here they maximise the small space with comfort and cute design, like a small hook under the table for your handbag or tote and a timber-top bar. I adore the cute portrait illustration on the glasses, too. The illustration is also the neon sign marking the entrance of this hip bar with its completely black painted façade. You won't miss it.

They also sell merch with the illustrative logo on clothing, such as hooded sweaters and T-shirts. Graphic designers who love interesting identity branding might also like to pick up a shop card in the shape of the Sour portrait illustration.

It's the perfect place to pop in for a quick drink before or after dinner. And be sure to check out the website for some fun music events hosted by Sour bar.

32 SHIMAYA STAYS
シマ屋ステイズ

w   shimayastays.com
A   431-3 Kamibenten-cho, Higashiyama-ku,
    650-0822

STAY/MACHIYA | This renovated two-storey machiya (traditional house) in Kamibentencho (Benten West) is the perfect place to relax after a day exploring Kyoto. My favourite part is the amazing large genkan (entrance area) with a beautiful stepping stone into the residence. This calm oasis is in the middle of the Higashiyama area, which is just a short stroll from Kiyomizu-dera (temple, see p. 74) and the historic town. It's the ideal Kyoto haven for families and couples alike.

Shimaya Stays has two bedrooms (both upstairs), one a traditional tatami room that can be set up with futons for sleeping, and the other with twin single beds for a more Western-style sleeping arrangement. Complete with espresso machine, washing machine, full kitchen, lounge and dining area, you will really feel at home here. When a friend of mine picked me up one evening, I was able to play make-believe house, opening the genkan as if it were my own little home.

On the ground floor, just outside the lounge area, you will find a small terrace garden with a harmonious balance of stones and ikebana-like trees. Spend your morning coffee break looking out at the shapes of the delicate trees, and, as night falls, enjoy watching the shadows cast onto the cement backing wall. This garden is also viewable from the bath, and I can't tell you just how relaxing this is! You will also find a lovely tatami room – a relaxing space for drinking tea, sunbathing or meditating. You might like to spend the afternoon here in the sunlight journalling and scrapbooking with all of your cute Kyoto memorabilia, or pen some letters or postcards to loved ones.

32

31

32

34

33

33 HOTEL SHE

W   hotelshekyoto.com
A   16 Higashikujo Minamikarasuma-cho,
     Minami-ku, 601-8041
T   075-634-8340

STAY/HOTEL | Reasonably new on the Kyoto hotel scene, Hotel She is such a fantastic place. From the moment you arrive in the lobby, you are hit with just how hip, and at the same time incredibly comforting, it is.

Both the rooms and hotel lobby are designed with smart fittings, such as plush blush-pink velvet lounges, copper light fittings and an iridescent wall in the shared guest kitchen. There is even an ice-cream parlour next to the reception desk. Each room comes complete with a record player and records in your room, and the knowledgeable staff will help you select vinyl to your listening needs. I asked for Showa-style music and was not disappointed. Additional records can be borrowed free of change from the reception desk.

Although only a 10-minute-walk from Kyoto station, it's located in a residential area, and from my 3rd-floor room I was able to sleep with the window open and wake up to local residential sounds. Sometimes when you stay at cheap and cheerful hotels, your room might be on a high floor or without a view, or you might not even be able to open your room's window, so I can't tell you how lovely it feels when your hotel room has a nice view to really set the mood that you live in the area.

The staff here, especially Taku-san, are all incredibly kind and helpful. Taku-san went above and beyond for me – making phone calls and arranging an appointment for me, and when I was a little late back to the hotel, he said he was worried about me. What a sweetheart!

They even have their own Spotify playlist, which will help with withdrawal symptoms when it's time to check out. Oh, and they also sell merch, like tote bags and cute tees!

34 ANTEROOM HOTEL
ホテルアンテルーム

W   hotel-anteroom.com
A   7 Higashikujo Aketa-cho, Minami-ku,
     601-8044
T   075-681-5656

STAY/HOTEL | Run by the folks behind Tokyo's famed Claska hotel, Anteroom is a designer hotel at a cheap and cheerful price point. The single rooms are often offered at a ¥4,700 rate, and the hotel is a convenient 15-minute walk south of Kyoto station (or if you have luggage, you might want to jump into a cab). I've stayed here on many a trip to Kyoto.

The classic designed single and double rooms are simple and small, but the design details are on point. Open the desk drawer to find the beautifully designed Anteroom newspaper and notepaper. Hang your camera on one of the cute knob hooks and relax in your bed with its simple fabric headboard. The single rooms have a grey linen theme with a singular canary yellow stripe detail, for which the minimalist in you will be glad.

The terrace room offers a slice of luxury, or you can select from one of the artist designed themed rooms if you're feeling playful. Perhaps you've watched *Followers* on Netflix? The show is directed by Japanese contemporary artist Mika Ninagawa, who has also designed a room in this eclectic hotel.

The hotel has an amazing ¥1,000 breakfast in a beautiful open-space cafe on the ground floor, or you can have a glass of Japanese craft beer at the hotel's bar while you're waiting for your coin laundry to finish. Anteroom also has a gallery and a small design store, not to mention rental bikes for you to explore the area. This really is a one-stop shop for travellers to Kyoto.

35 KOKINSE (KINSE INN)
こきんせ

W   Airbnb.com, property 17819697
A   79 Nishishinyashiki Tayu-cho,
    Shimogyo-ku, 600-8827
T   075-351-4781

STAY/MACHIYA | If you can only stay
at one place during your time in Kyoto, it
absolutely has to be Kokinse. This beautifully
renovated machiya (traditional house),
owned by the most delightful couple,
Seanacey and Kojiro, has everything you
could ever imagine needing – and more. If
there wasn't so much to see in Kyoto, you
could easily just spend the entire day here,
watching the sun fall over the tatami through
the Showa-era (1926–89) patterned glass
sliding doors.

Located in a quiet little neighbourhood
south-west of Kyoto station, Kokinse is
walking distance from the UNESCO World
Heritage Site Nishihonganji Temple and is
also well connected to the rest of the city via
train. The neighbourhood was previously
a geisha district, and some atmospheric
buildings, such as Sumiya, which is open to
the public for tours, still remain.

This machiya is separated into two
private spaces by a divine Japanese garden
courtyard in the middle, so if you're travelling
with a large family or group, it could be
perfect to rent both and be close and have
privacy at the same time.

The smaller machiya has a twin-style
Western bed set-up, with open-plan living/
dining/sleeping. The larger machiya is
a two-storey space, with a modern and
Western-style 1st floor where you will find
the living and dining, and the 2nd floor is the
most beautiful three-bedroom traditional
machiya with enough futons to sleep six
guests comfortably. I stayed in the larger
machiya where I slept on a futon on tatami,
and one morning I awoke to the sound of
chanting monks!

No matter your plans for the day, when
you stay at Kokinse you can wake up and
enjoy the space as you pour beautiful
complimentary coffee from the owners, play
your favourite playlist on the bluetooth Tivoli
speakers and relax on the gorgeous green
couch. If you feel like cooking food, this is
indeed the ideal place. Seanacey has collected
a beautiful range of local ceramics to use for
your dining purposes.

There's nothing quite like feeling at home
in Japan. Kokinse is so gorgeous, and you can
also do an ikebana workshop here (*see* p. 68)
and there's a cafe (*see* p. 99). You just might
not want to leave.

35

OSAKA

SUPER CHILL AND
RELAXED WITH
FRIENDLY LOCALS

34.672° N
135.502° E

04

大阪

The vibrant city of Osaka appeals to many travellers. With its relaxed atmosphere comparative to Tokyo, friendly and chatty locals who won't hesitate to strike up a conversation in a standing bar or izakaya (small bar), incredible local food like famous okonomiyaki (Japanese savoury pancakes) and takoyaki (fried octopus), Osaka has a laidback quality that is particularly unique to this city. Not surprisingly, many of Japan's famous comedians come from Osaka.

Osaka's shotengai (undercover shopping streets, *see* p. 115) have such a retro appeal, and the Horie district (*see* p. 115) has a lovely slower pace than most areas of the city. Some of my favourite stationery stores are in Osaka, like Retro Jam Insatsu (*see* p. 121) and Tools (*see* p. 118), as well as Tsutaya Bookstore (*see* p. 118).

Like the relaxed pace of the city, so too are the locals. I was surprised when a taxi driver in Osaka played The Beatles loudly over his speakers during a ride back to my hotel. He was chatty and fun, but I have never experienced something like this carpool karaoke in any taxi in my 10 years of living in Tokyo.

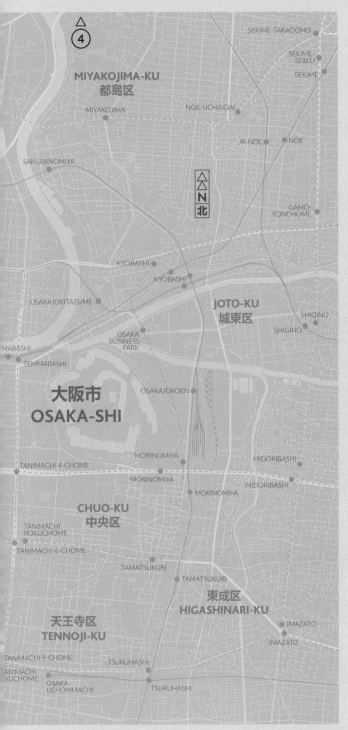

1   Dotonbori | **ATTRACTION**
2   The National Museum of Art Osaka |
    ATTRACTION/MUSEUM
3   Ichioka Motomachi Park | **ATTRACTION/PARK**
5   Shotengai shopping streets | **SHOPS/DISTRICT**
6   Horie District | **SHOPS/CAFES**
7   Amemura Area | **SHOPS/CAFES/DISTRICT**
8   Craftholic | **SHOP/HOMEWARES**
9   Tsutaya Bookstore (Umeda Branch) |
    SHOP/BOOKSHOP/STATIONERY
10 Tools | **SHOPS/STATIONERT/ART**
11 Retro Jam Insatsu | **SHOP/STATIONERY**
12 Super Tamade | **SHOP/SUPERMARKET**
13 Biotop | **SHOP/CAFE/RESTAURANT**
14 The Rendez Vous | **SHOP/BAR**
15 Wired Cafe | **CAFE**
16 Hi! Sandwich | **CAFE**
17 Madura | **CAFE/KISSATEN**
18 Mon Cheri | **CAFE/KISSATEN**
19 Kissakoko | **CAFE/KISSATEN**
20 Chikara Mochi Shokudo | **RESTAURANT/SOBA**
21 Matsuba Sohonten | **RESTAURANT/**
    STANDING BAR
22 King of Kings | **BAR**
23 Kamon Hotel Namba | **STAY/HOTEL**
24 Hotel She | **STAY/HOTEL**

OFF THE MAP

4   The Tower of the Sun Museum |
    ATTRACTION/MUSEUM | 22.5km (14mi) N of
    Osaka Station

1 DOTONBORI
道頓堀

A   1-9 Dotonbori, Chuo-ku, 542-0071

ATTRACTION | Perhaps the first image to
come to mind when people think of Osaka is
Dotonbori, Osaka's famous canal area, which
spans the area between the Daikokubashi
and Nipponbashi bridges. If you look down
the Dotonbori canal towards Ebisubashi
bridge, you will see the famous neon signs
of the Glico running man and Asahi beer,
among others. In the evening time when the
neon are illuminated, they cast a dreamlike
reflection on the water, and it's quite the
hotspot for visitors to take photos. You will
spot boat cruises passing along, too.

This bustling area is surrounded by
restaurants and shops. I recommend trying
okonomiyaki, a Japanese savoury pancake
consisting of flour, egg and cabbage along
with toppings of your choice. My favourite is
prawn, cheese and pork, but you can select
any ingredients you like. One of Osaka's
most famous restaurants in this area is Kani
Doraku, which is an extremely popular crab
restaurant. You'll easily spot it with the giant
moving crab sign on its shopfront.

To access the Dotonbori entertainment
area, you can catch the train to Namba
subway station and take a short 5-minute
walk from there.

2 THE NATIONAL MUSEUM OF ART OSAKA
国立国際美術館

A   4-2-55 Nakanoshima, Kita-ku, 530-0005
T   06-6447-4680

ATTRACTION/MUSEUM | The National
Museum of Art Osaka is one of Osaka's
best galleries. It was designed by architect
César Pelli and showcases exhibitions and
artworks by both international and Japanese
contemporary artists. The architecture is
a work of art in itself, with its stainless
steel and glass depiction of a Japanese
bamboo grove.

The permanent collection here boasts
over 6,000 pieces of artwork, including
work by Paul Cézanne, Pablo Picasso, Andy
Warhol, Max Ernst, Yayoi Kusama, Yasuo
Kuniyoshi and Tsuguharu Foujita.

The museum is located on Nakanoshima
Island in central Osaka. To access it, you
can take the Yotsubashi subway train line
to Higobashi station, from where it's only a
10-minute walk. Admission is only ¥430 for
the permanent collection, and additional fees
are charged for special exhibitions. If you
just feel like popping into the auditorium or
restaurant and gift shop, you can do so free
of charge.

The National Museum of Art is in the
same building as the Osaka Science Museum,
dedicated to space and energy, and the
planetarium here was renovated in March
2019. A trip to both these museums would be
such a fun day out for the whole family and is
sure to be especially enjoyed by kids.

えびす橋

3 ICHIOKA MOTOMACHI PARK

市岡元町公園

A   12 Ichioka Motomachi, Minato-ku, 552-0002

ATTRACTION/PARK | I always seek out cute and colourful urban architecture when travelling. Affirming yet again to always take the backstreets, I happened to stumble across Ichioka Motomachi Park on my way to Bentencho station from Hotel She (*see* p. 135).

This park is so fantastic – it's something halfway between an art installation and an urban park, making it a must-visit for those who share in this interest. In the centre of the park is a large installation of pastel pink, almost Memphis-meets-'80s style cement play equipment. The play equipment walls have a variety of different shapes, such as curved, straight and stair–shaped forms, which are super fun for kids to climb onto. The walls also have small windows cut out in various shapes and sizes, such as squares, circles and L-shapes, and each is painted with a vibrant colour, think canary yellow, red, navy and powder blue. There are also circular stepping stones painted in a mix of pastel and primary colours.

In addition to the colourful play equipment, the park also features a range of sakura (cherry blossom) trees, so it must be divine to visit during the hanami (cherry blossom viewing) season – if you happen to be so lucky.

4 THE TOWER OF THE SUN MUSEUM

太陽の塔

A   1-1 Senribanpakukoen, Suita, 565-0826
T   06-6877-7387

ATTRACTION/MUSEUM | The Tower of the Sun Museum, designed by famous Japanese artist Tarō Okamoto, was originally constructed as part of the theme pavilion for the 1970 Japan World Expo in Osaka. Located in the beautiful Osaka Expo Park, the tower features four faces: Golden Mask, Face of the Sun, Black Sun and the Underground Sun. The tower itself stands at an impressive 70-metres (230-feet) tall with one arm's length of approximately 25 metres (82 feet).

You can also visit the Tree of Life in the exhibition space inside the Tower of the Sun, a quirky and colourful sculptural exhibition that displays depictions of almost 300 models of living organisms, such as jellyfish and dinosaurs. Kids will love it here!

The entry price for adults is ¥720 and children are ¥310 (children younger than school age are free), and you can book your tickets online. Tours of the museum are held in groups of approximately 10–16 people.

You will also have the chance to climb five staircases to enjoy the exhibition throughout the inside of the tower. But if you prefer you can take the elevator to the 3rd floor and view the exhibit from this level.

4

3

5

6

5   SHOTENGAI SHOPPING STREETS
商店街

w   shinsaibashi.or.jp
A   14-5 Nanbasennichimae, Chuo-ku,
    542-0075 (Sennichimae Doguyasuji
    Shotengai)
    2-22 Shinsaibashisuji, Chuo-ku, 542-0085
    (Shinsaibashi-Suji Shotengai)

SHOPS/DISTRICT | Osaka is fascinating and unique with its rows and rows of shotengai (undercover shopping streets). Not only do they have an adorable retro charm, but they're perfect for protecting oneself from all sorts of weather. Filled with restaurants and shops in the central city area, you can find a range of shotengai that house international luxe labels positioned right next to cheap and cheerful stores. Such an eclectic mix. You can easily spend a full day exploring Osaka's shotengai.

There are shotengai dedicated to particular types of stores. For instance, the Sennichimae Doguyasuji shotengai is dedicated to shops selling household goods, kitchenware, pottery and cooking tools. Perhaps one of the most famous shotengai is the Shinsaibashi-suji shotengai, which is just a few minutes' walk from Dotonbori, where you can find a wide range of high-end tax-free shops that even have airport delivery, so be sure to pack your passport. Here you'll find stores like Gucci, Daimaru department store, United Arrows, Onitsuka Tiger, Uniqlo and Gap, as well as cafes such as Hoshino Coffee.

6   HORIE DISTRICT
堀江

A   1-13 Minami-Horie, Nishi-ku

SHOPS/CAFES/DISTRICT | Osaka's Horie district, located in the west side of Shinsaibashi, is a peaceful and hip area filled with vintage clothing stores, fashion labels, homewares stores, speciality boutiques and cafes. Horie has a very different and somewhat slower paced, less bustling feeling than other areas of the city, and it can be a nice relief after some of the more touristy areas.

The closest station is Shinsaibashi on the Midosuji subway line, from where you can take a short walk from exit 8. I suggest starting your Horie exploration by walking along Orange Street and expand off the side streets, where you will find more hidden-away stores.

As you explore the area, keep an eye out for Acme for American vintage home collectables; Jam, a three-level used and new clothing store; and Kind, a cute 'buy and sell' vintage clothing store. You will find Biotop cafe in this area (*see* p. 124), and don't miss Westwood Bakers. Craft beer lovers will love Craft Beer Works Kamikaze.

You might also like to visit The Flavor Design flagship store, where you can make your own fragrance for approximately ¥4,500. You select your favourite fragrances from the range of twenty unique scents, and the staff will assist you to mix your customised fragrance. A cute personalised label is attached to your bottle, making it a must-have memorabilia of your time in Osaka.

7 AMEMURA AREA
アメ村

w   vancy.co.jp
A   2F 1-7-2, Nishishinsaibashi, Chuo-ku,
    542-0086 (Vancy)
T   06-7493-8098 (Vancy)

SHOPS/CAFES/DISTRICT | Amemura could be described as the area where all the cool kids hang out, and it is bustling with shops and cafes. Its lively vibe makes it worth a trip, even just to wander around to soak up Osaka's fun and vibrant atmosphere.

You'll come across streets and streets filled with cute select shops full of youthful clothes for both men and women. In addition, you'll find local vintage clothes stores and stores that specialise in imported vintage clothing. A lot of the vintage clothes in Japan come from the USA, so expect to find some cute items from American brands.

Located in the middle of the Amemura area, you can find one of my favourite vintage clothing stores called Vancy. You won't miss it with its cute and colourful sign, and when you head up the outdoor stairs to the store, you will find so many used printed T-shirts. Vancy also print its own limited-edition branded unisex T-shirts from time to time, which make for a lovely keepsake from Osaka. You can check out Vancy's Instagram page and online store to see if there are any limited-edition T-shirts in stock.

8 CRAFTHOLIC

A   2-10-4 Nishishinsaibashi, Chuo-ku,
    542-0086
T   06-6226-7930

SHOP/HOMEWARES | Craftholic is a cute Japanese-brand shop selling original toys, loungewear, slippers and small homewares.

I've taken friends with babies to this store and they adored the character cushions, bibs, pillows, rattles and the cutest animal character towels with hoods. The caps are also adorable, with their little teeny ears.

If you're not in the market for baby items, it has a wide range of other products, including stationery, stickers, kitchen items, purses, smartphone accessories and even cleaning items. I mean, where else would you find striped sloth slippers? Oh, Japan! They've also added Kyoto tea to their range, too. What a fantastic one-stop shop!

And fear not, the needs of your little furry loved one are also covered at Craftholic, with this quirky brand offering soft toys, blankets, mats and pet food bowls. The design seems to be quite popular for the sensibility and taste of foreigners and Japanese alike.

This Osaka store is super conveniently located just a 1-minute walk from Amemura station, making it extremely easy to access during your shopping and exploring day. There is also a store located in Harajuku in Tokyo and some international branches, too.

9 TSUTAYA BOOKSTORE (UMEDA BRANCH)
梅田 蔦屋書店

A Lucua Osaka department store, 9F, 3-1-3 Umeda, Kita-ku, 530-0001

T 06-4799-1800

SHOP/BOOKSHOP/STATIONERY | Japanese book design is one of my favourite aspects of all design in Japan. And if you also happen to love Japanese book design, you'll love Tsutaya.

With branches all over Japan, the Umeda branch is located in the Lucua Osaka department store, and when you arrive on the 9th floor, you will instantly smell that sweet scent of Japanese paper and printing ink! Although most of the books at this branch are in Japanese language, the vast collection of design, architecture and art books makes this a fantastic place to come and get inspired by Japanese design. Fear not, they do stock a very small range of English books.

You can also find some lovely stationery here. I also love popping into Tsutaya for local travel magazines and 'mooks', which, as the name suggests, are a mix of a book and a magazine. These will point you to the latest cafes and shops, and, even if you can't read Japanese, they often have maps and/or websites that can help you navigate the city. I recommend popping into this store at the start of your trip in Osaka to pick up some mooks to help enhance your travel experience.

Enjoy spending a relaxing time here soaking up Japanese book design!

10 TOOLS
トゥールズ

A B1F/B2F, 1-1-3 Shibata, Kita-ku, 530-0012 Hankyu Sanbangai

T 06-6372-9272

SHOP/STATIONERY/ART | Tools is one of Japan's best stationery and art supply shops, and has stores in both Osaka and Tokyo. It sells an amazingly well curated selection of art and stationery supplies, such as papers, pens, paints, sketchbooks, pastels, markers and paint brushes. Whatever your creative medium, you're sure to find it at Tools.

I recommend buying the small travel watercolour paint set, which comes complete with a paintbrush that holds water inside the stem of the brush so you can easily paint on the go. Perfect for capturing moments on location or easy craft at your hotel. You might also like to purchase a set of watercolour postcards to make original postcards for your friends back home. You can also find a range of COPIC markers here. I love the Japanese fine ball pens, such as 0.38, perfect not only for writing Kanji but for writing and drawing fine elements, too. Be sure not to miss the basement 2nd level for the art supplies, and you will find the stationery on the level above.

This branch is conveniently located right at Osaka Umeda train station. If you exit the ticket gate by the Midosuji line near exits 1 and 2, you will have arrived already!

12

11 RETRO JAM INSATSU
レトロ印刷

A   6-6-23 Toyosaki, Kita-ku, 531-0072
T   06-6225-8186

SHOP/STATIONERY | Retro Jam Insatsu (printers) is always top of my list when I visit Osaka. Designers and creative types alike will love this famous printing company, known for its riso prints, and the small shop that sells paper products. I love the factory and warehouse style of this building, and the scent of printing ink drifting down from the 2nd floor takes me back to my days of working in magazines.

Keep in mind that riso print orders can only be placed in Japanese language via Retro Jam's website. It might be a good time to pull in that favour with your Japanese friend – wink wink!

Although this is quite simply a printing company, and so basically a factory space, the small shop on the ground floor sells cute stationery and other handmade paper goods. The curated collection of stationery is selected by paper lovers, and it is, after all, a printing company, so you can imagine the cute things you will find here.

If you are incredibly lucky, you might be able to catch the amazing paper market that is held from time to time, where you can buy assorted paper offcuts.

12 SUPER TAMADE
スーパー玉出

A   2-9-28 Minamihorie, Nishi-ku, 550-0015
T   06-6534-5700

SHOP/SUPERMARKET | This Osaka-founded supermarket is well known, not only for its incredibly low prices but also for its amazing neon signage. Obviously, the latter is why I visit every Super Tamade supermarket when I come close to one! My Google Maps on my iPhone is full of pins of Super Tamada locations, just in case I happen to be in the area!

The cheap and cheerful prices are especially apparent in the bento and snacks area. The bentos are the cheapest supermarket bentos I've ever seen in Japan. Of course, they have all the regular essentials like onigiri (rice balls), katsu and edamame, but I recommend getting the 'only in Osaka' bento box with takoyaki (fried octopus) and okonomiyaki (Japanese savoury pancake)! It's so fun trying new bento in different regions. Those Kansai region kids really know how to make delicious (albeit carb-heavy) food. Take your bento to a nearby park, and you've got yourself an authentic and super cheap lunch or dinner.

But let's get to my favourite aspect of Super Tamade. Have you ever seen such cute neon signage in a supermarket before? Each store has different neon signs, so that's why it's fun to visit several different stores. Double check with the staff if it's okay to take photos. The bento section in one store features a neon smiling onigiri and a piece of smiling seaweed peeking out of a bento box. You might also spot some neon tempura, pickles, eggplants, rainbows or even cute cityscapes with smiling planes flying overhead. Oh, I wish we had Super Tamade in Tokyo!

FUN & GAMES

MOCO MOCO

W karaoke-mokomoko.com
A various locations

KARAOKEKAN

W karaokekan.jp
A various locations

MORERU MIGNON

W ikspiari.com/shop/
    shops/1746
A 1-4 Maihama, Urayasu-ku,
    Chiba, 279-8529

One of the unique aspects of popular culture in Japan is the game parlours. These are usually bright, colourful and noisy places, where you can experience both new and retro arcade-style games. Then there's the karaoke! Japan has no shortage of ways to enjoy yourself and have a fun time!

During the day, you can pop into any game parlour (there are many dotted all over the country in busier nightlife and shopping areas) to play claw catch games, taiko drumming games (as seen in Sofia Coppola's *Lost in Translation* film) and various other cute games. You can win anything from a plush soft toy to a phone accessory. You can enter most of the game parlours without payment, but you pay a few hundred yen per game. There are many skill-based dancing games and musical rhythm games, which are fun to watch even if you prefer not to participate.

You might also like to pop into a purikura (sticker print store) to have your photo taken and spend time decorating it. Each purikura photo session will cost ¥400 per photo strip, and the booths are often found inside gaming arcades. For an extra special experience, head to Tokyo's pink Moreru Mignon parlour (*see* p. 26).

Karaoke is an all-time favourite of the Japanese locals – and of mine! You can find some impressive deals during the day, when the parlours are less busy. Moco Moco karaoke locations sometimes offer a ¥10 room charge for 30 minutes! Drinks are required to be paid on top of this cost. As the night falls, the karaoke room prices rise, and you can generally expect to pay from ¥2,000 to ¥5,000 for an all-you-can drink, all-you-can sing night of karaoke! I recommend requesting the Joysound brand of machine for the large selection of English-language songs, and also because it can be operated in English.

13 BIOTOP
ビオトープ

A   Mebro 16th Bldg 1/2/4F, 1-16-1 Minamihorie,
Nishi-ku, 550-0015
T   06-6531-8223

SHOP/CAFE/RESTAURANT | Biotop
is a cute homewares, clothing and plant
store with a lovely little cafe attached. It also
has a rooftop terrace restaurant, making it
a one-stop shop. You can come in here for
lunch, dinner or just a coffee or refreshing
drink. The pizzas are the popular go-to, as is
the coffee.

    The rare-in-Japan open-air rooftop
seating and lots of plants makes you feel as
though you've stumbled across a real hidden
gem. If you're looking to take cityscape
photos, however, this is not the high vantage
spot for you, as this rooftop has high walls
that don't offer any city views. For a view
over Osaka, you might like to try Abeno
Harukas, Tsutenkaku Tower or Umeda
Sky Building.

    In addition to being a fantastic spot for
Western-style dining, the shop features some
divine fashion by local Japanese designers.
On my last visit there was a unique fragrance
pop-up. You can also find accessories,
handbags and assorted homewares on the
ground floor.

    Although they have branches dotted
around the city, I recommend this particular
one in the fashionable Horie district
(*see* p. 115) for a perfect spot to break up your
day of shopping and exploring.

14 THE RENDEZ VOUS
レトロ古着ランデブー

A   Azito Bldg 1F, 4-13 Kurosaki-cho, Kita-ku,
530-0023
T   06-6136-8995

SHOP/BAR | The Rendez Vous is a vintage
clothing store selling items mostly from
the '60s and '70s, and it also has a tiny
4-seater bar. It is run by a husband-and-
wife team; she runs the vintage shop during
the day, and he runs Bar Yatchi Natoru
in the evenings.

    You won't miss it with all of the clothing
racks of colourful patterned vintage dresses,
jackets and shirts outside the store. Each
part of this small shop is jam-packed with
retro treasures. Everywhere you look you'll
find something unique. Scarves hanging
from racks, bags and beads hanging from the
ceiling, and treasure chests full of jewellery.
The prices are very reasonable, with dresses at
approximately ¥5,000 and T-shirts priced at
around ¥3,000. This is a retro lover's dream
come true! It also has an online shop in case
you can't make it to this dreamy store in
real life.

    Once you've perused the clothes and
vintage jewellery, then you can ponder your
purchases over a gin and tonic at the cute
retro bar, where you can listen to fun retro
music. It's the perfect place to step back
in time and enjoy the feeling of the '60s
and '70s.

14

13

13

15 WIRED CAFE
ワイアードカフェ

A   NU Chayamachi, 2F, 10-12 Chayamachi,
    Kita-ku, Yubinbango, 530-0013
T   06-6377-2399

CAFE | Wired Cafe is located on the
2nd floor of the NU Chayamachi building,
a department store full of fashionable
apparel shops.

Featuring large windows letting in an
abundance of light, the interior of Wired
is casual and comfortable with a range of
seating styles – sofas, tables and bench seats.
This makes it comfortable for any situation,
such as a date, a lunch with small children or
just a solo break while shopping.

The menu is extensive and offers salads,
sandwiches, pastas and a range of Japanese
food. But I like to pop in here for Japan's take
on taco rice – a famous dish from Okinawa.
I can also recommend the fresh mojito and
iced-coffee, depending on your mood.

If your phone is running low on battery,
you might want to sit at the counter seats,
where you can relax and charge up using the
power points. Wired has an English menu
and offers free wi-fi, making it the perfect
little spot to relax in the middle a busy day
of exploring.

16 HI! SANDWICH
ハイサンドウィッチ

A   4-19-6 Minamihorie, Nishi-ku, 550-0015

CAFE | Okay, so how could I not include
this adorable play on Hello Sandwich in this
book! Opened in late 2018, Hi! Sandwich
serves incredibly delicious sandwiches in a
cool and hip cafe located in the fashionable
Horie district (*see* p. 115). You won't miss it
with its red ribbon signage.

Each of the sandwiches on the menu
have playful names, such as the Mummy
Cheese grilled sandwich and the Nick Daddy.
The Nick Daddy is ¥1,280, and the melting
mix of slow-cooked beef, red cheddar
and natural cheese grilled on homemade
campagne rye bread is not to be missed.

The interior has a modern wooden
vibe with an open kitchen and feels nice
and cosy, with space for only a handful of
customers to dine in. You can also have your
sandwich to take away. Be sure to get there
early, as Hi! Sandwich is incredibly popular
and the sandwiches sell out once the bread
has finished!

The friendly staff of the cafe and I chat
a lot on Instagram direct messages, so if
you visit, please be sure to say hello from
Hello Sandwich! Definitely don't miss this
cute sandwich place during your Osaka trip!

16

17 MADURA KISSATEN
マヅラ喫茶店

A Ekimae No.1 bldg, B1F, 1-3-1 Kita-ku, Umeda, 530-0001
T 06-6345-3400

CAFE/KISSATEN | Madura is one of Osaka's cutest kissaten (retro coffee houses), and when I think back on my time in Osaka, I always miss this impressive hidden-away place!

Located in the basement of the Ekimae building, the interior is filled with mirrors and powder blue and white partitions that look like something out of a Pan Am aircraft. The bone-coloured '60s-style seats are so retro they give the impression they might just have been white once upon a time, and that the smoke-filled air aged them authentically over the years. That's one thing about kissaten – they are great places for people to come and have a coffee, sandwich and a cigarette (or five) on their breaks (although a lot of places in Tokyo have now banned smoking indoors, and I heard that Osaka will follow). Kissaten are often filled with salarymen and each table is adorned with an ashtray, so if you are sensitive to smoke, please leave this one off your list. Otherwise, if you're a retro lover, you will absolutely love this kissaten.

The sandwiches here have that 'only-in-Japan' softness that make you feel like your grandmother made it, and the cream sodas are Japanese Showa-era (1926–89) perfect!

18 MON CHERI
モンシェリー

A 2-4-1 Shibata, Kita-ku, 530-0012
T 06-6372-9385

CAFE/KISSATEN | A short walk from Umeda station into an otherwise almost industrial-vibe area, you will find yourself at a little unassuming building on a corner with an understated green box light sign. Fear not if you can't read Japanese, just look out for the little graphic of a coffee cup on the sign box. Then, take the stairs down to the basement level, and you will find yourself stepping into a super cute little kissaten (retro coffee house) in a time-warp style. Think olive green Showa-era (1926–89) lounge seats, red brick walls, and, just in front of the kitchen, a feature divider wall of two arches with illuminated pot plants and '70s-style blue design elements.

Pop in here for omuraisu (omelette rice) and a coffee or cream soda. To really fit in like a local, sit at the back where you can watch Japanese TV or read some of the manga found hidden next to the seats. With its basement vibe with no windows, it's easy to lose track of time in this relaxing cafe, so keep your timepiece handy if you're on a strict Osaka schedule!

A visit to Mon Cheri is truly a beautiful and retro experience that will leave you wondering if it's indeed really the 21st century.

19 KISSA KOKO
喫茶ココ

A   3-3-27 Minato-ku
T   06-6582-0214

CAFE/KISSATEN | Kissa Koko is an adorably retro kissaten (coffee house), serving curry and coffee and homestyle Japanese sandwiches. Once you open the door, you will be greeted by an interior so authentically retro you will wonder if you perhaps might just have walked through a dokodemo door from the famous Doraemon animation.

Opened in 1963, Kissa Koko appears, remarkably, virtually untouched decor-wise. The walls are lined with a cream leather–style finish with a graphic diagonal mustard stripe, which is set off by the cobalt blue–coloured transparent coating on the glass door. And, as a finishing touch, orange hanging pendant lights hang low above the various seating areas. This place is so authentic that, incredibly, the cash register is the original one from the day it opened in the '60s.

My visit was quite early in the morning, and the owner made me a sandwich that tasted just like something my Japanese grandmother would make. But I imagine if you visit at lunchtime the curry would be the recommendation to order.

It's located about 200 metres from Bentencho train station and is also just a short walk from Hotel She (*see* p. 135), which is rather convenient for those who happen to be staying there.

20 CHIKARA MOCHI SHOKUDO
力餅食堂

A   1-9-2 Nakazaki, Kita-ku, 530-0016
T   06-6372-1458

RESTAURANT/SOBA | Chikara Mochi Shokudo is an incredible and famous soba shop that has been running for over 100 years! Located on a quiet street, this restaurant is frequented by locals and has a friendly community vibe. It is a lovely place to chill and relax while you watch the instore TV or chat with your family or friends. The interior has a retro Showa-era (1926–89) vibe with beige and brown tiles, and charming timber walls covered in handmade menu posters.

On the menu is curry-flavoured soba! You can also have plain soba with curry sauce; however, the curry-flavoured soba is so unique (I've never seen it anywhere else in Japan) and is definitely worth trying for the experience. There is also a four-flavour set of various types of soba for the more adventurous. One of the four flavours is coffee! Can you imagine coffee-flavoured soba? This set also includes the curry flavoured soba, so you can have a well-rounded experience trying both the curry and coffee soba. Most of the soba dishes are served cold with a dipping sauce.

The menu is in Japanese only and is displayed on signs stuck to the restaurant walls, but at the front of the restaurant there are some display foods that you can point to and smile to place your order. The owner is so kind and will try his hardest to explain the dishes and make sure you enjoy your time at Chikara Mochi Shokudo.

21 MATSUBA SOHONTEN
松葉総本店

A　9-20 Kakudacho, Kita-ku, 530-0017
T　06-6312-6615

RESTAURANT/STANDING BAR |
Matsuba Sohonten is a cheerful and cute little kushi katsu standing bar under the train tracks of Osaka station, and it is a great place to pop in and try cheap kushi katsu (food deep-fried on sticks), one of Osaka's famous foods.

Here you can try a range of kushi katsu, such as lotus root, mini sausages, fish and even quail eggs. My favourite is always the ebi (prawn), which is juicy underneath the crispy fried coating. In between each stick, you can refresh your palate by dipping the readily available cabbage into the house-made sauce and enjoy the crisp and refreshing taste.

The L-shaped standing counter here is always busy with a buzzy clientele. You can stow your handbag or stack of shopping bags on the mini shelf below the counter bar to save space at this always busy restaurant. When you've enjoyed eating enough kushi katsu, you ask for the bill and they count the sticks left on your plate to work out the amount.

Matsuba has three stores in Osaka, but the main branch, the Sohonten, is my recommendation, as the vibe is extremely chilled, no fuss and thus perfectly Osaka-style. It's the perfect place for when you just need a quick bite to eat on your way home.

22 KING OF KINGS
キング オブ キングス

A　Osaka Ekimae 1st bldg, B1F, 1-3-1 Kita-ku, Umeda, 530-0001
T　06-6345-3100

BAR | King of Kings is an incredibly cute and retro-style whisky bar hidden underground on the basement level of the Ekimae 1st building. The charming interior here combines period features from the '70s and '80s. Not to mention the ornate, decorative stained-glass feature wall – the entire bar is separated by a silver sculptural-like 'wall' made of thin curved poles. At the time of my visit, white lillies were featured on a table covered with white linen cloths, adding to the special time-warp aspect of this bar. Did I mention the flooring is apricot velvet carpet?

In case that hasn't already got you pinning this place on Google Maps, the bar section at the back allows guests to purchase a bottle of whisky and leave it in one of the cute whisky lockers for future visits. If you're lucky, and visit during the evening, you might be treated to a live piano performance.

I recommend ordering one of the various gin-based cocktails that cost ¥600. They have a lilac-coloured mixer for one of these cocktails that is ever so pretty, and delicious, too. If you are hungry, you can order items from the quirky menu, such as spaghetti, wiener sausages, sandwiches and bar snacks, such as mixed nuts, caviar and anchovies and cheese.

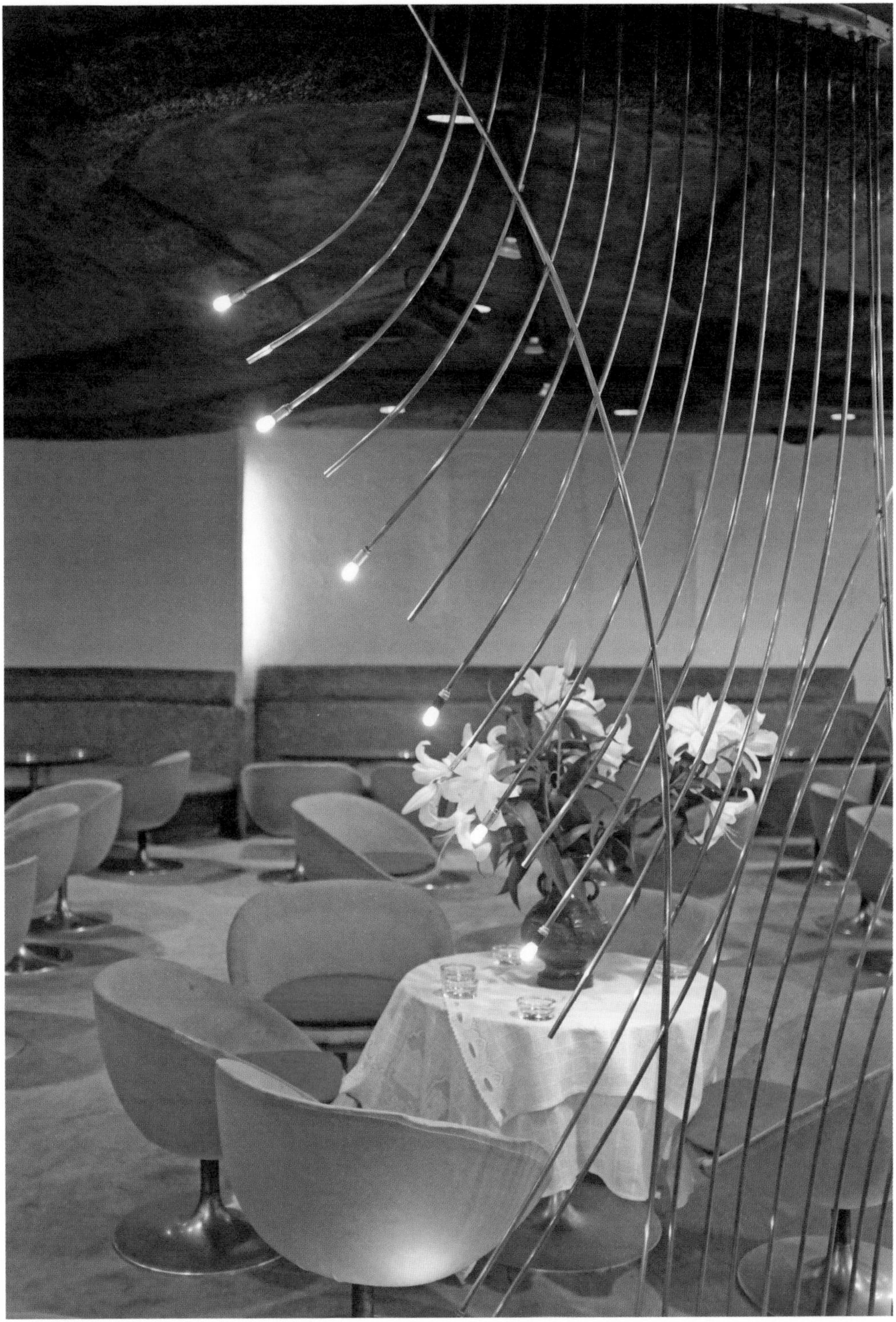

24

23

23 KAMON HOTEL NAMBA
カモンホテルなんば

A   2-3-33 Sennichimae, Chuo-ku, 542-0074
T   06-6632-3520

STAY/HOTEL | Fantastically located right in the city centre just near Namba, Kamon Hotel Namba is perfect for those in search of a cheap stay with a design focus. The hotel's fantastic location makes it easy to walk to all types of shopping and nightlife locations.

There are various styles of rooms to select from, but I chose the white 'less is more' room, with its simple white linen, white walls and stylish timber finishes. Next to my bed was a tiny triangle shelf that was the perfect size for an iPhone and a coffee cup. These tiny and well thought–out details enhance the experience and add a sense of high quality to your stay.

The youthful staff here are cheerful and helpful, but please note that there isn't a phone in your room, so if you need to chat with the front desk, you will have to walk to the elevator where there is a phone or go down to the reception. I would recommend adding the breakfast buffet to your reservation, and it's also worth noting that the hotel runs events such as matcha ceremonies.

Kamon Hotel Namba is located in a renovated warehouse-style building with painted cement floors, which kind of reminds me of the floors at my art university! It also has an incredible rooftop open-air deck where they often host events, or you can buy a beer from the reception desk and enjoy it on the deck.

24 HOTEL SHE

A   1-2-5 Ichioka, Minato-ku, 552-0012
T   06-6577-5500

STAY/HOTEL | Hotel She opened in the Bentencho area in September 2017 and is a super cute place to stay. Although it's approximately thirty minutes via train from the centre of the city, this hotel has a special charm that is worth experiencing if you don't mind the extra travel time.

Emerald blue is featured throughout the hotel. The entrance lobby features blue bricks, which mixes an industrial vibe with current trends, referencing Bentencho's port town history. The common space, with its L-shaped emerald-blue velvet lounge, graphic striped timber floor and grid spotlights, gives a casual youthful feel to the place.

The blue continues into each room, with the walls painted in this bold colour. The rooms also feature other cute trend-forward features, such as the timber Eames-style hang-it-all hangers. The reception staff will be able to tell you about some cute Showa-era (1926–89) places, such as cafes, sento (public baths) and shotengai (undercover shopping streets), in the area for you to wander around during your stay.

Each room has a record player, and you can borrow records from the reception and play them in your room. I asked the staff for Japanese Showa-era records and was pleasantly surprised. You can also purchase the records if you fall in love with them, like, ahem, I did.

Oh, and a pro-tip: I found it easier to catch the bus into the city than the train.

NAGOYA

名古屋

DELICIOUS LOCAL
CUISINE JUST
A SHORT TRIP
FROM TOKYO

35.167° N
136.907° E

05

& GIFU 岐阜

Nagoya is a fun little stop and easy to access if you take the shinkansen (bullet train) between Tokyo and Kyoto. It's not a particularly large city, but its charm comes from enjoying local aspects, such as regional dishes at stylish Pecori (*see* p. 152) and the cute little kissaten (retro coffee houses) like Kissa River (*see* p. 150) and Bon Bon (*see* p. 150), which has cakes to die for!

One quick ekiben (bento lunch on a train) and a can of Sapporo, and you'll find yourself close to Sakae, one of the most central hubs of Nagoya. My favourite department store PARCO (*see* p. 140) is here.

You won't want to miss Only Free Paper (*see* p. 140) for free flyers and zines or On Reading Gallery (*see* p. 143) with its amazing selection of art books.

If your schedule allows, you should explore Gifu prefecture. I highly recommend a trip to the Site Of Reversible Destiny art park (*see* p. 156) – it's one of my favourite places in all of Japan. You can even get a Hello Kitty train from Nagoya! Then there's Shirakawa-go's villages (*see* p. 156), where you can experience 250-year-old thatched-roof houses and stay overnight at a minshuku (B&B).

1 URAMONZEN PARK
裏門前公園

A   3-3 Osu, Naka-ku, Nagoya,
Aichi, 460-0011

T   052-972-2492

ATTRACTION/PARK | Nagoya has its very own Mt Fuji, but it goes that extra mile in the kawaii (cute) department – it's pink and made from cement. It's a popular piece of play equipment for little kids and big kids alike, with a set of small stepping stones on one side so you can climb up to the top and sit at the very top of the 'mountain'. It's located in Uramonzen Park.

I first visited this Mt Fuji in the evening, and a bunch of hip young Japanese guys were sitting on the top of the mountain. I was so focused on taking a photo with my Fujifilm camera that I didn't notice that they were posing with the peace sign for my photo. I was sprung!

Of course, there are a few other small play equipment items in Uramonzen Park, like a slippery slide, as well as some benches to enjoy a picnic lunch or a take-away coffee from nearby cafe Mill (*see* p. 146). Japan is so playful with its playground equipment and this one always brings a smile to my face.

For the true experience of this park, I recommend visiting during the day, so that you can enjoy the pastel colour of gorgeous and unique pink Mt Fuji!

2 OSU SHOTENGAI AREA
大須 商店街

A   2-18 Osu, Naka-ku, Nagoya,
Aichi, 460-0011
3-14-43, Osu, Naka, Nagoya, Aichi
(Haneten store)

SHOP/CAFES/RESTAURANTS | Shotengai (undercover shopping streets) are the perfect place to explore shops and restaurants when the weather is less than perfect, and the area of Osu has no shortage of shotengai. Osu's lovely vibe makes it my favourite part of Nagoya. This shopping area is split into a neat grid-like area, so it's almost impossible to get lost – unlike in the streets of Tokyo's Shibuya!

The shotengai streets are full of vintage clothing stores (*see* p. 143), second-hand goods stores, restaurants and supermarkets. You could easily spend a day here, wandering the vintage clothing and knick-knack shops, popping into a cafe for lunch and then heading to a restaurant or izakaya (small bar) for dinner. The vibe is so chilled and charming that a friend of mine who lives in Nagoya likened Osu to Tokyo's Shimokitazawa area, stating that it's 'cool, but unpretentious'.

There is a range of eateries, including some cheap, quick snack places, such as Haneten, where they advertise a type of beer and snack set perfect for anytime – for example a nama (draft) beer and an assorted tempura set for a mere ¥800. Oso Shokudo Meek (*see* p. 152) is a perfect spot for a set lunch break during your Osu shopping, and for beautiful baked goods head to Osu Bakery (*see* p. 149).

Here is a local tip: if you're travelling on a pushbike, get off your bike and walk holding your bike, as riding through these shotengai streets is not permitted.

3 PARCO
パルコ

W nagoya.parco.jp/en
A 3-29-1 Sakae, Naka-ku, Nagoya, Aichi,
   460-0008
T 052-264-8111

SHOP/DEPARTMENT STORE | With branches all over Japan, PARCO is without doubt my favourite department store ever! Not only can you find incredible Japanese fashion, homewares, cosmetics and assorted living essentials, PARCO also features a range of excellent cafes and restaurants, where it's quite hard to go wrong! PARCO is separated into East building, West building, South building and midi sections.

You'll find Journal Standard, Ships, Tower Records, Muji and plenty of other stores. Food-wise you can find anything from Cheese Craft Works to Yakinuki (Japanese barbecue) and Eggs 'n Things, an ice-cream store. Plus the requisite sushi. There is even a club here, called Club Quattro, where you can see live music, as well as a sports stadium and sports club.

PARCO often hosts pop-up events, so be sure to check its website for details of upcoming happenings. Years ago, I was lucky enough to visit during a locally made ceramic pop-up event, where I was able to buy some small white plates with metallic silver handpainted polka dots. So keep an eye out for some very special keepsakes here.

In case I haven't already sold you on popping into PARCO, let me also mention that some of the stores have tax-free options, so be sure to bring your passport. They also offer free wi-fi in store. Enjoy!

4 ONLY FREE PAPER
フリーペーパー

W onlyfreepaper.com
A Horie bldg, 12-12 Tsubaki-cho, Nakamura-
   ku, Nagoya, Aichi, 453-0015
T 050-5532-3900

SHOP/STATIONERY | Only Free Paper is, quite frankly, an editorial designer's heaven. It's a 'store' that specialises in free flyers, free papers and free zines. Free flyers in Japan are next-level design and will provide you with more than enough inspiration to make your own little zine, collage or scrapbook, or you can fold them into handmade envelopes to send to your friends.

Here, you're welcome to take any of the papers and booklets from the tables and shelves for free! There's also a little locker-like cabinet wall full of gorgeous little zines and flyers. The presentation is so inspiring because it's like a little treasure hunt, peeking through all the teeny slots in the cabinet. Only Free Paper stocks approximately 100 new magazines a month, and the only thing you will need to spend money on is branded merchandise or a bag to carry your free papers in.

You'll enjoy exploring the different ways zines and free papers are created in Japan. From a folded poster-style zine to a small booklet. If you're anything like me, you'll leave wanting to make your own free paper!

Make sure you stop into retro-style cafe Kissa River (*see* p. 150) in the same Horie building, which is only a 4-minute walk from the Taiko street exit of Nagoya station.

4

4

6

5

5

5 ON READING GALLERY

w   onreading.jp
A   Kameda bldg, 2A & 2B, 5-19,
    Higashiyama-dori, Chikusa-ku, Nagoya,
    464-0807
T   052-789-0855

SHOP/BOOKSHOP/ART | On Reading is undeniably Nagoya's best and coolest bookshop and gallery. Run by the sweetest couple, it's an absolute must-see when you're in Nagoya. It's a little train trip away from the main part of the city, but I promise you it's well worth it (and open from midday to 8pm). It stocks a range of impeccably curated artists' zines, music, photography, art and architecture books. The shop features a feminine wall mural by a local Japanese artist that sets a whimsical tone as soon as you enter.

At the back of the bookshop, you will find a gallery to the left. I actually had a solo exhibition and have hosted a workshop here. On Reading often showcases various Japanese artists' work, ranging from painting to drawing and photography, so keep an eye on its website for details of upcoming shows and events.

The vibe here is unpretentious but ever so inspiring. You can feel free to enjoy the beautiful range of books without feeling the need to rush or any pressure. Previously, my own books have been stocked here, so if you happen to pop in, please say hello from Hello Sandwich. On the level below is a lovely little cafe where you can enjoy a drink or lunch after you're incredibly inspired from your On Reading visit.

6 VINTAGE CLOTHING STORES OSU
大須の古着屋

w   theotherosu.jp
A   3-42-6 Osu, Naka-ku, Nagoya
T   052-269-3113

SHOP/VINTAGE | In the Osu shotengai (undercover shopping streets, *see* p. 138), you will find a vintage clothing store on almost every street! My favourite is called The Other and specialises in colourful patterned clothes from the '60s and '70s. You'll notice the shop with its unique '70s-style circular bubble-like blue shopfront and painted blue floor. At the time of my visit, the front window was adorned with mannequins wearing cute '60s chequered skirts teamed with neck scarves and berets – making me want to immediately dress in retro clothing!

If you're after slightly more of an '80s vibe, pop into Sweet Monroe, where you'll find a range of denim jackets, patterned sweaters and floral dresses. Other vintage shops of note include Crunch, Rocat and Big Time, which are all worth heading into to find super-cute clothes. Hunky Dory is another gem and stocks menswear brands like J.Crew and Ralph Lauren.

You can also find a 2nd Street store, which has over 600 stores within Japan and is a buy/sell store where you can pick up brand items in fantastic condition at low costs.

7   KITSCH ET BIO
キッチュ エ ビオ

W   food-ikuta.co.jp/shop_bio
A   3-6-21 Marunouchi, Naka-ku, Nagoya,
    Aichi, 460-0002
T   052-265-5850

SHOP/SUPERMARKET | Sometimes
when you're travelling you miss cooking, or
you just want to eat in your hotel or Airbnb,
right? I love visiting Japanese supermarkets
to really get the vibe of the city – you can
tell a lot about a city or country from what
is on offer in the supermarkets. Kitsch et Bio
stocks essentials such as fresh vegetables,
cheese, cold meats, salads, fruits, breads
and wine. You can find a range of seasonal,
locally grown Japanese vegetables and fruits
here, such as daikon.

Kitsch et Bio also has quite a good
selection of premade sandwiches and bento
boxes. I recommend the bento boxes and the
Japanese curry bowls. And the sandwiches
are also delicious, although please be warned
that I bought a sandwich that looked like
cheese and ham, but when I bit into it, that
'cheese' was in fact butter! Oh, Japan!

Stock up on some Japanese condiments
to take home, too. It also has a little cafe
dining area upstairs for those who fancy a
snack on location.

7

8 EARLY BIRDS BREAKFAST
アーリーバーズ　ブレックファスト

w　earlybirdsbreakfast.com
A　4-14-20 Chiyoda, Naka-ku, Nagoya,
　　Aichi, 460-0012
T　052-265-9290

CAFE | One of the best things about living in Japan, for night-owls like me, is that places open late and stay open late. There's never any pressure to go on your morning run and get your green smoothie from a hip cafe all before 8am! Hardly anything opens until 10am or even 11am, so you can let yourself have slower mornings and escape the commuter train rush. There are a few exceptions, though, like Early Birds Breakfast, which opens at 7am. My friend Shawn from Lullatone (Nagoya's best music creator) took me here one morning. He knows all the best spots!

The interior is cosy with a range of table seats and counter seating. If you're lucky, you can also snag the outdoor table seating, which is divine in perfect weather. Dishes are served on colourful green plates and drinks in blue Yves Klein ceramic mugs.

The menu (in English and Japanese) is quite heavy on egg dishes, with a few salads, such as smoked chicken or grilled sausage salads, and sandwiches. You can also order from a range of omelettes, including a pork and spinach or a mushroom and cream cheese omelette. A Mexican food lover, I ordered the breakfast tacos from the specials menu, which were incredible. The tortillas were house-made and delicious.

The cafe is attached to a bike repair store that seems to employ only the hippest, hottest boys in Nagoya. So that's already worth a trip, but if you're craving breakfast before 11am, you'll want to pop in here.

Be sure to arrive early, unless you don't mind waiting for a table. While you wait, you could potter around the bike shop, which would hardly be torture – wink, wink.

9 MILL
コーヒーショップ ミル

w　milljapan.com
A　3-13-9 Osu, Naka-ku, Nagoya,
　　Aichi, 460-0011
T　052-265-5756

CAFE/COFFEE | Mill is a super-cute cafe for your morning caffeine hit, and the chic entrance sets a lovely tone for the start of your day. The interior is modern, with cement flooring, a minimal white slab counter, long timber bench seating along one wall and industrial white metal stools.

Pop into Mill for anything from a cold-brew coffee, cafe latte, iced-latte or hot cocoa. It also serves Australian brand Pranachai chai lattes or iced-chai. I recommend trying the cold-brew coffee, made to perfection, but if you're not in a coffee vibe, I recommend the Hojicha Japanese green tea, made by slowly roasting tightly rolled dried tea leaves; it has a bold, rich and smoky–sweet flavour. It's one of Japan's specialties! You can also select from the various range of teas, and for an additional ¥50, they will turn your tea into a tea latte.

Unlike many places in Japan that don't open until 10am or 11am, Mill is open from 8am! You can order your morning drink between opening time and 10.30am, after which they take a short break until they reopen in the evening.

8

9

8

11

10

10 OSU BAKERY
大須ベーカリー

w   facebook.com/osubakery
A   3-27-18 Osu, Naka-ku, Nagoya,
      Aichi, 460-0011
T   052-262-0075

CAFE/BAKERY | Japanese people take such utmost care and pride in almost everything, and as a result they tend to excel at pretty much everything. Baked goods are no exception! Pop into Osu Bakery for the most delicious baked goods.

Set in a rustic-looking shop with a timber board wall and large enticing windows, Osu is both warm and welcoming. It's located on a corner, so you won't miss it when you're exploring Osu's shotengai (undercover shopping streets, *see* p. 138).

For those who are craving something savoury, my recommendation is the mushroom croque monsieur, but you might also like to pick up a juicy frankfurt hotdog in a roll. So delicious! If a sweet-tooth option is more your cup of tea, try the lemon pie, which is new to the menu. For more basic options, you could pick up a loaf of shokupan (Japanese sweet white bread).

One of the many wonderful things about Japan is that bread often comes in small packets containing six or eight slices. This is probably put down to Japanese people eating rice and not requiring large loaves of bread, but it means that your bread is always super fluffy and fresh!

Osu is strictly take-away, so you can take your goodies to a nearby park to enjoy them.

11 KOMEDA'S COFFEE
珈琲所コメダ

w   komeda.co.jp
A   3-8-8 Sakae, Naka-ku, Nagoya,
      Aichi, 460-0008
T   052-243-2021

CAFE/KISSATEN | Komeda's Coffee is a classic Nagoya-based chain kissaten (retro coffee house). In Japan it's not uncommon for patrons to visit a cafe with their laptop and spend hours working there. I asked a few cool Nagoya locals where they usually go to do their work, and the answer was always Komeda's Coffee. Nagoya itself has approximately 20 branches, but branches can also be found in Tokyo.

My recommendation is to visit before 11am, so you can take advantage of the breakfast set. I recommend ordering the C-set, which consists of a piece of thick, Japanese bread with a small dish of sweet red bean paste served in a little basket. There is also the A-set, where the bread comes with a boiled egg instead of the sweet red bean paste. My friend Ai-chan put me onto this Nagoya specialty. The sets come with drip-filter coffee included, and the coffee is served in Komeda's original mug.

When ordering off the menu (rather than the sets), try the wiener coffee, which is served with whipped cream that melts into your drink in the most delicious and comforting way.

12 BON BON
ボンボン

w　cake-bonbon.com
A　2-1-22 Izumi, Higashi-ku, Nagoya,
　　Aichi, 461-0001
T　052-931-0442

CAFE/BAKERY/KISSATEN | This famous little Nagoya kissaten (retro coffee house) has been running since 1949! Bon Bon make incredible cakes that look far too pretty and perfect to eat! Think sweet potato mont blanc, a hazelnut and two-layer mousse chocolate cake, or the chestnut 'maron' cake, which is the number one most popular cake. All the cakes are house-made and can be enjoyed in the cafe, the take-away option is also extremely popular if you fancy a picnic or a dessert treat at your accommodation.

Be sure to check the menu for the lunch or breakfast set, depending on what time you visit, as it's often a lot cheaper than ordering off the regular menu. They'll often have a cake and drink set, or a sandwich and drink set. The sandwiches are standard for Japanese kissaten, such as ham and cucumber, or egg and mayonnaise.

On my last visit to Bon Bon, I ordered a mixed sandwich, which was presumably cut with a knife so sharp that my sandwich looked like one of those fake plastic display sandwiches! Rest assured though, the sandwiches here are very much real and have that sweet and soft 'made-with-love-by-a-Japanese-grandma' flavour specific to Japan.

The red leather bench seating and Showa-era (1926–89) decor, with timber walls and indoor plants, heightens the kissaten-style vibe. Soak up the retro feel of this popular establishment!

13 KISSA RIVER
喫茶 リバー

w　omyage.shop
A　Horie bldg, 12-12 Tsubakicho, Nakamura-
　　ku, Nagoya, Aichi, 453-0015
T　050-5532-3900

CAFE/KISSATEN | Once you've chosen your cute free papers and zines from Only Free Paper (*see* p. 140), head to Kissa River in the same building for lunch and a relaxing afternoon. It's a kissaten-style cafe (retro coffee house) and is charming and modern in style. It has a simple but relaxing interior with a turquoise feature wall, stainless steel seating and light timber tables.

Order one of the dreamy soda floats in a colour of your choice – green, blue, yellow or red. And for those who love fluffy pancakes, you won't want to miss the pancake stack here.

For the design savvy, you might notice the cute branding that adorns the coffee mugs, and you'll also love the cute coaster designs.

Kissa River is located in the back area of the 50-year-old Horie building, which is only a 4-minute walk from the Taiko street exit of Nagoya station. You will also find a rental gallery, NA2, and an independent shop, Omyage Nagoya, selling specialised souvenirs, such as Iwappen brand embroidered patches. It's a perfect one-stop building to spend an hour or three in.

12

14 PECORI
食堂ペコリ

W   marumitsu.jp/pecori
A   2-285-1 Fujimori, Meito-ku, Nagoya,
    465-0026
T   052-777-0678

RESTAURANT/TEISHOKU |
Recommended to me by Lullatone (Nagoya's best music creator), Pecori is an adorable and charming Japanese restaurant, where you can enjoy the most delicious organic teishoku (lunch sets). The feel is very Japanese *Kinfolk* magazine. I adore the white grid of windows that fill the entrance, and the beautiful rustic timber door. In summer, the entrance of the cafe is partially covered with greenery.

The teishoku include flavour combinations like grilled salmon and miso with a side dish of pickles. Pecori pays special attention not only to the taste but also to the nutrition and balance of each meal. You can be assured that you will be able to rest both your body and mind with a meal here. These beautiful lunch sets are priced at ¥1,700 and include a mini dessert, too.

Each teishoku is served on divine handmade ceramics, turning your lunch set into something of an artwork. They also sell their ceramic dishes for the most perfect take-home keepsakes. Can you imagine getting back home after your holiday and recreating some Japanese food and serving it on these dishes? Beautiful memories are sure to flow back if you do so.

Sweets, such as caramel cheesecake, lemon ginger poundcake and homemade ice-cream, are also available at Pecori for approximately ¥650. Of course, you can order delicious teas and coffee, but I recommend the homemade ginger ale or the matcha latte. Seasonal drinks are also available, including a homemade baked lemon squash float. So gorgeous!

15 OSU SHOKUDO MEEK
大須食堂 MEEK

A   3-34-9 Osu, Naka-ku, Nagoya, Aichi,
    460-0011
T   052-252-7815

RESTAURANT/BAR | Oso Shokudo
Meek is a great spot to come for lunch during your Osu shotengai shopping (*see* p. 138), if you're in the mood for a teishoku (meal set), often served with miso, rice, side dishes and a main dish. The extensive menu includes curry, pasta, karaage (fried chicken) and fish dishes. The side dishes include pasta salad, gobo (burdock) salad and potato salad, and tofu topped with leek and soy sauce. Even if you're not hungry, Osu Shokudo Meek is also a great place to stop for a quick drink, such as a nama (draft) beer or a sour (shochu-based Japanese cocktail). I recommend the refreshing lemon flavoured sour.

The overall vibe is slightly Western-meets-Japanese, with an industrial-style beamed ceiling teamed with timber seats and floorboards, and is family and couple friendly. They have a few outdoor seats, so if the weather permits, enjoy some lovely fresh air with your dinner and nama beer.

Meek is open for both lunch and dinner, and although there is no English menu, they have a range of photos of their dishes, so you can easily use the tried and tested 'point and smile' technique.

14

14

14

17

17

16

16 YAN BAR
やんバー

w   bar-navi.suntory.co.jp
A   Hibino bldg, 1F, 3–9–10 Chiyoda, Naka-ku,
    Nagoya, Aichi, 460-0012
T   090-8187-9194

BAR | Yan Bar is not to be missed. A little local gem located in an otherwise residential area, this atmospheric 20-seater bar opens at 7pm but doesn't get busy until around 9pm. If you can, try to get there before 9pm to snap up one of the cute seats in the cosy couch area by the window or at the fun counter seats. Yan Bar stays open until 4am, so better get your Uber app ready as you'll want to stay here until the trains have stopped running.

This little bar is known for its okonomiyaki (Japanese savoury pancakes), and it's quite surprising how such a small kitchen can produce such delicious okonomiyaki. You can also order yakisoba and small dishes like pickles, but the okonomiyaki is so delicious that I strongly recommend that you order it. The menu is only in Japanese, so just say 'okonomiyaki onegaishimasu', and you'll be set. For drinks, try a Shandy Gaff, recommended by Tane-san, a Nagoya local, or a gin and tonic.

The decor here is eclectic – think collector's home-meets Japanese bar. It's filled with books, quirky ornaments and retro paper lanterns hanging inside. Even if you are travelling alone, you could happily spend your time browsing the decor or reading one of the many books dotted around the bar. If you sit in the little couch area, you can chat with the charasmatic bar owner.

17 HOTEL ANDROOMS NAGOYA SAKAE
ホテル・アンドルームス名古屋栄

w   hotel-androoms.com/ans
A   3-6-8 Marunouchi, Naka-ku, Nagoya,
    Aichi, 460-0002
T   052-959-3211

STAY/HOTEL | Hotel Androoms is a wonderful place to stay. The rooms are cheap and cheerful but with design touches, and they are reasonably large by Japanese budget standards. The highlight is the amazing sento (public bath), free for guests to use.

The sento is on the same floor as the coin laundry machines and the vending machines, so it's a one-stop level. You can pop your laundry in, buy a cold can of Asahi and sit on the lounge while you wait for your washing, or better yet, relax in the bath. The sento has a large indoor bath and a small bath (comfortable for two people) outside. Men and women's bathing areas are separated, and you will need to follow the standard Japanese rules of public bathing, such as washing your body and hair and rinsing off before entering the bath. You must enter the bath naked with nothing but your body touching the bath. Your towel can be placed on your head while you're in the bath but must not touch the water.

The sento make-up counter has a wide range of facial washing products and toners, so it's also a great place to pamper yourself after a day of exploring Nagoya. In your room you'll find a cute little basket that you can use to take your towels to the sento, and then you can leave them in the laundry basket after you've finished your bath.

For breakfast, there's a restaurant on the ground level, or you can order a breakfast basket that will be delivered to your door. If you aren't quite ready for breakfast, fear not, because the coffee comes in a little thermos, so it's nice and hot for whenever you find yourself ready.

18 SITE OF REVERSIBLE DESTINY
養老天命反転地

W yoro-park.com/sp/en
A **GIFU** | Yoro Park, 1298-2 Takabayashi, Yoro, 503-1267

ATTRACTION/MUSEUM | The Site of Reversible Destiny is a mind-blowing art park: an architectural wonder, sculpture park and museum rolled into one, and it is one of my most favourite places in Japan! It's located in Yoro Park, which is situated at the foot of the Yoro Mountains in Nishimino of southwest Gifu. I recommend that you spend at least two hours in the art park itself, but you might want to spend longer in Yoro Park.

This art park is one of the many pieces by artists and architects, Arakawa and Madeline Gins. The pair make architectural artworks that deal with the perception of space, and they construct environments that challenge the body in ways to overcome death, thus reversing our destinies. As you enter the first room, the ceiling could easily be the floor, and vice versa, thanks to an array of sculptural elements that play with one's sense of perspective.

The vibrant colours both inside and out (think mustard yellow and hot pink) evoke a sense of playfulness. The park has many outdoor architectural artworks that ask the viewer to engage with them (such as climbing a large pile of giant rocks) to view the artworks from different perspectives. It's a wonderful place for creative types and kids alike who want to let off some energy.

Yoro Park can be accessed by a 15-minute walk from Yoro station, and if you're lucky, you might even get the retro Hello Kitty train when you take your journey from Nagoya to Gifu! Entrance into the Site of Reversible Destiny will cost adults ¥770.

19 SHIRAKAWA-GO
白川郷

W ml.shirakawa-go.org/en
A **GIFU** | Shirakawa, Ono, 501-5600

ATTRACTION/VILLAGE | Shirakawa-go is a mountain village in Gifu, listed as a UNESCO World Cultural Heritage. The village is filled with beautiful traditional thatched-roof homes, some of which are more than 250 years old. Shirakawa-go is divine and incredibly picturesque all year round. In summer the green is so vivid it almost looks as though you're looking through an Instagram filter, and in winter heavy snow covers the rooftops of the huts in this special little village. You will definitely want to charge your camera for this journey.

Ogimachi village nearby is the area's most famous village and the largest, and can be accessed via bus from Takayama. On my last visit I just did a daytrip, but there are many beautiful farm houses that you can stay at overnight, which operate as minshuku (B&B), where you live and eat with the owners of the farmhouse.

My recommended tour would be to start at the bus terminal and wander around the Ogimachi area to explore these thatched farm houses, and then head up to the Shiroyama viewpoint to get a view over the village. You can access the viewpoint via a walking trail, which takes approximately 20 minutes, but in winter when this trail is covered in heavy snow, jump on the shuttle bus.

If you feel like a coffee, pop into Mamekichi Honpo Shirakawa-go (240 Ogimachi, Shirakawa), which is a 1-minute walk from Shirakawa-go, or pick up some ice-cream from Shirakawa-go Aisu Kobo (321-1 Hagino, Shirakawa) while you explore.

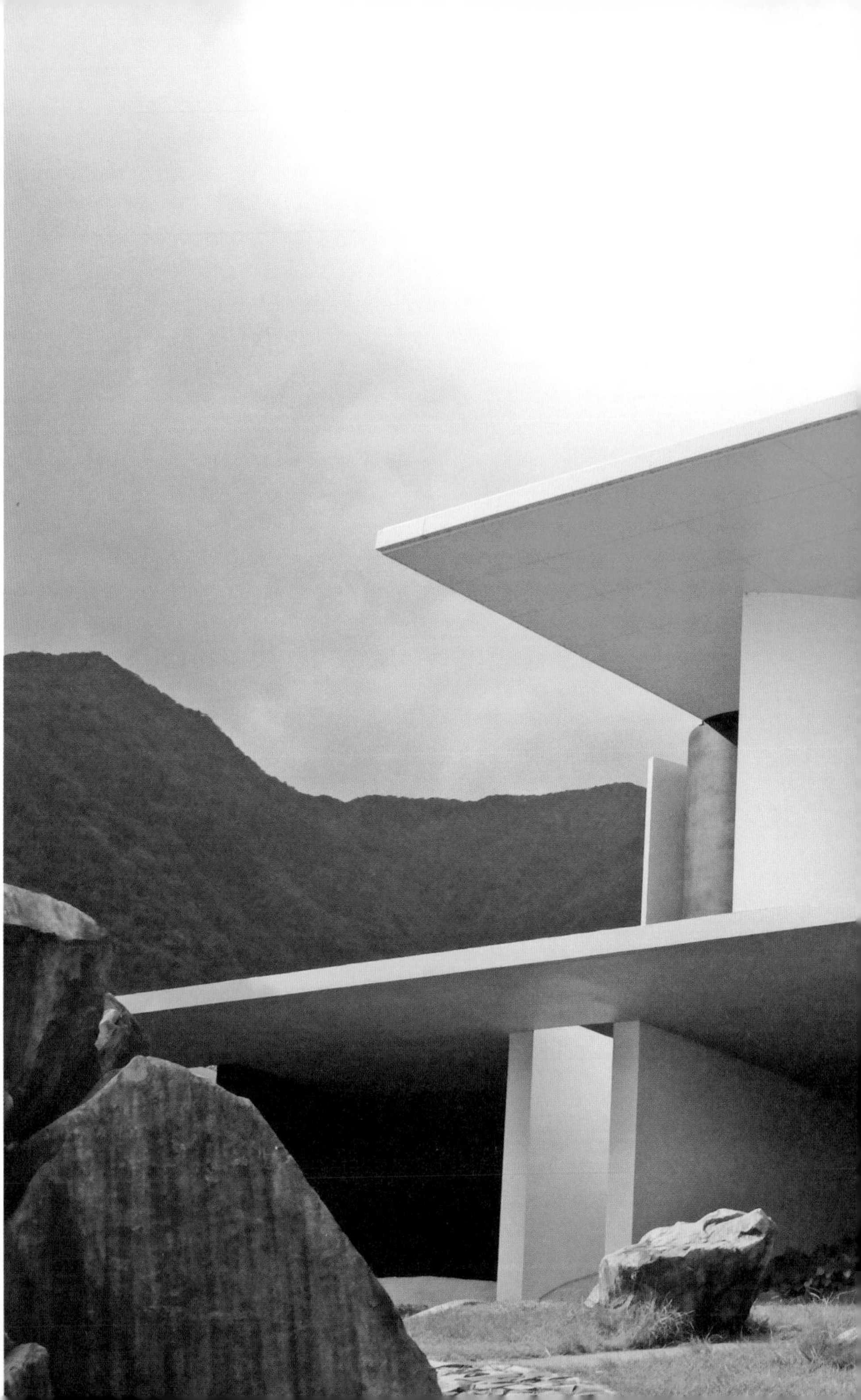

HIROSH

AN EXTREMELY
IMPORTANT
PART OF JAPAN'S
HISTORY

34.397° N
132.457° E

06

IMA

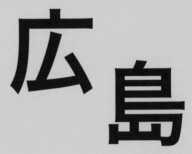

Hiroshima, geographically located in the south area of Japan, is an important historic city to visit for those who wish to witness the remains of the atomic bomb dome in Hiroshima Peace Memorial Park and learn more about World War II at the Hiroshima Peace Memorial Museum (*see* p. 162). Prepare for an extremely emotional visit, and keep those tissues handy (although bear in mind that blowing your nose in public is frowned upon in Japan, with citizens favouring sniffling to blowing their nose in a public space).

Hiroshima also has nightlife areas where you can debrief after your emotional day – head to the restaurants and izakaya (small bars) in Nagarekawa and Shin-Tenchi (*see* p. 167), you might even catch some live music. Or you can find inspiration in both the permanent collection and temporary exhibitions at the Hiroshima City Museum of Contemporary Art (*see* p. 162).

If you fancy a daytrip from Hiroshima, Itsukushima Shrine/ Miyajima (*see* p. 164) is a UNESCO World Heritage Site with a 'floating' torii gate that you might have seen in photos.

1 HIROSHIMA PEACE MEMORIAL PARK & HIROSHIMA PEACE MEMORIAL MUSEUM
広島平和記念資料館

W   hpmmuseum.jp
A   1-1 Nakajima-cho, Naka-ku, 730-0811

ATTRACTION/MUSEUM | Located in the centre of the city, the Hiroshima Peace Memorial Park and Hiroshima Peace Memorial Museum are dedicated to the legacy of Hiroshima as the first city in the world to be attacked by an atomic bomb.

The A-Bomb Dome is an important part of a visit to the Peace Memorial Park to see the impact the atomic bomb had at ground zero. This building was once the Hiroshima Prefectural Industrial Promotion Hall, until the atomic bomb was almost directly above it. The thick walls and steel dome escaped complete demolition, and the structure stands today as a UNESCO World Heritage Site.

The Hiroshima Peace Memorial Museum opened in 1955 and continues to be an extremely important part of both Japan's and Hiroshima's history. It aims to record the memories of the bomb victims, starting with accounts from people who witnessed the 6 August 1945 blast to the recovery efforts, and, heartbreakingly, includes exhibits on the effect of radiation damage on people. The displays have English information and entry is a mere ¥200. You can also rent an audio tour, which helps to give a vision of the scale and incredibly devastating impact of the bombing. I suggest allowing approximately two hours for a visit to the museum, but be sure to pack tissues for this incredibly important but overwhelming experience. Your trip to Hiroshima would not be complete without coming here.

If you need to gather your thoughts afterwards, it's only a short walk to Touka Tsuyu Coffee (*see* p. 167) for a coffee and curry.

2 HIROSHIMA CITY MUSEUM OF CONTEMPORARY ART
広島市現代美術館

W   hiroshima-moca.jp/en
A   1-1 Hijiyama-koen, Minami-ku, 732-0815
T   82-264-1121

ATTRACTION/MUSEUM | The Hiroshima City Museum of Contemporary Art, established in 1989, was the first museum in Japan dedicated exclusively to contemporary art. It hosts various changing exhibitions but also features some brilliant works in its permanent collection. Here you can expect to see all forms of contemporary art, ranging from paintings and drawings to sculptures and installation film work, by both international and Japanese artists. I recommend that you spend a couple of hours here to connect with pieces in the collection.

After exploring the museum, take a stroll in the sculpture garden and the open-air exhibition gallery to view works such as *Enclose with Stones* by Kishio Suga, which the museum recommends that you walk around to feel the rhythm of this stone artwork.

The museum is located in Hijiyama Park, which overlooks Hiroshima, making it a fantastic location to take some photos of the cityscape. If you happen to be lucky enough to visit during hanami (cherry blossom viewing) in March or April, you will be able to enjoy the most divine sakura (cherry blossom) experience.

If you have a Japan Rail (JR) Pass (*see* p. 310) you can access the museum via the free hop-on, hop-off bus, or you can pay to take the bus further up the hill. Entry to the permanent exhibits is ¥370 for adults, or ¥1,030 for entry to both the permanent and temporary exhibitions.

3 ITSUKUSHIMA SHRINE/ MIYAJIMA

厳島神社 / 宮島

W   itsukushimajinja.jp
A   1-1 Miyajima-cho, Hatsukaichi, 739-0588
T   0829-44-2020

ATTRACTION/SHRINE | Accessible in just one hour via train and ferry from Hiroshima station, Itsukushima Shrine, built in the Shinden-zukuri architectural style, is one sight not to miss when you're in Hiroshima. Famous for its seemingly floating red torii gate in the shallow water, which contrasts with the mountain backdrop, the shrine is one of Japan's most popular tourist attractions and also now a UNESCO World Heritage Site. You might have heard this shrine called Miyajima, which translates as 'shrine island'.

After the sun sets, the shrine is illuminated until 11pm and it's such an incredibly magnificent sight. Enjoy watching the lights reflect on the surrounding water, or you can take a special boat cruise for approximately half an hour, which also takes you through the red torii gate. When it's low tide, visitors can walk out and see the gate up close. However, it is most picturesque when it's high tide and the gate appears to be floating in the water.

To visit the shrine, take a short 10-minute walk from the Miyajima ferry pier and enjoy walking around the Asebihodo nature walk and Momijidani Park.

4 HIRA HIRA

ひらひら

W   coudre.shop-pro.jp
A   984-7 Kawanami, Kannabe-cho, Fukuyama-ku, 720-2124
T   0849-66-3719

SHOP/HOMEWARES /CLOTHING/ STATIONERY | Hira Hira is a lovely little zakka (homewares and lifestyle goods) shop selling items such as apparel, candles, handmade accessories, handmade ceramics, ornaments, shoes, tea and stationery. It is a perfect one-stop shop for goods by makers from Hiroshima.

Exploring the delicately crafted items is a reminder of the joy of handmade goods and a slower pace of life. I recommend the ceramic vases in the shape of the cutest little puppies by Japanese ceramic artist Tomoko Sakaguchi. You could use this so the flowers pop out of the head of the cute puppy like an adorable hat, or you could use it as a pen stand, a make-up brush holder or fill it with cotton buds or even toothpicks.

Cat or bunny rabbit lovers might like the chopstick rests made by Japanese artist Atelier Chie, who uses porcelain earth from Ehime prefecture to create these adorable handmade ceramic pieces. They come in a range of patterns and colours so you can mix and match. Your suitcase will be bulging after a stop at Hira Hira.

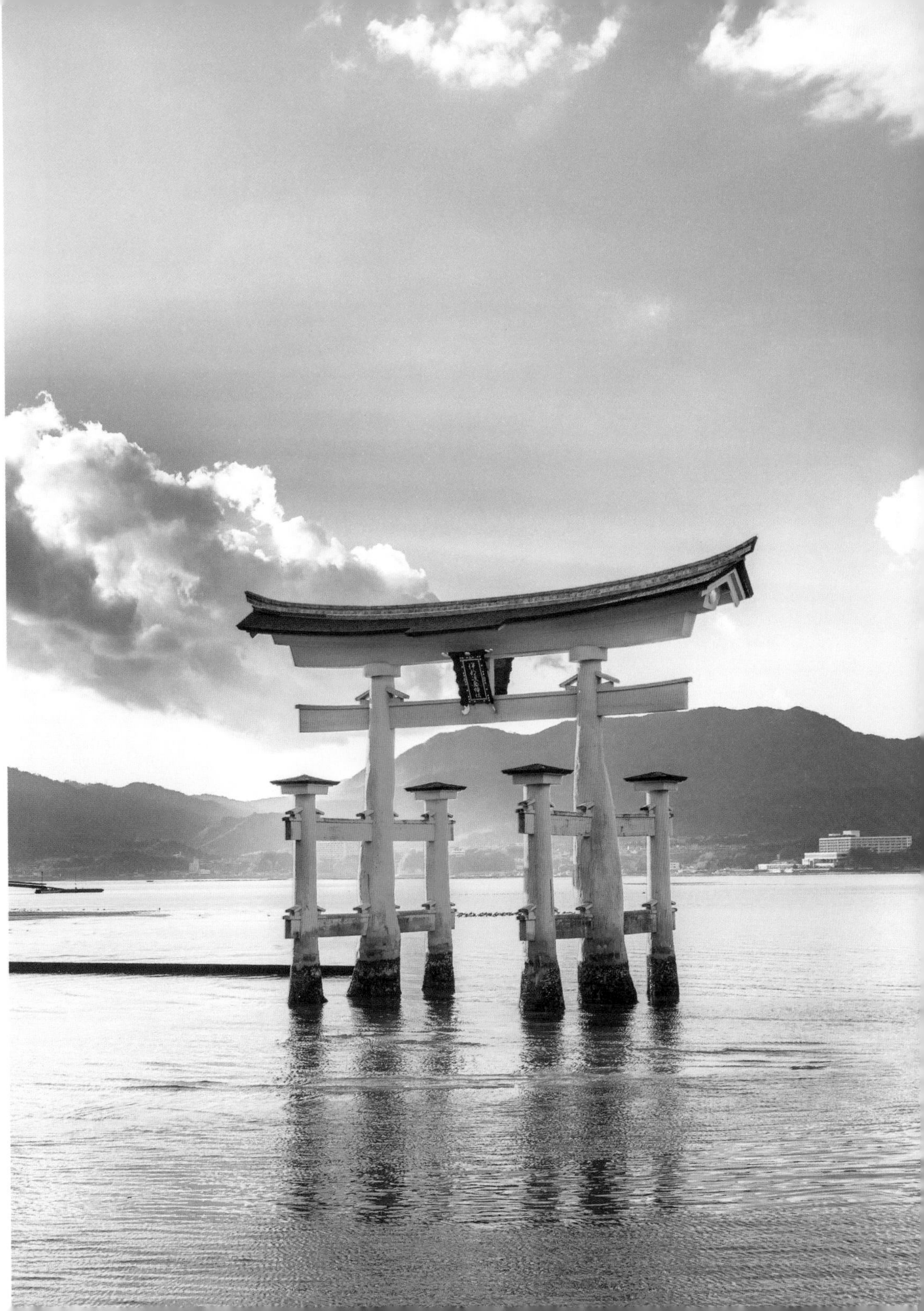

6

5 TOUKA TSUYU COFFEE
ツユコーヒー

A   2-3-3 Tokaichimachi, Naka-ku, 730-0805
T   080-7696-9333

CAFE/COFFEE | Touka Tsuyu Coffee, despite the name, serves not only coffee but also incredible curries and delicious cakes. The cosy atmosphere will warm your heart and soul. The interior style is modern with white walls, minimalist counter-stool seating and an exposed cement ceiling finished with warm touches, such as dried floral arrangements and timber finishes. It is definitely a recommended spot during your stay in Hiroshima.

The breakfast set is toast, soup and a soft-boiled egg, or enjoy a cake or delicious chocolate-chip scone in the afternoon. During regular meal times, don't miss the popular green curry. I also recommend the toast with the homemade ginger butter. The butter is made with chopped ginger mixed with sweet spices and will be certain to warm your heart. You can also buy coffee beans, cakes and cookies to take away! Imagine enjoying a take-away coffee with some cookies by the riverside. Divine!

The cafe is open early from 7.30am, and the lunch service runs from 11.30am until 2pm. At the time of research it had a 4.8-star rating online, which is almost unheard of.

Located beside the river and overlooking Sorazay Park, just a short walk from the Hiroshima Peace Memorial Park (*see* p. 162), it's a relaxing place to reset your mind after a visit to the site of the atomic bomb.

6 NAGAREKAWA AND SHIN-TENCHI BARS
流川・新天地のバー

A   2F, 8-27 Nagarekawa, Naka-ku, 730-0028 (A.M bar) & Ondo Onsen bldg, B1F, 6-3 Tanakamachi, Naka-ku (Ondo Ongaku Shokudo)
T   082-249-6677 (A.M bar) & 082-245-9563 (Ondo Ongaku Shokudo)

BARS | When it comes to nightlife in Hiroshima, look no further than the streets lined with small bars and dining venues in the Nagarekawa and Shin-Tenchi areas. Here you will find many small izakaya (small bars) and restaurants to fulfil any type of craving. Enjoy walking along these streets and pick whatever options take your fancy.

If you're after a late-night drink, head to A.M., a tiny bar with a fantastic atmosphere and draft beer for ¥400. You can snack on a panini sandwich or a simple pizza, and they also have a range of live music events – if you're lucky enough to happen across one.

If you are looking for a more substantial meal, look no further than Ondo Ongaku Shokudo. Located in the basement space of Ondo Onsen, this is a wonderful place to enjoy a teishoku (meal set) with a main dish, rice and miso soup. Ongaku means music and, as the name suggests, this is a big part of the appeal of this restaurant. The cafe walls are lined with records upon records. It even hosts the occasional flea market. This is really your one-stop shop!

A.M. and Ondo Ongaku Shokudo are only a 2-minute walk away from each other in the Nagarekawa area. From there you can walk 5 minutes towards Shin-Tenchi, where you will find other bars along the way. Walk a few minutes further, beyond Shin-Tenchi, and you will find Okonomimura, where you can try Hiroshima-style okonomiyaki (Japanese savoury pancake), which traditionally has noodles in it.

SEASONS

WINTER

Japan is truly a country of four distinct seasons. My favourite season is winter, when cafes hand out blankets for your lap and serve hot wine, and convenience stores are filled with winter specialties, such as oden and nikuman (steamed pork buns).

While Christmas is mostly celebrated by couples on Christmas Eve, New Year's Day is the most celebrated family holiday in Japan. Most shops close from 31 December until around 7 January. Houses are often decorated with New Year's wreathes and special bamboo and pine tree decorations to welcome a fresh, happy and healthy new year. Before 31 December, Japanese households busy themselves by cleaning their house extremely thoroughly. Blinds, windows, even those pesky places, such as under the fridge and so on, are scrubbed. This means that people are able to start the new year fresh. Just moments before the clock strikes midnight, it is customary to eat toshikoshi (literally to cross over the year) soba. The soba should be eaten in long pieces to symbolise longevity and good fortune. On the morning of 1 January (or 2 January, if the first day is not possible), many Japanese go to hatsumode (the first visit to the shrine for the year) and make a wish for good fortune for the coming year.

Winter is the perfect time to enjoy sitting under kotatsu (low heated Japanese coffee tables), eating nabe (hotpot), frolicking in the snow, trying the heat pads that you can buy from the pharmacy that keep your hands warm, and is also the best time for the sales when the stores open back up after the New Year holidays.

Please keep in mind that most things are closed between 31 December and 7 January.

SPRING

Spring is divine in Japan. Schools reopen as the flowers bloom. If you're lucky you might catch the very fleeting hanami (cherry blossom viewing). There are some early blooming ume (plum trees) that flower in February in some parts of Japan, which, although more sparse on the trees than the sakura (cherry blossom), are a more vibrant pink colour and very beautiful. A fantastic place to see these is Hanegi Park in Tokyo's Umegaoka (literally plum blossom hills), which is only a 10-minute train ride from Shinjuku station or an even shorter trip from Shimokitazawa. Take the stairs to the top of the park and you will see tables to sit at to enjoy watching the blossoms.

Once the sakura come into bloom, there are a range of places that I recommend to enjoy hanami parties. Tokyo's Yoyogi-koen (park) is a popular one and is always crowded with an incredibly festive atmosphere. Everyone brings a picnic sheet (like a tarpaulin mat that can be bought from many convenience stores, supermarkets or ¥100 stores) and enjoys drinks and snacks under the beautiful blossoms. You should take your shoes off before standing or sitting on the picnic sheets. I love walking around the park seeing the neat little rows of shoes all lined up. Oh, Japan! For a less busy atmosphere, try Inokashira Park in Tokyo's Kichijoji area (*see* p. 6). I like to visit this park at the end of sakura season, when the petals start to fall into the lake and create a sakura petal lake.

Yozakura (night sakura) is popular in Tokyo's Nakameguro area (*see* p. 30), when the canal is lit up with pink and white lanterns, each with the name of a local shop who have sponsored the payment of the lantern. And my pro tip is to catch the train to Nakameguro and stand near the end of the train platform, where you can get a photo of all of the sakura trees over the canal.

There are often many photographers there when the trees are in full bloom.

If you're in Kyoto during spring, Kiyomizu-dera (*see* p. 74) temple grounds has over 1500 sakura (cherry blossom) trees and is very beautiful. When you're in Hiroshima, you must not miss Hijiyama Park (*see* p. 162) for both its hanami (cherry blossom viewing) and its views over the city.

SUMMER

Summer is a difficult season for me. Every year I say that I am going to move to Hokkaido from May to October, because the humidity in Tokyo (and most of Honshu) is unbearably humid. Heat-strokes are common in summer and many people die from them every year. You'll see people walking with sun-protecting umbrellas, large stores let off a mist to try and cool down the streets and businesses relax the dress code to 'cool biz', where short sleeves and tie-less attire is allowed. If you look at the temperature it doesn't look so bad, but I promise you the humidity is unbearable. Unless you love free hot yoga vibes for months on end, or plan to only visit Hokkaido, I suggest travelling out of these months.

If you do find yourself in Japan in the summer months, you can enjoy summer festivals, such as Awaodori, where the streets of local neighbourhoods are filled with traditional Japanese dance. Each suburb has a different weekend date for these and the most popular in Tokyo is Koenji Awaodori, which gets extremely crowded. You can also find street vendors selling summer snacks, like cucumbers dipped in miso on sticks, and festival favourites like karaage (fried chicken) and takoyaki (fried octopus). Many stores also have a summer sale, so if you are in need of some air-conditioning, you can spend your time inside shopping complexes.

AUTUMN

Autumn is my second-favourite season in Japan. That relief that summer is finally over! It's also a beautiful time to travel to nature-filled places such as Hakone (*see* p. 52) or Mt Takao (*see* p. 54) and see the changing colours of the leaves. Tokyo's Yoyogi-koen (park) is also a beautiful spot to see the changing of the leaves. Japanese people love Halloween, so the shops and celebrations for Halloween and all things pumpkin are big during these months. You can find seasonal pumpkin flavoured drinks and sweets at cafes, and chestnuts are cooked into rice and served in bentos available during the autumn months.

NAGANO

THE DREAMIEST
NATURE SPOT EVER

36.643° N
138.189° E

07

長野

If you adore nature and fancy a getaway from Tokyo, Nagano is a beautiful must-visit while you're in Japan. Lake Kizaki (*see* p. 174) is where you can fish, picnic and canoe, and you can even stay lakeside in one of the cute, retro timber cabins (*see* p. 182) and wake up inspired to draw or write about nature.

Enjoy soaking in Nagano's plethora of onsen (hot springs), some of which are even free of charge, such as Nozawa Onsen (*see* p. 179). Nozawa Onsen village is also a fantastic place for snowboarding and skiing in winter. Don't miss Ch. Books (*see* p. 179) for local Nagano zines, and Marking Records (*see* p. 180) for its collection of independent music from around the globe.

Those with an international driver's license can drive to Nagano or rent a car upon arrival. This way you're able to visit the less populated mountains and cities.

1 LAKE KIZAKI
木崎湖

W   kizakiko.com
A   10521 Tairamori, Omachi, 398-0001

ATTRACTION/NATURE | Lake Kizaki
is one of Nagano's most beautiful lakes. Here
you can enjoy fishing, sightseeing, canoeing
and even sitting on the jetty and having
a picnic, like I did. I've visited this park
numerous times, and it's such a special place.
I highly recommend you come here, and you
might even like to stay in the lakeside cabins
(*see* p. 182). Surrounded by mountains, the
beautiful lake is a peaceful spot to have a
meditative rest.

I recommend packing a picnic rug, some
snacks and a thermos of coffee, and spending
a delightful afternoon dangling your feet off
the edge of the jetty and soaking up nature.
On one of our visits a dragonfly came and
joined our picnic and it sat right on my
friend's fingertip. This little dragonfly must
have known she was a local!

Like many things in Nagano's nature,
the lake is most easily accessed by car, and
you can find an entrance where you are able
to park just near the jetty. However, if you
can't rent a car, it's also accessible via three
stations near the lake: Shinano-Kizaki, Inao,
and Uminokuchi, all on the JR Ōito line.

This mesotrophic lake is approximately
2.7km (1.7 miles) long and is so special it even
features in the anime series *Onegai Teacher*
and *Onegai Twins*. Definitely one to add to
your Nagano list!

2 TOGAKUSHI JINJA
戸隠神社

W   togakushi-jinja.jp
A   3506 Togakushi, Chusha, 381-4101

ATTRACTION/SHRINE | Togakushi
Jinja is one of Nagano's most famous shrines
and has a history spanning over 2,000 years.
The entrance to the main shrine, on Okusha
road, is lined with sugi trees that have stood
strong for over 400 years. This dreamlike
walkway continues for about 500 metres
(1,640 feet). It's the type of grand entrance
that is spiritual and picturesque at all times
of the day. If you visit in the morning you
will notice the strong light beams through
the middle of the sugi trees, but if you visit
on a misty day, it's absolutely spectacular and
mystical to watch the fog drift between the
massive tree trunks. On the day we visited, it
was clear-ish weather upon arrival, however
as time passed, the most incredible mist
flowed over us and turned our experience and
photos into moments seemingly captured
from a Ghibli film.

Originally, Togakushi Jinja was known
as a place of worship for the god of good
harvest, and even today some people bring
rice with them to offer them to the god.

The shrine can be accessed by bus
number 70 from Nagano station (bound
for Togakushi Kogen via Loop Bridge) and
takes approximately one hour. During winter
the route changes, so be sure to check the
website for the access details as it involves
taking a taxi from Chusha.

2

2

1

3 ZENKOJI TEMPLE
善光寺

W   zenkoji.jp
A   491 Naganomotoyoshi-cho, 380-0851
T   0262-34-3591

ATTRACTION/TEMPLE | Zenkoji is Nagano's most famous Buddhist temple and is located in the centre of the city. This beautiful temple was built in the 7th century, and the modern city was actually built around it. It was founded before Buddhism split into two different sects in Japan, and it still belongs to both the Tendai and Jodoshu schools of Buddhism. Over 30 priests take pride in looking after this temple, and it includes a main hall, a history museum, statues and gates.

Be sure to enjoy the beautiful grounds, especially the stunning weeping tree, and during hanami (cherry blossom viewing) season you can enjoy the sakura (cherry blossom) trees. The lead-up to the Sanmon gate is lined with small shops and restaurants which are interesting to peek into but you may just find a lovely and special Nagano keepsake here, or try a snack from one of the street-food vendors.

The temple is the perfect way to spend a day when you need a break from snow sports! It's said to be the third-largest temple in Japan, so there is plenty to see here!

It's accessible from Nagano station via a 30-minute walk or a city bus that runs directly from the station to the temple.

4 JIGOKUDANI MONKEY PARK
地獄谷野猿公苑

W   jigokudani-yaenkoen.co.jp
A   6845 Hirao, Yamanochi, Shimotakai, 381-0401

ATTRACTION/NATURE | A popular tourist attraction in Nagano is the Jigokudani Monkey Park (although it might not be for everyone), located in the valley of Kokoyu River in north Nagano. With an altitude of 850 metres (2,788 feet), this special place is covered by snow for almost one-third of the year, and the hot springs are a paradise for Japanese Macaques (known as snow monkeys), who love bathing and playing in the warm water. These snow monkeys are accustomed to humans, so they can be observed from a very close distance without being bothered. Be careful not to touch or feed the monkeys, though, as this is strictly prohibited.

The monkey park is open all year round, with varying hours depending on the season and weather. There are a couple of options to get to the park, one with a 40-minute walk through the forest after a bus trip to Kanbayashi Onsen, and the other is a 15-minute walk from the parking area of Jigokudani Monkey Park. Admission costs ¥800 for adults.

If your travel schedule doesn't allow you to visit in real life, you can view the monkeys on the live camera available on the website.

3

4

4

5

6

5 NOZAWA ONSEN
野沢温泉

A   Nozawa Onsen village

**ATTRACTION/SKI RESORT/ONSEN/
VILLAGE** | Nozawa Onsen is one of Japan's
most beautiful and popular ski resorts
and onsen villages. Actually, it is home to
Hello Sandwich's very first snowboarding
lesson. Needless to say, the onsen came in
very handy for relaxing after all of those
snowboarding falls!

In fact, there are 13 free onsen in this
village, and they are the perfect way to
unwind after a day on the slopes. Many of
them are housed in beautiful, traditional
Japanese buildings scattered all around
the town. Some of the onsen have a few
baths with various temperatures. I learnt
the hard way many, many years ago, well
before I moved to Japan, that quite often
the bath with no one in it is the one that is
unbelievably hot! So please be warned!

Not only is this town perfect for skiing,
snowboarding and onsen, but it has a lively
festival and community feel with shops,
ryokans (traditional Japanese inns), bars
and restaurants.

Ogama hot spring is also a lovely place to
visit to treat yourself and warm up your feet
after exploring this charming village.

6 CH. BOOKS
チャンネルブックス

W   chan-nel.jp
A   1069 Minami Agatamachi, 380-0836
T   0262-17-5687

SHOP/BOOKSHOP | Ch. Books is a new
bookstore focusing on the theme of 'travel
and art' and is undeniably Nagano's hippest
bookstore, full of art books and handprinted
zines. It's a wonderful place to be inspired on
your Japan journey, and many of the zines
feature local Nagano photography.

If you take one look at the entrance to the
shop, you will instantly notice the eclectic
and creative nature of this store. Think cute
potted plants, flyers and free papers for
local creative events scattered on a bench
for people passing by to collect, and also
the windows are covered with posters of
publications, films and music events.

It even has a morning cafe open from
11am until 6pm on weekends, catering to
those who love starting their weekends with
some creative inspiration. I recommend
trying the original blended black tea.

On my last visit, I had such a relaxing
time here and stocked up on local travel
photography zines capturing the small but
beautifully significant details of everyday
life in Japan. A local souvenir that one can
absolutely cherish for ever.

The 2nd floor of the store, although not
accessible to visitors, is a working space for
designers, editors and writers.

7 MARKING RECORDS

w markingrecords.com
A 3-12-8 Chuo, Matsumoto-ku, 390-0811

SHOP/VINYL | Record lovers won't want to miss Marking Records, a small but impeccably curated store that collects the best independent music from all over the world. It also sells a range of zines, cassette tapes and CDs. It's a one-stop shop. Oh, and did I mention there is also a bar counter so you can enjoy a lovely break while you sip on a coffee or something a little stiffer!

The interior is like the shop: cool and modern but unpretentious. The people in Nagano are among Japan's kindest, and this shop is no exception. Flick through the records in the timber boxes or enjoy looking at the CDs on display in the cute timber purpose-made stands. And just behind the counter you will find a selection of cute tote bags that are super handy to carry your vinyl home in!

Marking Records regularly updates its Instagram with new vinyl so you don't miss out on any gems!

8 MIASA CAFE
美麻珈琲

w miasacoffee.com
A 14902-1 Mima, Omachi-ku, 399-9101
T 0261-23-1102

CAFE | Miasa Cafe is a heavenly little coffee shop hidden in the middle of an open grassy field at the base of a beautiful mountain park. The building, with its white textured surface and timber chateau-style roof, makes it feel as though you have stumbled across a fairy tale. Something more akin to the alps in Austria than in the middle of Japan, the atmosphere is just so dreamy!

Head up the rustic timber stairs, which are like something out of a ski lodge, and take a seat by the window to overlook the park greenery and mountains. My friend who took me to this special place is a local and adores nature, so you can be assured that this is one of the best hidden spots in Nagano.

If the charm of the building and the surroundings are not enough for you, the food is also delicious here. The cheesecake is incredible, as is the chai.

Enjoy walking around the park outside the cafe after your treat. Just to the left of the cafe is a little timber hut that looks so enchanting! Have your camera ready and be sure to dance in the fields like they do in *The Sound of Music.*

9 HIRANO COFFEE
平野珈琲

A 981 Tatema-chi, 380-0864

CAFE/COFFEE | Those who love timber interiors, slow time and black-drip coffee will love Hirano Coffee. Located less than a kilometre from Gondo station, it's the perfect place to escape the snowy weather in winter or cool down with a refreshing iced-coffee in summer. Its location is right near Zenkoji Temple (*see* p. 176), making it a fantastic place to relax after your temple visit.

It is set in a machiya (traditional house) full of beautiful timber beams and sliding doors with Showa-era (1926–89) glass. The interior features rustic timber with spot lighting that creates an even cosier feel to the already warm space and is decorated with dried floral arrangements. Even the coffee bean jars and various coffee-making apparatus become beautiful decorations in themselves.

Head up to the 2nd floor and sit near the window to overlook Nagano passing by. Enjoy sweets, cakes or toast with your coffee. Time stands still at Hirano Coffee. Enjoy the divine peace and tranquility.

w n45cafe.com
A 1-7-7 Minami Chitose, 380-0823

w kizakiko.com
A 10521 Tairamori, Omachi, 398-0001
T 0261-23-3939

CAFE/COFFEE/BAR | N4.5 opened in January 2020 in the Minami Chitose area, just a 6-minute walk from Nagano station. You won't miss it with its almost completely black, chic exterior and interior. This new hip place really offers it all, with the cafe open from 11am until 11pm (lunch 11am to 2pm, dinner 5pm to 11pm).

You can enjoy espresso here and select from two different types of coffee beans, and have the most relaxing coffee break with a homemade cheesecake, pudding or a lemon cake. For lunch, I recommend trying one of the three types of hot dogs: plain, cheese or chilli sauce. There's also a range of alcoholic drinks. During summer you can also find kakigori (shaved-ice dessert). It's definitely something to try if you haven't before!

Be sure to check N4.5's Instagram for various pop-up events. They also sell some original merchandise, such as eco tote bags. I recommend picking one up and supporting this new business.

STAY | If you love Lake Kizaki (*see* p. 174) so much and all that your heart desires is to wake up to the soft sound of the lake, the bright sun and birdsong, then you might like to stay here. It is such a dreamy way to wake up! Can you imagine sipping your morning coffee overlooking this beautiful lake! The experience is beyond words in such a simple and perfect way.

The campground has rental tents for two to four people for ¥2,000. My personal favourite, however, are the adorable timber cabins that vary in size, accommodating from two to eight people. The cabins would be the perfect artist's retreat, waking up and drawing or journalling all day, or even writing some poetry or playing a guitar. Prices range from ¥1,500 to ¥2,000 per person. While no reservations are required for the tent sites, you will need to make a reservation for the cabins – either online or over the phone.

There are showers at the campground, and it has a range of barbecue facilities, so you can cook on location! The campground is only open April to November.

SHIOGAM

塩竈

QUIET AND
PICTURESQUE
SEASIDE TOWNS

38.317° N
141.022° E

08

A & MATSUSHIMA

松島

Shiogama and Matsushima are towns to be explored for a less touristy and quieter experience than in the cities. These towns are close to Ishinomaki, and all were strongly hit by the 2011 Tohoku earthquake and tsunami off the Pacific Coast. The seaside villages are slowly rebuilding, and I strongly encourage visiting the Tohoku region to help with the recovery of these beautiful towns.

Shiogama (*see* p. 189), located close to Sendai train station where the shinkansen (bullet train) stops, is a town I adore because of its slow seaside port feel, and you can also visit the beautiful Shiogama Sugimura Jun Museum of Art (*see* p. 190) and the gallery and shop Birdo Flugas (*see* p. 190). In Matsushima, you must go to Fukuura Island (*see* p. 186) for an amazing view of Matsushima bay. These locations are best explored with a car but are also possible without.

1 FUKUURA ISLAND
福浦島

A   **MATSUSHIMA** | 39 Matsushima, Miyagi,
    981-0213
T   022-354-3457

ATTRACTION/NATURE | When in
Matsushima you should visit Fukuurajima
(Fukuura Island), which is accessible by
walking across the 252-metre (826-foot)
Fukuura Bridge. This beautiful red bridge
was damaged in the 2011 tsunami but has
since been repaired. It costs ¥200 to cross the
bridge, but once you reach Fukuura Island,
you can enjoy one of Matsushima's few pine
tree–covered islands.

The island is a fantastic place to view
Matsushima Bay. I also love the view of the
tiny little islands, imagining hiding away on
one of these treasure island type places. If
you walk along the trail through the island,
you will see the delightful natural botanical
garden, featuring more than 300 species
of flowers, trees and plants. The walk will
take approximately one hour at a slow
and peaceful pace.

You can visit the island year-round from
8am until 5pm, although it closes 30 minutes
earlier in the winter months (Nov–Feb) when
it gets dark earlier. I recommend taking
a moment to enjoy some slow nature life
during your trip to Matsushima, and Fukuura
Island is the perfect place to do so!

And fear not, your ¥200 will cover your
round-trip back over the bridge, so you won't
get stuck on Fukuura Island and have to 'live
off the land', as the saying goes.

2 NATURAL PIER UMANOSE IN RIFU
天然の桟橋 馬の背／利府町

A   **MATSUSHIMA** | Hitsugasawa Akanuma,
    Rifu, Miyagi, 981-0101

ATTRACTION/NATURE | This
incredible natural pier juts out into Rifu
sea and is a must-see when in Matsushima!
Formed by years of waves carving out the
amazing geological shape, this natural pier
can be walked along very, very carefully. It
gets very narrow at one point, so hold onto
your phones and handbags, people! My
advice is to walk like when you're riding a
bike through a skinny section – rather than
focusing on hitting the poles on the side, you
have to look forward, otherwise a wrong step
could easily end up with a foot in the water.

To access this beautiful natural pier, you
can take the Senseki train line from Hamada
Rikuzen station, and then it's a 25-minute
walk. Or if you're already in Matsushima you
can easily take a taxi to the entrance area. If
you're driving, take the 45 route and stop at
Umanose (Japanese for horseback). Although
very close to Matsushima town, you will feel
miles away in this little hidden oasis.

芭蕉コース巡り

3

4

3

3 SHIOGAMA
塩竈

A   5 Higashitamagawa-cho, Shiogama,
Miyagi, 985-0036

ATTRACTION/TOWN | Located
between Sendai and Matsushima is a lovely
little seaport town called Shiogama. I've
visited this town a number of times to host
workshops, and I absolutely adore it, partly
because of the beautiful local people that
have showed me around. I also love to try
and help bring tourism back to places that
were hit hard by the 2011 tsunami. That's not
hard in this charming, retro town, which
is the kind of place that time left behind in
many ways.

On one visit, after my workshop was
finished, I spent the day walking around
in the rain with my Japanese see-through
clear plastic umbrella, taking photos of
the beautiful Showa-era (1926–89) retro
shopfronts and local neighbourhood.
Although there is a range of galleries,
restaurants and shrines, the real charm here
for me are the people and the shopfronts.

If you're travelling between Sendai and
the popular tourist area of Matsushima,
I absolutely recommend a little stop in
Shiogama. It's heartbreaking to imagine the
tsunami hitting this gorgeous town, but the
seaside here is so divine it's absolutely worth
a visit!

Make sure you pop into the Shiogama
Sugimura Jun Museum of Art (*see* p. 190) and
Birdo Flugas (*see* p. 190).

4 SHICHIGAHAMA
七ヶ浜町

A   Ohyama, Hanabuchihama,
Shichigahama-machi, Miyagi, 985-8577

ATTRACTION/TOWN | Shichigahama
is a small, quiet seaside town in Miyagi
prefecture. With a population of less than
20,000 people, it's set in beautiful nature.
Shichigahama, which means 'seven beaches'
is one of the seven seaside villages that make
up this lovely little area.

The area is famous for its stunning
beaches and the popular fishing industry.
Table Beach is one beach definitely not to
miss, and I also recommend the striking red
torii (gate) by the seaside in Gotenzaki.

With its close proximity to Ishinomaki,
this town was hit badly by the 2011 tsunami.
Many homes here were destroyed, and over
95 per cent of the town's rice fields were
flooded with water. After a long period of
rebuilding, many of the locals were able to
rebuild their houses and resume daily life
in Shichigahama.

This area is unique in the freestanding
rock formations that are scattered organically
along the coast. Coming from New South
Wales in Australia and doing weekend trips
to coastal Culburra, this is an uncommon
sight that for me makes the experience even
more unique. There's something quite special
about looking out over the sea in a foreign
country thinking about places on the other
side of the ocean and how different the
seascape is there.

5 SHIOGAMA SUGIMURA JUN MUSEUM OF ART

塩竈市杉村惇美術館

W   sugimurajun.shiomo.jp
A   8-1, Honmachi, Shiogama-ku,
    Miyagi, 985-0052
T   022-362-2555

ATTRACTION/MUSEUM | The Shiogama Sugimura Jun Museum of Art is Shiogama's most beautiful gallery. It's a divine historic museum with the most stunning architecture, featuring an almost 10-metre (32-foot) high curved timber ceiling. Built in 1950, the museum itself opened in November 2014.

It features a permanent collection of works by Jun Sugimura, and also a range of temporary exhibitions featuring the work of Japanese artists, such as Akiko Abe.

The main hall is used not only as a public hall and art museum, but as a space to connect citizens and visitors alike through various cultural activities like markets and a range of workshop events, where you can learn skills like lacquerware and weaving. In addition, the museum aims to foster a friendly and cultural environment by hosting various live music events, swing dance parties and historic photo exhibitions. It is a wonderful place for those who would like to engage in the creative arts, but also for those who are interested in the history of Shiogama, which, unfortunately, was hit strongly by the 2011 tsunami.

The cinema lounge is an area where visitors can engage in a discourse session about movies whilst enjoying coffee and sweets.

It's clear that this local museum is run by a forward-thinking contemporary team of staff, and it's absolutely worth visiting during your Shiogama trip.

6 BIRDO FLUGAS

ビルドフルーガス

A   2-3-11 Minatomachi, Shiogama-ku,
    Miyagi, 985-0016
T   080-3198-4818

ATTRACTION/GALLERY/SHOP | Birdo Flugas is a small gallery and shop located on the ground floor of a residential space in Shiogama. This lovely little gallery showcases work from a wide range of Japanese artists, including sculptors and painters.

At the front of the gallery space, you will find a little shop selling cute handmade items, such as stationery, homewares, artworks and a range of locally made zines by Japanese artists.

Birdo Flugas gallery also hosts various pop-up events, such as the mt masking tape workshop that I hosted a few years back. There is the most divine light coming in through the large windows at the back of the gallery space that open onto a cute terrace, which gives a peaceful vibe to your overall experience. When I hosted the workshop here, I noticed just what an incredible community spirit Shiogama and Birdo Flugas has, with everyone knowing each other and kids meeting their friends at this creative space. It was so heartwarming!

You can access the gallery via a 7-minute walk from Hon-Shiogama train station. Please do yourself a favour and visit this gorgeous space while you're in Shiogama. And say hello to Aya-san from me at Hello Sandwich!

7 SHIOGAMAKOU SUSHI
塩釜港寿司

A 18-1 Noda, Shiogama, Miyagi, 985-0035
T 022-367-3838

RESTAURANT/SUSHI | Just a 10-minute walk from Shiogama station, you will find Shiogamakou Sushi, one of Sendai's most famous sushi restaurants. Although it's a conveyor-belt sushi restaurant, the sushi here is incredibly fresh, and the fish are sourced mostly from the coastal waters off Shiogama, which are some of the best fishing waters in all of Japan.

I was taken to Shiogamakou Sushi by the co-organiser of a workshop that I ran on mt masking tape. She brought her friends along, and it felt incredible to be sitting with my new friends in such a lively sushi restaurant. There was even a queue to enter, which is always a great sign of a quality restaurant. Visit early to avoid having to queue.

Not only is the flavour and freshness of this sushi incredible, it is also cheap, ranging from ¥140 to ¥650 per plate of two sushi pieces. You can sit at tables along the conveyor belt, but there are also tables scattered throughout the restaurant. And no matter where you sit, you are free to order off the menu. Green tea is served free of charge with your sushi. Enjoy the fresh sushi of Shiogama!

AKITA

A WINTERY
WONDERLAND
WHEN IT'S COVERED
IN SNOW

39.717° N
140.129° E

09

秋田

Travel in Japan during the cooler seasons and a trip from Tokyo to Akita is the perfect winter getaway. It is so easy to be transported into the depths of the snowfields with only a one-hour flight from Tokyo. It's almost as simple as popping your snow boots into an overnight bag and heading to Haneda airport (*see* p. 309). Akita offers a wintery white wonderland, where you can enjoy that amazing swish of snow beneath your feet and snowflakes falling softly upon your nose. You can also experience beautiful temples, steaming hot bowls of udon and local hospitality. If you visit in February, you can step inside a snow globe during the kamakura (igloo) festival at Minkaen Kido Gorobei village (*see* p. 198).

If you're a manga fan, you should head to Yokote Masuda Manga Museum (*see* p. 196) and, even if you're not into manga, it's a retro-cool place to step back in time to the '80s. In Akita, you can also experience a special Kanto lantern balancing performance at the Kanto Festival Center (*see* p. 201), see a maiko (geisha in training) dance performance at Akita Maiko (*see* p. 202) and have a traditional obento lunch at the Akita Cultural and Industrial Facility afterwards (*see* p. 207). Akita prefecture has unique udon, and a tour of Yosuke Sato Sohonten (*see* p. 204) will show you how it's made. You might also like to vist Takashimizu Sake Brewery (*see* p. 202) for sake tastings.

1 YOKOTE MASUDA MANGA MUSEUM
横手市増田まんが美術館

W   manga-museum.com
A   285 Shinmachi, Masudamachi, Masuda, Yokote, 019-0701
T   018-245-5569

ATTRACTION/MUSEUM | Established in 1995 and known as Japan's first manga-themed art museum, the Yokote Masuda Manga Museum houses more than 220,000 original drawings by approximately 179 manga artists. The museum is not only a fantastic spot to soak up some manga, but also a brilliant place to feel as though you have stepped back in time to an '80s amusement park. The bright red and pale blue upholstery is a perfect backdrop to the Akita manga displayed so colourfully on the many shelves.

The museum includes work by Leiji Matsumoto, the creator of *Galaxy Express 999*; Yōichi Takahashi, the creator of Captain Tsubasa; and Shigeru Tsuchiyama, author of *Kuishinbo!* The original artworks are stored in temperature and humidity safe glass cases for the protection of these historic artwork gems.

The museum also features a manga cafe on the 1st floor, which serves dishes such as sandwiches, pastas, desserts and drinks. There is also a dedicated vegan menu. You need to order your food through a ticket machine, but the menu can be changed to English and also features photos, which makes ordering that little bit easier. Don't forget to pop into the museum shop and pick up a tote bag or postcard as a gorgeous keepsake, too.

The museum is located about 30 minutes by taxi or car from Yokote station in the Masuda area, which is full of interesting warehouses and timber homes that were constructed between 1850 and 1920.

2 AKITA MUSEUM OF ART
秋田県立美術館

W   akita-museum-of-art.jp
A   1-4-2 Nakadori, 010-0001
T   018-853-8686

ATTRACTION/MUSEUM | Akita Museum of Art used to be in a nearby retro building, but now the collection is housed in a new building designed by renowned architect Tadao Ando. The grand minimalistic entrance showcases a large staircase set against concrete walls and a triangular roof. The museum aims to serve by connecting Akita's local citizens and visitors with easy access to artworks. It is located in the centre of Akita in front of Senshu Park.

On display is a painting by Léonard Tsuguharu Foujita, which illustrates Akita life during the four seasons. This extremely large work remarkably escaped damage during World War II and is the focal point of the museum's collection.

After enjoying the artwork, you may like a cup of coffee or tea in the peaceful museum cafe, which overlooks the former museum building. The museum shop offers a range of art and design books, and also a small library of books featuring both Japanese and international artists.

The museum's aim of being accessible to all is reflected in the entry fee admission, which is a mere ¥310. It's such a lovely way to spend a few hours (and also a great way to keep warm if you're visiting in the snow season).

2

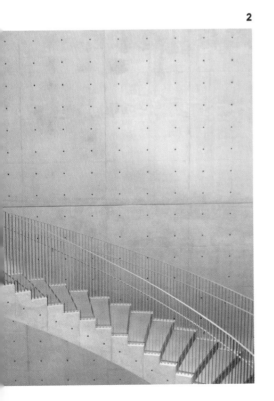

2

1

3 MASUDA TOWN
増田町

W masudakanko.com/en/uchigura
A 53 Masuda-Kamimachi, Masuda-machi,
Yokote-shi, (Masuda Tourist Information
Center/Hotaru)
T 018-223-6331

ATTRACTION/NEIGHBOURHOOD |
Take a stroll around the beautiful
neighbourhood of Masuda, an incredible
historical area – not unlike a movie set –
known for being one of the places in Akita
where the snow falls heaviest. It's easy to
grasp a sense of Akita's history through
the traditional architecture in Masuda,
although, in true Hello Sandwich fashion,
I am particularly drawn to the Showa-era
(1926–89) buildings here, with their faded
signs and retro qualities.

Once a bustling shopping area, Masuda
now stands as a preserved area of a bygone
time. Take a short walk around and you will
discover many uchigura-style storehouses,
as well as approximately 40 uchigura homes.
The uchigura style means the homes have
quite modest façades compared with the back
area of the homes – called uchigura.

Some of the homes and stores, such as
the sake breweries, offer tours, so you might
like to start your walking tour at the Masuda
Tourist Information Center (called Hotaru),
where they can show you the range of homes
and shops, and you can select those of
interest to you.

Masuda is located in the south-east area
of Yokote city, where the Naruse and Minase
rivers merge.

4 MINKAEN KIDO GOROBEI KAMUKURA FESTIVAL
横手の雪まつり{かまくら}

W akitafan.com/hands_on_sightseeing/en
A Yokote Park, 4 Shiroyamamachi, Yokote,
013-0012

ATTRACTION/FESTIVAL/VILLAGE |
If you're in Akita in February, plan your
itinerary around Minkaen Kido Gorobei
village, where on 15–16 February you can
experience the kamakura (igloo) festival.
These igloos are mind-blowing in their
construction and stature, and my absolute
favourite part of exploring Akita was a visit
to the kamakura.

The setting itself in Yokote Park, with the
temple in the background, is also extremely
memorable. Just imagine the incredible
whiteness of snow, the pitter-patter of falling
snowflakes and the crunching sound of ice
underneath your snow boots. So divine!

During the festival, some of the
kamakura are displayed with rugs, cushions,
cooking utensils and hanging decorations
tucked deep into the igloos, so that visitors
are comfortable sitting inside them.
Surprisingly, the kamakura are warm, often
because of a hot stove placed in the centre.
Foods, such as oshiroko (red bean soup
with mochi), are cooked on the stoves to
help you keep warm, and the obaachans
(grandmothers) who serve it are so lovely
(see p. 201). It is a warm and comforting
homestyle cooking dish that many Japanese
people might associate with their childhood
or grandmother.

At 5pm the kamakura are illuminated
with lights, making for an impressive vision
and quite the photo hotspot. Pretty please
be careful walking in the snow, especially as
night falls.

I can't recommend this festival enough.
It's one of my fondest memories in Japan
to date.

4

4

5

6

5 KAMAKURA OSHIROKO
鎌倉もちとおしるこ

W   akitafan.com/hands_on_sightseeing/en
A   Yokote Park, 4 Shiroyamamachi, Yokote, 013-0012

ATTRACTION/FESTIVAL | During the February kamakura (igloo) festival (*see* p. 198), the city opens up one of the beautiful traditional buildings in the village of Minkaen Kido Gorobei, and you can sit and be warmed by the in-floor fire built into the tatami flooring. On my visit, a team of volunteer obaachans (grandmothers) were buzzing around and serving pickles and oshiroko (red bean soup with mochi). It was my first time tasting oshiroko, and I doubt that I will ever taste a more delicious one. When the food is served in such a beautiful environment, by such friendly obaachans, it's hard to top.

I was invited to look in the kitchen, and I was overcome by the wonderful sense of community. The obaachans were calling to each other, 'Bring out the pickles!' and 'Quick, pass the chopsticks', and it was obvious that they were working hard and loved the buzz of this special event. The ladies were gathered around a large retro washbasin and chattered as they cleaned. Other ladies were kneeling down on the timber floor and stirring large vats of red bean paste. And then, hidden in the corner, were two ladies making a hotpot of amazake (hot sweet rice wine), which I was fortunate enough to try.

I wish I could live with these lovely obaachans and learn from their incredible cooking skills, warm spirit and outlook on life. What a dream that would be!

6 KANTO MATSURI FESTIVAL (KANTO FESTIVAL CENTER)
秋田市民俗芸能伝承館

W   city.akita.akita.jp
A   1-3-30 Omachi, 010-0921
T   018-886-7091

ATTRACTION/FESTIVAL | The Kanto Matsuri is a pole lantern summer festival held every year in August (generally from 3 to 6 August). If you happen to visit in another month, fear not, as you can still experience elements of the festival at the Neburinagashi kan, or Kanto Festival Center. It is conveniently located just a 15-minute walk from Akita station.

Here you can enjoy a special Kanto lantern balancing performance, where trained performers display the impressive art of balancing Kanto lanterns on a long stick on not only their hands, but in their belts and even on their foreheads as well. If you're lucky, after the performance they might allow you to try balancing them yourselves – which is nowhere near as easy as it first appears.

The Kanto Festival Center showcases information and exhibits about Akita's three largest festivals: Bonden festival, Tsuchizaki Shinmeisha festival and Kanto Matsuri itself, with a small exhibition of costumes and awards from the Kanto Matsuri festival.

It is an incredible cultural place to visit if you are interested in the special festivals that make up this city. Make sure you book ahead online.

7 AKITA MAIKO
あきた舞妓

w   akitamaiko.com
A   1-3 Chiaki Park, Akita-ku, Matsushita
T   018-827-3241

ATTRACTION/EXPERIENCE | If you enjoy tradition (or history), you shouldn't miss this incredible experience and chance to see traditional Japanese dance performed by maiko (geisha in training) at the Akita Cultural and Industrial Facility in Matsushita (*see* p. 207). The Akita maiko-san's posture, elegant movements and kimono dress will leave you mesmerised.

Take special note of their matte white foundation make-up, red lips and red-toned eye shadow, teamed with colourful kimono and ornate floral and metallic head dress. Although maiko dedicate their work to hospitality, they also aim to convey the charm of Akita prefecture's history and culture through cultural tourism for visitors.

The beautiful building where the maiko perform features traditional craftsmanship, such as ceiling beams made from one piece of timber – a craft that is almost non-existent in the work of today's Japanese architects. The windows are handmade retro-patterned glass. Simply stunning!

During the performance (book online), you are usually allowed to take photographs (please check first), and afterwards you might be able to chat and ask questions of the maiko-san about their art and specialised practice.

8 TAKASHIMIZU SAKE BREWERY
高清水醸造元

w   takashimizu.com
A   4-12 Kawamoto Mutsumi-machi, 010-0934
T   018-864-7331

ATTRACTION/EXPERIENCE | Takashimizu Sake Brewery was founded in 1944, when 12 of the local sake breweries joined together to form one. It is proud of its history and unique sake with a delicious aroma and umami (taste) – smooth and with a refreshing aftertaste. The brewery offers tours where you can taste and buy.

On my visit in the cold, my guide turned the heaters on and kindly pointed them our way as he played a DVD about how to make sake. It was fascinating to learn about the cross-fermentation in sake brewing, where rice is turned into yeast and sugar at the same time. The flavour of the pure local water plays a large part in sake brewing, and it was interesting to begin the tour with a glass of the local water. 'Don't worry, you'll get to drink sake later', laughed the guide.

Refreshed by the sip of pure water, it was time for me to cover my odango (hair bun top-knot) with a protective hair net and take off to the top floor of the brewery. After peerimg into 5-metre (16-foot) tall vats bubbling with sake in the making, the guide scooped a taste of sake directly from the tank, serving up perhaps the freshest sake I will ever try. The taste was clean and pure, and I appreciated it more than I have ever done so before.

The tour concluded with a sake tasting, followed by a spot of sake shopping. The brewery also produces sake hand cream and lotion, both of which are a must-buy to take home with you.

The brewery is open for tours three times a day (weekdays only) at 10.30am, 1.30pm and 3pm, and online bookings are required.

7

8

8

9 YOSUKE SATO SOHONTEN

佐藤養助　総本店

W   sato-yoske.co.jp/shop/akita
A   80 Inaba, Yuzawa-ku
T   018-343-2911

ATTRACTION/EXPERIENCE |
On a tour of Yosuke Sato's udon factory
(book online), you can observe how Akita
prefecture's unique Inaniwa udon is kneaded,
twisted and stretched by udon craftsmen.
Inaniwa udon is a special type of udon
only made in Akita, and its history dates
back to the start of the Edo era in the early
17th century. It is slightly thinner than
regular udon. After you have learnt the ins
and outs of udon making, you can taste test
the special udon.

    I recommend ordering the seasonal
tempura udon set, especially if it's a snowy
day. The delicious thin udon with salty
broth topped with delicate mitsuba (a
fresh green Japanese leafy herb) is the
perfect way to warm up in the gorgeous
Akita snow. Enjoy slurping the udon and
savour the crispy tempura dipped into the
accompanying tempura sauce.

    Launched in 1986, this famous udon
factory also has a fantastic shop where
you can pick up some udon and lacquered
handmade bowls produced in Kawatsura
village to take home. Yosuke Sato has seven
branches in Akita, two in Tokyo and one
in Fukuoka.

9

10

10 AKITA CITIZENS MARKET
秋田市民市場

w   akita-yulala.jp/en/see/akita-citizens-market
A   4-7-35 Naka-dori, 010-0001
T   018-833-1855

SHOP/MARKET | This colourful and textured market is such a visual treat. It's a great place to pick up vegetables, meat, fish, kitchenware, fresh flowers and Akita keepsakes. You can also find a selection of local sake.

I love the inventive and often retro-style merchandising. Divine Japanese citrus fruits are carefully wrapped in protective mesh and sit in cobalt-blue plastic display bowls alongside strawberries so vibrantly red that you could easily plan your seasonal wardrobe with the colour combinations spotted here. The display techniques come with age and a clever use of space. Every area is packed with products and merchandise, arranged from floor to ceiling, and even on colourful s-hooks hanging suspended on poles from the ceiling.

The market is conveniently located a few minutes' walk from Akita station. The morning market with seasonal products and fresh seafood is open from 5am until 8am, but the overall market is open until 6pm. It is closed on Sundays. If you're a bit peckish after visiting the market – understandably so – you will find restaurants, such as conveyor-belt sushi beside the market.

11 AKITA CULTURAL AND INDUSTRIAL FACILITY IN MATSUSHITA

w   matsushita-akita.jp
A   1-3 Senshukoen, 010-0876
T   018-827-3241

CAFE/TEA HOUSE | This incredibly atmospheric restored tea house offers the most exquisite obento lunch. The obento is served on small lacquered tables sat on tatami flooring. As you sit on the tatami and smell the fibres from it, if you're anything like me, you might find the whole experience so overwhelmingly divine that it'll be hard to hold back the tears. Watch the light shine through the patterned Showa-era (1926–89) glass, casting soft shadows on the timber floorboards and tatami as you sip your Japanese tea and enjoy your special obento.

The locally produced obento comes wrapped in a simple red elastic tie and contains delicacies such as prawn, oinarisan (sweet-tofu wrapped rice), takikomi gohan (mixed rice), tamagoyaki (omelette) and vegetables. Each part of your bento box is kept fresh with divided sections. Enjoying a special bento box like this, in this traditional setting, is a beautiful experience. You should also book a dance performance by Akita Maiko (*see* p. 202).

Matsushita tea house is so well preserved that it feels like a privilege to dine in this historic space. You will want to document it, so be sure to pack your camera or ensure your phone is charged.

After you've enjoyed your lunch experience, you might like to take a stroll in the nearby park and shrine, and then have a coffee or sake at Shubo, which is located just outside Matsushita. In winter, you can enjoy sitting by the cosy kerosene heater and watch the snow from the window. In my opinion, life doesn't get much better than this.

—ON & ART

DESIGN, FASHI

AO BUILDING

A 3-11-7 Kitaaoyama, Minato-ku, Tokyo, 107-0061

PRADA

A 5-2-6 Minamiaoyama, Minato-ku, Tokyo, 107-0062

SUNNY HILLS

A 3-10-20 Minamiaoyama, Minato-ku, Tokyo 107-0062

NEZU MUSEUM

A 6-5-1 Minamiaoyama, Minato-ku, Tokyo, 107-0062

TOKYO OLYMPIC STADIUM

A 10-1 Kasumigaokamachi, Shinjuku-ku, Tokyo 160-0013

DIOR

A 5-9-11 Jingumae, Shibuya-ku, Tokyo 150-0001

The creative scene in Japan is one of the main reasons I moved to this incredible country. The high skill level, attention to detail, craftsmanship and creativity of artists here is out of this world.

Architecture lovers might like to start their experience in the Omotesando neighbourhood of Tokyo where they can view the AO building by Sakakura Associates; the Prada shop by Herzog & de Meuron; Sunny Hills by Kengo Kuma, who also designed the nearby Nezu Museum and the Tokyo Olympic stadium; and the Dior store by Tokyo's SANAA firm, founded by Kazuyo Sejima and Ryue Nishizawa. SANAA also designed Shibaura House, which is a must-see for architecture lovers, as you are able to enter this co-working space. Incidentally, I also hosted regular workshops here when I first moved to Japan.

Shibuya's PARCO shopping complex, recently renovated and re-opened in 2019, is a fantastic spot to immerse oneself in Japanese fashion, showcasing brands such as Issey Miyake, A.P.C., Comme des Garçons and Junya Watanabe Men. Shibuya PARCO also has galleries and pop-up shops that feature the work of Japanese artists. Head up to the rooftop for COMMUNE, an amazing bar where you can order gin by selecting an emotion!

Fashion lovers should also head to Issey Miyake's Pleats Please store in Aoyama, for the incredible textural pleating technology used by this fashion label, and to the nearby Tsumori Chisato, for a more whimsical approach to Japanese fashion design.

Japan is blessed with so many incredible art galleries, such as Mori Art Museum (*see* p. 8), Yayoi Kusama Museum (*see* p. 11), but also features a range of impressive commercial galleries, my favourite of which is Tomio Koyama gallery, which showcases the work of Japanese micro-pop artists, such as Yoshitomo Nara, Shintaro Miyake and my all-time favourite artist, Hiroshi Sugito. The gallery is located in the Complex 665 building in Roppongi along with various other commercial galleries.

If you happen to have a free day, and even access to a rental car (although you can also access this gallery via bus), I cannot recommend the Kawamura Memorial DIC Museum in Chiba enough. Hosting both temporary and permanent exhibitions, including works by Robert Ryan, the last time I visited this gallery I cried tears of joy and beauty. At that time, work by Hiroshi Sugito was showing, so emotions were high, but the space located in Chiba in a large park and tree-filled area was also equally as tear-jerkingly beautiful. The room that hosts the Robert Ryan works features a curved wall with large windows looking out to swaying forest trees, almost installation-like. And so much attention is paid to detail that the artwork is guarded by the most beautiful pastel pink tape. The attention to detail and respect for art is so indicative of Japanese sensibility in all creative forms.

HELLO SANDWICH JAPAN

NAOSHI

ART AND NATURE
ISLAND FOR
CULTURE LOVERS

34.460° N
133.985° E

10

M A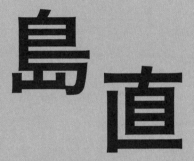

Art lovers won't want to miss Naoshima Island, commonly known as 'Japan's art island'. If you have a day or two to visit, I highly recommend it. Not only is the art of an incredible standard, so too is the natural beauty, which includes seaside bays and an array of natural gardens. Naoshima is arranged in a way in which the art, architecture and nature work together forming one overall immersive experience.

Yayoi Kusama's iconic yellow pumpkin (*see* p. 212) is installed on a jetty where you can experience it up close, and Chichu Art Museum (*see* p. 212) features James Turrell's artworks, as well as works by Claude Monet and Walter De Maria. Art House Project (*see* p. 215) is another must-see that showcases site-specific artworks, including an art house designed by Tadao Ando specifically to house works by James Turrell. Those who have seen Kusama and Turrell's works elsewhere will still find the island inspiring, due to the way that nature impacts and changes the viewing experience of each of these site-specific artworks. Once you've soaked up all the artwork, soak in a sento (public bath) at I Love Yu (*see* p. 215).

The island is accessible via ferry from Shikoku Island.

1   YAYOI KUSAMA'S YELLOW PUMPKIN

草間彌生黄色かぼうちゃ

A   3419 Kagawa, 761-3110
T   087-892-2030

ATTRACTION/ARTWORK | Yayoi Kusama's yellow pumpkin with black dots sculpture, created in 1994 from fibreglass, is perhaps one of the most famous pieces of art that comes to mind when people think of Naoshima Island. The piece is so iconic that during typhoon season it's transported from its display on a jetty by the water to a safe shelter.

When you first arrive on Naoshima Island at Miyanoura Port, you will see a cute red pumpkin sculpture, also by Yayoi Kusama. This red pumpkin is particularly special as you can enter the hollow inside and peek out through its little face-sized window cut-out holes.

However, the yellow pumpkin, located about 40 minutes away from the port, has become the more famous artwork. It's free to view, and you can walk right up to it to experience the sculpture close up and have your photo taken with it. You can take the free shuttle bus from the port or even hire bikes and ride, although there are a few steep hills.

It's fun walking around the ocean side near this sculpture, and you can enjoy the grassy area and sit under a tree, relax with a cold drink and take a moment to absorb this Japanese art island.

2   CHICHU ART MUSEUM

地中美術館

A   3449-1 Kagawa, 761-3110
T   087-892-3755

ATTRACTION/MUSEUM | Chichu Art Museum is a must-see when you're on Naoshima Island. The museum was built in 2004 and is mostly underground, so as not to disturb the spectacular view of the Seto Inland Sea.

Artworks on permanent display include works by Claude Monet and Walter De Maria, but perhaps the most famous work here is the installation by James Turrell. Although Turrell's work can be viewed during the usual museum opening hours, you can also arrange a 45-minute evening sunset viewing of his work, where you will experience elements of nature and his artwork, *Open Sky*, in the immersive light.

No matter when you visit the museum, the light and seasons change the appearance of the works and the space itself, so even if you've visited once before, I recommend visiting again to capture a unique and different experience. Museum admission is ¥2,100.

Relaxing at the museum cafe is a wonderful way to spend some time reflecting on the artworks as you overlook the sea. The menu includes items such as burgers, vegetable plates, steak, bagels and a range of cakes and drinks. I recommend ordering one of the Setouchi local drinks, such as the olive cider or lemonade.

1

2

2

4

4

3 ART HOUSE PROJECT
家プロジェクト

A   Honmura, Kagawa, 761-3110
T   087-892-3223 (Benesse House)

ATTRACTION/ARTWORKS | Art House Project is a fascinating and evolving art installation in Naoshima's Honmura area. With the first project commencing in 1998, artists have taken over abandoned houses in this otherwise residential area and created site-specific artworks in the houses. At the time of writing, seven houses were part of the project.

As you walk between each house, you pass by everyday residential areas, combining local architecture with art in an exciting way that challenges the norms of thinking.

Start at the Honmura Lounge, which sells tickets to the Art House Project. This building used to be a co-op supermarket and was renovated by Japanese architect Ryue Nishizawa. Admission is ¥1,050 for six houses (excluding Kinza), and ¥420 for admission into Kinza, a unique art house by Rei Naito. Reservations are required to access Kinza and only one person can enter at a time in order to fully experience the artwork.

One of the art houses, called Minami-dera, was designed by famed architect Tadao Ando in 1999 to house the works of James Turrell. Another divine art house is Appropriate Proportion (2002) by well-known Japanese artist Hiroshi Sugimoto, who often works in the field of photography. Also not to be missed is Shinro Ohtake's 'Haisha', which means dentist in Japanese and was formally a dentist office.

This incredible Art House Project is absolutely not to be missed during your trip to Naoshima. You will be inspired beyond belief!

4 I LOVE YU
直島銭湯「I♥湯」

W   benesse-artsite.jp/en/art/
    naoshimasento.html
A   2252-2 Kagawa, 761-3110
T   087-892-2626

ATTRACTION/SENTO | I Love Yu is an old and quirky retro sento (public bath) covered in tiles and mosaics, making it part public bath and part art installation. In Japanese, 'Yu' stands for bath/hot water. So the name 'I love Yu' is a fun play on words, showcasing the quirky side of this public bathhouse.

It was designed by Otake Shinro, whose eclectic artwork style often incorporates recycled materials. The artist, a graduate of the prestigious Musashino Art University, is based in Tokyo and has published various books, designs record and book covers, and paints and creates installations, too. The outside of the public bathhouse is covered in a patchwork of quirky, mismatched colourful tiles, and when soaking in the bath, visitors can look up at the brightly painted ceiling glass and tile murals. It's definitely a unique art-meets-sento experience!

Admission costs ¥660 and can be purchased through the ticket machine located inside the entrance. I Love Yu also sells shampoo, body soap and self-branded sento towels that make such a lovely keepsake to remember your special experience here. The usual sento rules and etiquette of bathing apply (*see* p. 93). I Love Yu is only a few minutes from the ferry terminal at Miyanoura Port.

5 BENESSE HOUSE MUSEUM
ベネッセハウス美術館

A　Gotanchi, Kagawa, 761-3110
T　087-892-3223

6 SHIOYA DINER
シオヤダイナー

A　2227 Kagawa, 761-3110
T　087-892-3290

ATTRACTION/MUSEUM/STAY/ HOTEL | Benesse House Museum, designed by Tadao Ando and opened in 1992, overlooks the Seto Inland Sea and is a museum with a luxury hotel, built with the concept of combining art, nature and architecture. Tadao Ando's concrete architecture is not only an artwork in itself, but becomes a canvas for other artworks, such as Yoshihiro Suda's *Weeds* (2002) where greenery pops through the concrete walls. In addition to a range of paintings, sculptures and photographic works, many site-specific installations are located outside in the museum park with a spectacular ocean view.

One particular work of note is the site-specific *Cai Guo-Qiang Cultural Melting Bath*, where every Sunday since 1998 a limited group of guests can have a private bathing session soaking in a herbal medicine bath overlooking the sea. You can also expect to find works by Andy Warhol, Gerhard Richter, David Hockney, Hiroshi Sugimoto, Tadao Ando, Kazuo Katase and Robert Rauschenberg.

For those who want to treat themselves, book a divine stay at the hotel and immerse yourself in art and nature in a luxurious manner. The great news is that even if you aren't staying at the hotel you can still visit the museum, which is ¥1,050 for entry. Kids under the age of 15 can enter for free.

RESTAURANT/DINER | Seriously, you must stop in here if you're in Naoshima! It's run by the sweetest owners, and you can order American diner-inspired food, such as hot dogs (which come with French fries), hamburgers, toasted sandwiches, tacos and steak. Naturally, everything here is served on super-cute retro-style plates.

You'll enjoy listening to cute rock 'n' roll music and gazing at all of the lovely retro ornaments. The interior is a mix of '50s and '60s Americana, with patterned laminex tables, a turquoise wall with a gallery of retro artworks and shelves filled with vinyl.

After a long day of exploring the art in Naoshima, Shioya Diner is a fantastic place to relax in a friendly and quirky atmosphere before you head back on your ferry. Shioya also has free wi-fi, so you can check your ferry times while you're enjoying your meal.

During the busy seasons in Naoshima, especially during the Setouchi Triennale (July and Aug), it's best to book ahead at this diner. You can do this by messaging them on their Facebook page.

You'll feel as though you've stepped back in time at this cosy little Naoshima Island diner.

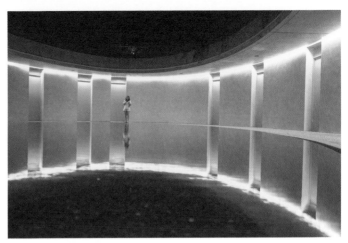

5

LIVE AND DIE	LIVE AND LIVE	SING AND DIE	SING AND LIVE
DIE AND DIE	DIE AND LIVE	SCREAM AND DIE	SCREAM AND LIVE
SHIT AND DIE	SHIT AND LIVE	YOUNG AND DIE	YOUNG AND LIVE
PISS AND DIE	PISS AND LIVE	OLD AND DIE	OLD AND LIVE
EAT AND DIE	EAT AND LIVE	CUT AND DIE	CUT AND LIVE
SLEEP AND DIE	SLEEP AND LIVE	RUN AND DIE	RUN AND LIVE
LOVE AND DIE	LOVE AND LIVE	STAY AND DIE	STAY AND LIVE
HATE AND DIE	HATE AND LIVE	PLAY AND DIE	PLAY AND LIVE
FUCK AND DIE	FUCK AND LIVE	KILL AND DIE	KILL AND LIVE
PEAK AND DIE	SPEAK AND LIVE	SUCK AND DIE	SUCK AND LIVE
LIE AND DIE	LIE AND LIVE	COME AND DIE	COME AND LIVE
HEAD AND DIE	HEAD AND LIVE	GO AND DIE	GO AND LIVE
CRY AND DIE	CRY AND LIVE	KNOW AND DIE	KNOW AND LIVE
KISS AND DIE	KISS AND LIVE	TELL AND DIE	TELL AND LIVE
RAGE AND DIE	RAGE AND LIVE	SMELL AND DIE	SMELL AND LIVE
LAUGH AND DIE	LAUGH AND LIVE	FALL AND DIE	FALL AND LIVE
TOUCH AND DIE	TOUCH AND LIVE	RISE AND DIE	RISE AND LIVE
FEEL AND DIE	FEEL AND LIVE	STAND AND DIE	STAND AND LIVE
FEAR AND DIE	FEAR AND LIVE	SIT AND DIE	SIT AND LIVE
SICK AND DIE	SICK AND LIVE	SPIT AND DIE	SPIT AND LIVE
WELL AND DIE	WELL AND LIVE	TRY AND DIE	TRY AND LIVE
BLACK AND DIE	BLACK AND LIVE	FAIL AND DIE	FAIL AND LIVE
WHITE AND DIE	WHITE AND LIVE	SMILE AND DIE	SMILE AND LIVE
RED AND DIE	RED AND LIVE	THINK AND DIE	THINK AND LIVE
YELLOW AND DIE	YELLOW AND LIVE	PAY AND DIE	PAY AND LIVE

SAPPORO

HOKKAIDO'S
CAPITAL CITY,
PERFECT FOR
THOSE OFF TO THE
SKI FIELDS

43.067° N
141.352° E

11

札幌

Sapporo, located on Japan's northernmost island, Hokkaido, is yet another entry port city to one of Japan's most picturesque nature-filled islands. Of course, for those who love snowboarding or skiing, Sapporo might be a fantastic first stop on your way to the popular ski fields like Niseko, but it also serves as an amazing wintery wonderland for those who prefer a city-style winter experience.

If you visit Sapporo during the snowy winter months, you'll find sandbags in small boxes at many pedestrian crossings. These sandbags can be used freely by anyone to scatter over the roads' slippery surfaces so you can walk across safely. Another way to stay safe in the slippery icy streets is to take the Sapporo Ekimae-dori Chi-ka-ho underground walkway that connects Odori and Sapporo stations. The walkway is lined with clothing shops, everyday stores like pharmacies, cafes and restaurants, and is a warm and fun way to stay safe and warm from the icy streets. Sapporo also has some unique cuisine, and you must try 175°Deno's (*see* p. 228) dandan noodles, the famed yakinuku (barbecued lamb) at Daruma (*see* p. 230) and soup curry at Soul Store (*see* p. 230).

Pretty please don't slip on the black ice under all of that beautiful Sapporo snow. Enjoy this cosy city and stay safe, Sandwiches!

1 MT MOIWA
藻岩山

W   moiwa.sapporo-dc.co.jp
A   Moiwayama, Minami-ku,
    005-0041

2 NAKAJIMA KOEN
中島公園

W   sapporo-park.or.jp/nakajima
A   1 Nakajima-koen, Chuo-ku, 064-0931
T   011-511-3924

ATTRACTION/EXPERIENCE | Head to Mt Moiwa for an incredible 360-degree view over Sapporo. Not only is the view from the rooftop observation deck breathtaking, but you will also love the experience of taking the ropeway (cable car and gondola) up the mountain. Try to time your visit for the late afternoon, so you can see both the day view over the mountains and the glistening night lights over the city after the sun sets.

If you visit in winter, be sure to pack enough spare change to buy a can of hot chocolate from the vending machine on the observation deck. I visited in December and my fingers froze taking photos! If I could step back in time, I would pack some fingerless gloves. To help you withstand the cold weather while you wait for sunset, you can treat yourself to a hot drink or beer at Jewel Restaurant below the observation deck and then pop back up to take a shot of the city's glistening night lights. It's so pretty you're likely to forget how utterly freezing it is.

Many tourists love to have their photo taken inside the diamond-shaped sculpture and ring the bell for good luck, but, to me, this seems gimicky. You can also climb the mountain via one of five popular walking trails. The shortest is 2.4 kilometres (1.5 miles) and the longest is 4.5 kilometres (2.8 miles). For stargazers, visit the Super Planetarium and see five million stars projected.

ATTRACTION/PARK | Nakajima Koen is a lovely expansive park close to the centre of the city to get your intake of nature close to the centre of the city. Take some snacks or a coffee and enjoy walking around the pond and soak up the beautiful scenery. Just be sure to watch your step – this is home to the Hello Sandwich broken ankle incident, which I wouldn't recommend.

In addition to all the park essentials, it also has some super-cute kids, play equipment, which is just in front of a colourful, graphic mural on a nearby building. If it's snowing, this makes for the most gorgeous pops of colour set against the whitest snow. You can also enjoy looking at Sapporo's Mt Moiwa in the background as you walk around this special park.

Nakajima Koen is a wonderful place to make snow-people in winter, or have a drink on a park bench in summer. The park is also divine in autumn when the leaves start to change colour. And in spring, you can enjoy hanami (cherry blossom viewing). Oh, and did I mention it has a pond, a baseball ground, a tennis court and a golf course! It's a one-stop park! But ... because I broke my ankle in this park, please promise me you will be careful and wear snow boots with proper grip! The boots with metal spikes might not be 'on-trend' but certainly will help keep you safe.

The park is accessible via the Namboku train line, and if it's snowing you can select from a few different exits from the Nakajima Koen train station to land you exactly where you'd like to visit in this park.

1

2

3 FABULOUS
ファビュラス

w rounduptrading.com
A NKC bldg, 1F, 2-3-1 Minami, 1 Johigashi,
   Chuo-ku, 060-0051
T 011-271-0310

**SHOP/CLOTHING/HOMEWARES/
STATIONERY/CAFE** | Fabulous is exactly
that: a one-stop fashion, stationery and
homewares shop with a cafe. It's the perfect
place to spend half a day. I met one of the
staff members of Fabulous at The Lots (*see*
p. 234), where he was enjoying a drink with
a Nagoya-based accessory designer who was
having a pop-up shop at this shop. I guess
this is my roundabout way of saying that
Fabulous is well connected, and you can be
guaranteed that the selection of items in the
store and the cafe are well chosen from all
over Japan.

Stock up here on jewellery, homewares,
furniture, camping accessories, stationery,
bags and a range of Made in Hokkaido
essentials, such as wood carvings and vases
made from Sapporo soft stone. The hand
towels with a forest motif reference Sapporo's
beautiful nature. You will find an amazing
selection of men's and women's fashion
labels, as well as interior brands like Costa
Nova ceramics, Chemex coffee makers, La
Rochere glassware, Merchant & Mills textiles
and Danish designer Kay Bojesen.

After you've finished shopping, pop into
the spacious cafe area (open early from 8am
which is rare for Japan) and enjoy a coffee
and a delicious sandwich to fuel your day of
travel. Depending on the time of your visit, a
sandwich and drink set will only cost around
¥1,000. There is a range of salads and pasta
dishes available for dinner. And why not treat
yourself to a cocktail – you're on holidays
after all!

4 SABITA
サビタ

w sabita.jp
A MOMA Place, 1F, 28-2-35 Kita 1 Jonishi,
   Chuo-ku, 064-0821

SHOP/HOMEWARES/CAFE | Nestled
into a strikingly minimalist white building,
this homewares shop and cafe is a gorgeous
place to pick up some Japanese ceramics
made by local artisans. Entering the shop
is like entering a peaceful and tranquil
meditative state; it's quiet and filled with
homewares and clothes in a soothing,
neutral colour palette. Even the afternoon
light in this store is something like an art
installation. The peaceful tranquility gently
encourages you to replace everything in your
kitchen and home. Be warned!

Here you can find beautiful linen
tableware, baby clothes, women's clothing,
delicate, unique and locally made gold and
silver jewellery, and an extensive range
of plates, mugs and assorted dishes. After
you've browsed, pop upstairs for a coffee in
this beautifully relaxing space.

You might like to follow your shopping
with a stroll in the nearby picturesque
Maruyama Park, just a few minutes' walk
from Sabita store.

4

4

3

OBENTO

Obento (or bento, informally) are deeply instilled in Japanese culture. From a young age, parents send their children off to kindergarten with these handmade boxed lunches, and office workers pop to convenience stores and supermarkets to pick up obento for a convenient lunch or dinner. You can even buy ekiben (eki is the Japanese word for station and ben is short for bento) at train stations where the shinkansen (bullet train) departs from. Even oshogatsu (New Year's) food is set in compartments like a bento box. Eating small pieces of various foods is typical in Japanese culture, not just with bento boxes but with most Japanese meals comprising of side dishes, a main, rice and miso.

There are many and various types of obento, but it usually consists of rice (sometimes topped with a sour ume plum placed in the centre, not dissimilar in design to the Japanese flag), a protein, such as fish, chicken or meat, and an assortment of side dishes and pickles. Obento are often as colourful as they are delicious and are generally very reasonably priced. Convenience stores and supermarkets sell obento from ¥300 to ¥1,000.

ISETAN SHINJUKU

w   isetan.mistore.jp

A   3 Chome-14-1 Shinjuku,
Shinjuku City, Tokyo,
160-0022

T   8133-352-1111

TOKYU FOOD SHOW

w   tokyu-dept.co.jp/
shibuya_foodshow

A   1 Chome-12-1 Dogenzaka,
Shibuya City, Tokyo,
150-0043

T   8133-477-3111

For a special obento, I recommend visiting a fancy department store basement level, such as ISETAN Shinjuku or Tokyu Food Show, where you can find slightly more expensive obento ranging from ¥500 to ¥2,000. These are delicious and fresh, and one of my favourite ways to treat myself after a long day of work when I don't have the energy to cook. A little pro-tip for buying at the basement markets: steer away from buying the obento with the plastic displays, instead select from the extensive range of obento where the actual product is displayed. Some obento are wrapped in pretty paper, with a simple string tie, or come packaged in pretty bamboo boxes. The food is always artfully displayed, often using the five bento rules:

FIVE WAYS OF COOKING — niru (simmer), musu (steam), yaku (grill), ageru (fry), tsukuru (create – often also raw)

FIVE FLAVOURS — shiokarai (salty), suppai (sour), amai (sweet), nigai (bitter), karai (spicy)

FIVE COLOURS — aka (red), kiiro (yellow), midori (green), shiro (white), kuro (black)

FIVE SENSES — miru (sight), kiku (hearing), kyukaku (smell), ajiwau (taste), fureru (touch)

FIVE OUTLOOKS OR VIEWPOINTS — a set of Buddhist principles for the best frame of mind when consuming food.

In addition to obento, Japanese convenience stores are also fun places to explore cute food. Here you can expect to find:

· Boiled single eggs
· Soft-serve cones in the ice-cream section (the whipped shaped ice-cream is made in a certain way so it holds its shape)
· Cute chu-hi (alcoholic canned drinks) usually made from shochu (Japanese potato-based liquor) adorned with patterns such as polka dots or ribbons
· Various flavoured onigiri (rice balls) with fillings such as sour ume plum, tuna and mayonnaise or kombu (seaweed).

5

6

6

5 MILL
ミル

W ile-sapporo.jp/mill
A 1-13 Odorinishi, Chuo-ku,
   060-0042
T 011-213-0903

SHOP/HOMEWARES | Mill is a gorgeous homewares and accessories store located inside the Odori Bisse department store, near the famous Sapporo clock tower. This shop has a very well curated selection of the best homewares in Japan. Think locally made accessories and linen from Japanese brand Fog Linen, which makes divine tablecloths and napkins, as well as many other items using Lithuanian linen. I recommend buying one of the beautiful timber bento boxes to recreate your Japanese experience at home. You will also find some international brands, such as Baggu, that release limited-edition ranges for Japan only.

Pick up some local coffee, divine handwoven baskets, greeting cards, stationery items, vases, ceramic vessels, room fragrance and even fairtrade chocolate. Mill is really your one-stop shop for small gifts and treats for yourself.

As Mill is located inside a department store, you can also enjoy wandering around the other stores. And, if you're a little peckish, you might like to treat yourself to a snack from the popular bakery, Donguri, located on the ground floor. Either dine in or buy some sweet and savoury bread treats and bring them to enjoy in the neighbouring Odori Park overlooking the clock tower.

6 MORIHICO COFFEE
森彦コーヒー

W morihico.com/en
A 26-2-18, Minami 2jo nishi, Chuo-ku,
   064-0802
T 011-622-8880

CAFE/COFFEE | This beautiful red-roof two-storey traditional Japanese house-turned-cafe is the perfect place to have a cosy cup of coffee, a cake or a savoury bread snack. Opened in 1996, Morihico is in the lovely, quiet residential area of Maruyama. The company has a range of stores, but this little cosy shop is my favourite and my recommendation for your Sapporo trip.

As you enter the cute cafe you reach the counter where the staff will show you to your table. Turn left and you find a cosy room perfect for a large group around the communal table and a small bench seat ideal for solo diners or two people. The cafe is filled with Japanese antique-style ornate lantern-like lamps and other charming natural-style furnishings, such as dried flower arrangements.

On my visit, I sat on the ground floor by the bookshelf and watched the afternoon light cast geometric shadows over the collection of vintage books. The staff will help you select from the range of black coffee beans, according to your taste preferences. I selected the house blend, which was dark and smooth and, quite frankly, the perfect afternoon pick-me-up. I recommend ordering the croque monsieur for a home-cooked comfort lunch.

You can also request to be seated on the 2nd storey, but pretty please be careful on those old timber stairs – they're so steep and narrow, and we don't want any broken ankles.

You can purchase some locally roasted coffee beans to create that perfect brew in your own home.

7   & EAT.BY SUU
アンドイートバイスー

W   suu.life
A   16-1-27 Ōdorinishi, Chuo-ku, 060-0042
T   011-676-9664

CAFE | & Eat.by SUU dining is the sister cafe to a zakka (homewares and lifestyle goods) store by the same name in the same area. The decor is charming and rustic meets modern, with timber and metallic finishes meshed with arrangements of soft, dried flowers and low-hanging lamps. Even the music is sweet and charming.

The owner, who is also a food stylist, is so incredibly charming and lovely, and her food arrangement is something like the beautiful ikebana art form. Watching her from over the counter was like watching an artist at work. The way she arranged seasonal produce in layers of colours and artfully placed lettuce leaves dotted with spots of pink pickled daikon and seasonal citrus was almost spiritual. Depending on seasonal produce, the one-plate lunches will often include a curry with assorted vegetables and salad in a Japanese-meets-French-and-Italian-style. You can select from bread or rice to accompany your dish.

This 20-seater cafe has both upstairs and ground floor dining options. I sat at the spacious counter so I could chat with the staff as they prepared my lunch. It's the perfect place to spend a slow lunch.

8   175°DENO

W   175.co.jp
A   6-20 Minamijojo Nishi, Chuo-ku, 060-0061
T   011-596-8175

RESTAURANT/RAMEN | 175°Deno's dandan noodles are a must-eat when in Sapporo! After many visits to Chendgu, in Sichuan province in China, the Japanese owner started this fusion of Japanese ramen with the spices of China – and these dandan ramen noodles were born!

The special flavour comes from the combination of spices and sauces, such as sardine oil with Sichuan pepper mixed with a secret sesame sauce. The noodles are served with stir-fried soy beans or minced meat in a chicken flavoured broth with homemade umami (taste) seasoning. The most popular dish is the soup-less ramen. Also delicious is the spicy ramen, where you can add various toppings like eggs and coriander. You can customise your noodles and broth almost to the point where it's too much choice. But trust me, the work you do here will be worth it when you take your first slurp. They also offer a range of local craft beers to accompany your dandan noodles.

With five stores in Sapporo, 175°Deno also has branches in Tokyo and Fukushima. This main branch in Sapporo is unpretentious and located down a narrow side entrance of what looks like a commercial building. On our visit, my friend Kay and I sat at the counter seats and warmed up with spicy ramen.

8

7

7

9 DARUMA
成吉思汗だるま本店

A   4 Crystal bldg, 1F, Minami 5 Jonishi, Chuo-ku, 064-0805

RESTAURANT/YAKINUKU | Daruma is one of the most famous and popular lamb yakinuku (barbecued lamb) restaurants in Sapporo. Here you can order your choice of lamb pieces and vegetables to grill on the shichirin (personal barbecue) for each group of diners. Expect to queue for at least 30 minutes, but the wait is well worth it.

Upon entry, you will notice that there are no coat hangers for your winter woollies, but fear not, each stool has a removable lid so you can store your clothes inside, which is not only super convenient but also helps keep that barbecue smell off your clothes.

The focus here is definitely on the delicious food. The small restaurant only seats a few diners at a time and is always buzzy and crowded. Get used to saying 'sumimasen' (excuse me) as you brush past other diners to make your way around the curved counter seating to the bathroom.

My friend Kay and I ordered the assorted cut meat set, which was incredibly delicious, especially on a cold and snowy winter's evening. The staff will assist you by giving instructions on how to cook your meat, or you can simply take a peek around at other diners and follow their lead. Generally though, you lightly grill the meat on the top of your shichirin and then use scissors to cut the meat in half or to size before serving onto your plate. If you order an alcoholic drink, you will be given a small 'alcohol charge set' side dish, which is often a plate of pickles.

It's more of an in-and-out restaurant, so it's not the best place if you're looking for a slow dinner where you can have a leisurely chat between dishes. This fast-food vibe is largely due to its popularity and the long queue outside.

10 SOUL STORE
ソウルストア

A   F-DRESS7 bldg, 7-3-2 Minami 3 Jonishi, Chuo-ku, 060-0001

RESTAURANT/SOUP CURRY | Soul Store, with its rustic wooden interior, is the perfect place to enjoy soup curry, one of Sapporo's famous cuisines. The atmosphere is cosy, with both table and counter seating options. I suggest sitting at the counter so you can enjoy the buzz of watching the kitchen in action.

The chicken and vegetable soup curry is one of its top sellers and comes with a range of vegetables, such as pumpkin, broccoli and shiitake, all artfully presented around a deep-fried tempura gobo (burdock) root. The chicken is so soft it melts off the bone, and you can customise your broth, rice size and even your spice level. I love spicy food and selected moderate hotness, but perhaps I could have handled a spicier option. The broth is light and soup-like, and is perfect teamed with rice. I paired my chicken curry with one of my favourite Japanese beers, Heartland beer. If you like beer, I recommend you try it.

It's also a great place to stop in for lunch or dinner if you're a solo diner, as the counter seats are perfect for enjoying your meal alone in peace.

10

9

11 KAMADA SARYO
かまだ茶寮

W   kamada-saryo.com
A   25-1-31 Minami 2 Jonishi, Chuo-ku

RESTAURANT/SUSHI | Set in a cosy little Japanese house tucked down the side laneway off the main road, you'll find this lovely little popular spot. Kamada Saryo is famous for its picturesque and colourful sushi and side dish teishoku (meal/lunch sets). The interior is classic Japanese dark timber and spans from the floors and walls to the tables and chairs.

The special sushi lunch set includes side dishes, tempura, chawanmushi (Japanese savoury pudding) and dessert. The sushi toppings, such as raw salmon, raw scallop, omelette and pickles, are served with a bowl of rice and seaweed so you can assemble your own sushi. You will also find wasabi and mustard on your plate.

To find the restaurant, which is located down a small side path, keep an eye out for the Kamada Saryo sign and image, and then walk down the path. It's a quiet little restaurant frequented by mostly women speaking in soft hushed voices. If you're looking for a peaceful, slow and quiet dining place, look no further.

As this restaurant is extremely popular, I recommend making a booking and at the same time requesting the special sushi plate, as the seats fill up fast and it only serves a limited number of sushi plates each day. If you miss out on a booking, fear not, enjoy a matcha ice-cream in the traditional Japanese house cafe setting.

12 MENYA YUKIKAZE
麺屋雪風

A   4-2-6 Minami 7 Jonishi, Chuo-ku, 064-0807

RESTAURANT/RAMEN | Like all good ramen places, expect to wait in line at this famous local establishment. I lined up in the snow for at least 30 minutes, but the anticipation and the long queue made it fun.

The interior is like all of the best ramen places – tiny, old, dusty and filled with laminated photos that have faded and are turning brown. Menya Yukikaze's (literally meaning 'snow wind') walls are covered with autographs of persons of note who have previously dined here.

It has an English menu, which explains the delicious options. The most popular dish is the miso ramen, but for those who like a bit of added spice, you should try the chilli ramen. On my visit, I tried the miso ramen and, let me tell you, it did not disappoint. The vibe of local diners teamed with the retreat from the snow outside and steamy hot miso ramen is one memory I'll never forget. When you take that first sip of soup and first slurp of noodles, you can't help but smile.

This is the best cheap and cheerful ramen for less than ¥1,000 that you can find!

13 THE LOTS
ザ ロッツ

W   Instagram.com/the.lots
A   Social Hall bldg, 2F, 2 Minami 5 Jonishi,
     Chuo-ku, 064-0805
T   011-213-0201

BAR | The Lots is undeniably my favourite place in Sapporo. I visited alone at about 10pm on my last night in Sapporo, and as I entered through the warehouse-like building, climbing up the industrial-style stairs filled with small rooms/bars, I got the feeling that I'd stumbled across a real gem. At the end of the 2nd floor corridor, I spotted the cute neon 'The Lots' sign, and I could just tell it was going to be a cute bar.

The owner sat me at the counter next to a row of super-cute guys. Although there isn't an English menu, the owner was so kind that he helped me with anything I needed. Behind the counter I spotted some fruits in an open refrigerator and ordered a fresh citrus fruit sour (shochu-based Japanese cocktail). I was a little peckish and ordered the spicy edamame and house-made nikomi soup, which was incredibly delicious and perfect for a snowy evening.

By the end of the evening, I had made friends with not only the owner but all of the guys as well, who were so surprised that I had found this cool local hotspot. The guys were so friendly and took me to another bar afterwards. It's a fun place to make some new friends – and they do karaoke here! Enjoy and say hello from Hello Sandwich!

14 & SEIS.INC
酒と銀シャリ せいす

W   andseis-inc.com
A   6–5-3, Minami 2 Jonishi, Chuo-ku,
     060-0062

BAR/SAKE | & SEIS is a large modern sake bar in the centre of Sapporo's shotengai (undercover shopping streets). You'll notice it instantly because the shop façade is adorned with graphic noren (traditional Japanese fabric dividing curtains) featuring geisha in vibrant patterned kimono. This sake bar, part of a chain of four stores, has a casual and buzzy vibe.

Seating options range from table seating to counter seats. You'll love the shop-branded plates and timber sake cups. You can even pick up a packet of shop-branded matches as a sweet little take-home memory. The interior is open plan with an industrial vibe, with cement and spot lighting on black railings.

One of the specialties at & SEIS is oysters, so be sure to order a plate of these. Also popular is the assortment of grilled fish cooked on skewers over a hot flame, giving them a crispy coating. Being a sake bar, it places utmost respect on the production of rice (the ingredient used to make sake), so it offers six different types of rice, and you can enjoy the lustre, fragrance and stickiness of each.

This bar is in a fantastically convenient location, making for an easy quick drink, lunch or dinner – you won't regret it.

13

13

14

15 UNWIND HOTEL
ホテルアンワインド札幌

W   hotel-unwind.com/en
A   289-111 Minami 8 Nishi 5, Chuo-ku,
     064-0808

STAY/HOTEL | Unwind Hotel is a
gorgeous lodge-themed hotel to relax and
unwind in at the end of a day. From the
moment you walk in, the attention to detail
in the design and furnishings is so spot
on. A log fire warms up the reception area,
and upon check-in guests can select from a
special menu of welcome drinks. I picked the
hot apple cider, which was served in a glass
mug with slices of citrus.

Inside your cabin-themed timber room,
you will find thoughtful details, such as an
earthy room fragrance, copper gold light
fittings and a Balmuda brand kettle complete
with a coffee-pouring spout – a perfectly
considered touch for the complete enjoyment
of your stay.

A breakfast of hearty Sapporo soup stew
and fresh bread is included and is served at
the time of your choice in a basket delivered to
your room door. The rooms have oven toasters
that you can warm your bread up in.

Guests can also enjoy complimentary
all-you-can-drink Hokkaido wine from
5pm–7pm at the hotel's rooftop bar. In the
cooler months, before it starts snowing,
the rooftop fire-pit is lit and guests gather
around the lovely view over Sapporo. I highly
recommend staying here.

15

15

15

FUKUOK

A RELAXED CITY
ON JAPAN'S KYUSHU
ISLAND

33.589° N
130.397° E

12

Fukuoka, Kyushu Island's main city, is a comfortable size where you can expect to find all the shopping, restaurants and other traveller needs that you might require, and there's good transport infrastructure. It's filled with unpretentious and kind locals, and you won't be hard pressed to find a cute cafe, fun izakaya (small bar) or a late-night karaoke bar. You can't miss Shochu Bar Mogura (*see* p. 252), with over 500 types of shochu (Japanese potato-based liquor), or Fukuichi Ramen (*see* p. 251), one of my favourite ramen shops. If you're in need of caffeine, the city has great cafes, such as Coffee County bean roasters (*see* p. 248).

Fukuoka also has an energetic art scene with residencies and galleries, like Konya 2023 Project (*see* p. 240), scattered throughout the city, as well as the not-to-be-missed stationery stores of Linde Cartonnage (*see* p. 245) and Hightide (*see* p. 245). And, if you visit during hanami (cherry blossom viewing) season, you shouldn't miss beautiful Ohori Koen (*see* p. 240).

If you visit Kyushu, you might find yourself stopping by Fukuoka for a few days as a base or port of entry on your way to Beppu (*see* p. 256) and Nagasaki.

1 OHORI KOEN
大濠公園

A   1 Ohori-koen, Chuo-ku, 810-0051
T   092-741-2004

ATTRACTION/PARK | Ohori Koen is one of Fukuoka's most famous parks and has so many areas to explore. It's beautiful and spacious and is set across almost 400,000 square metres (500,000 square yards). The park was constructed between 1926 and 1929 and designed after the classic garden style of the West Lake in China.

You can rent boats to enjoy the large pond and wander around the stepping stones of the Japanese garden, and you will also find a children's amusement park, a wild bird forest and even a Noh theatre. The park has an outer moat surrounding it, which is gorgeous to take a leisurely walk around. In fact, Ohori is Japanese for 'moat'.

Ohori Koen is especially special during hanami (cherry blossom viewing) season, when people flock here for parties under the floating cherry blossom petals. I spent one hanami party here with my 'Tokyo sister', Ame-chan (an Australian who now lives back in Melbourne), and we had such a special pink hanami picnic with pink Asahi beers and bento boxes. If you happen to be in the city during hanami, the best place to sit under the petals is near the Fukuoka Castle ruins inside the park. You can also walk up to the nearby lookout here and take some photographs overlooking the park.

The park can be accessed from Ohorikoen and Tojinmachi stations on the Fukuoka City Subway Kuko line. It's a 7-minute walk from both stations.

2 KONYA 2023 PROJECT
紺屋2023

W   konya2023.travelers-project.info/en/about-2
A   Daiichi Matsumura bldg, 1-14-28 Daimyo, Chuo-ku, 810-0041
T   092-984-6292

ATTRACTION/CREATIVE SPACE/ GALLERY | Fukuoka is well known for its vibrant art scene, and Konya 2023 Project is no exception – it is a gallery space and artist residency rolled into one, and a fantastic spot to see local art. The space has been running since 2008 and is on a 15-year lease until 2023. Here you can see artwork by a diverse range of artists working with various mediums. Artists of all nationalities and ages exhibit here. I first learned of it when my best friend, Rhys, did an artist's residency here and made some interactive artwork.

Its location a little off the street can be tricky to find, so once your phone's GPS takes you to this location, just head down the little laneway right to the back, and then take the stairs to your right up to the gallery. The space is set in a warehouse building with a vibe that reminds me more of Sydney's Surry Hills than Japan. If you're lucky, you might run into one of the artists doing a residency to have a chat to discover more about their artworks.

Just before the entrance to the gallery is a fantastic collection of free papers, so be sure to pick up some of these for information about Fukuoka. The space is a 10–15 minute walk from either Tenjin or Akasaka stations.

3 YATAI
屋台

A 8 Nakagawa-dori, Nakasu, Hakata-ku, 810-0801

SHOP/MARKET | Open any guidebook on Fukuoka and it'll recommend you visit these waterside yatai (open-air food stands). They're probably one of the best-known attractions in Fukuoka. However, I've visited these yatai on two occasions and, although they're fun to walk past and peek at, they are rather touristy, and I'm not sure I'd dine at them again. So if you do happen to go, be prepared about what to expect. It is, however, lovely to walk along the riverside and watch the lights glisten in the reflections.

These yatai are mostly frequented by tourists and, unlike most yakitori (grilled skewers) bars, many of these yatai have a minimum amount of sticks per person rule. In addition to yakitori, you can also find foods such as oden (hotpot), hakata ramen and various alcoholic drinks.

Nearby is a mall called Canal City that I adore for its '80s-retro vibe and an outdoor water park. So you might like to walk up to this mall if you find yourself somewhat underwhelmed by the yatai.

The Fukuoka yatai are most popular on Saturdays and are generally open from 6pm to around 2am. Each yatai usually takes one day off a week (this varies per shop but is often Sunday), and they will close in bad weather when it's not fun to sit outside in the rain.

4 KAGOYA
カゴヤ

A 3-13-21 Yakuin, Chuo-ku, 810-0022

SHOP/HOMEWARES | If you've been to The Basket burger restaurant (*see* p. 251) – and you really must – this cutest little basket store is run by the owner's mother! This store actually used to be in the location of where The Basket is now, but she moved around the corner when her son returned to Fukuoka to let him use the space for his burger restaurant. It's such a sweet story. While I was dining at The Basket, the owner had one of his staff members walk us to his mother's store and introduce us to her beautiful work.

Kyushu Island is well known for basket weaving, and here in this shop there is such a fantastic collection of locally-made baskets in all shapes and sizes, for all purposes. You'll delight in wandering around the store and choosing display, decorative or carry baskets.

Although the owner doesn't speak English, she will absolutely explain through her heart and hands the details about each basket. She has such a beautiful energy, and I can't recommend popping in here enough for a divine keepsake.

4

3

3

5 LINDE CARTONNAGE
リンデ

w   linde-cartonnage.com
A   Sanfuruno bldg, 2F-B, 1-8-11 Otemon,
    Chuo-ku, 810-0074
T   092-725-7745

SHOP/STATIONERY | This gem of a stationery shop is hidden upstairs in a warehouse-like building near Fukuoka Art Museum. It's absolutely Fukuoka's best riso printing store, and it also stocks a range of classic-style calligraphy pens and inks. Naturally, you can also find divine paper to use with these calligraphy tools.

I discovered that the owner of this store used to work as an editor and speaks perfect English, which will be helpful if you plan to order your own personalised riso printed cards. Imagine writing postcards to your loved ones on cards you designed and had printed locally. The cards can be printed with an extremely fast turnaround, so this could be the most memorable take-home good from your trip to Japan.

A range of the store's original postcards are also for sale if you just want to pick up something premade. The cartonnage boxes are perfect not only for storing items in but also for creating a little stationery set.

If you're a paper lover, this is one store that you won't want to miss out on. When you hear the owner describe paper as having a 'certain magic that makes the person holding it smile unconsciously', you'll understand what I mean!

6 HIGHTIDE
ハイタイド

w   hightide.co.jp/shop
A   1-8-28 Shirogane, Chuo-ku, 810-0012
T   092-533-0338

SHOP/STATIONERY/CAFE | Hightide is one of Fukuoka's must-see stores. It's a Fukuoka-based stationery brand that opened this retail flagship store at the start of 2017. Situated in a quiet residential area, you might wonder if you're heading the right way, but once you're there you can't miss this all white warehouse-style building.

Before you even enter the store, there's a large covered outdoor area full of tables and chairs where you can enjoy a sandwich, cake or beer or a coffee made from a special blend from nearby Coffee County (*see* p. 248), all ordered from the little cafe window.

Entering the stationery store is what dreams are made of for stationery lovers. Rows and rows of coloured pens, pencils, papers, notebooks and also homeware items, such as trays, cups and some apparel items. They also have a small area for pop-up stores.

One of my favourite things about this flagship store is that you can make your own customised notebooks here. You can select everything from the cover to the binding colour and even the elastic band. Hightide's philosophy is that they consider stationery and notebooks as part of fashion that expresses ourselves, so they aim to create products that enrich people's lives by making work and study fun.

Pop in here, buy some stationery, then have a coffee in the cafe area and do a little sketching or journal writing.

7 COMO ES
コモエス

w Instagram.com/como_es_imaizumi
A 2-1-75 Imaizumi, Chuo-ku, 810-0021
T 092-516-3996

CAFE/MUSIC | Como Es is a Fukuoka favourite. Hidden down a pebbly street off the main road in a renovated 50-year-old building that looks like a residential house, you should come here if you adore donuts, coffee and records. Or if you just feel like visiting a lovely place to have a break while exploring Fukuoka.

There is an English menu, so fear not! Some of the menu items include coffee, chai, Heartland beer and, of course, some delicious donuts – I recommend trying the kinako (soybean flour) one. You can also order lunch sets for ¥1,000 that include hayashi rice and a salad. Potato salad can be added for an additional ¥250. In summer, you can order a fresh house-made lemonade that is as picturesque as it is delicious. I also recommend the rum chai ginger cocktail.

The manager, Nishida-san, plays records from his record collection of over 20,000 vinyls! You can enjoy sitting at the counter seats next to the DJ booth, which plays music through Electro-Voice and Klipsch speakers, but there are also tables upstairs if you're after a bit more space to relax.

Come night time, Nishida-san mans the DJ booth and the space turns into a fun bar. You can also chance upon music events and various types of workshops here. From time to time you can find pop-up stores, like fashion stores, so be sure to check its Instagram for upcoming events. Como Es also hosts music nights, which are a fun way to meet some locals! The space is non-smoking and it takes cash only, so be sure to have some yen handy.

8 COFFEE & CAKE STAND LULU
コーヒー＆ケーキ・スタンド・ルル

w Instagram.com/cacs_lulu
A Loire Mansion 2, 3-26 Yakuin,
   (room number 2-103) Chuo-ku, 810-0022

CAFE/COFFEE | This is perhaps Fukuoka's coolest coffee shop, and you'll feel it from the moment you step in. The interior is minimal with industrial and copper details mixed in. Concrete walls are teamed with plush carpet and seating is either at the counter or at small gold tables surrounded by clear plastic stools. There are even small golden wall fixtures just large enough to hold your coffee cup, so you can choose to stand if all the seats are taken or if you're just after a quick caffeine fix.

I visited in summer and ordered an iced-coffee, which was the perfect brew. If you're feeling peckish, I absolutely recommend trying one of the incredible cakes. Not only are they delicious but they're beautifully presented and topped with fresh fruits or nuts for decoration. I recommend the fig chiffon shortcake, which is a delicious, light and fluffy cream-filled cake. There are also seasonal cheesecakes, such as a cheesecake topped with homemade peach jam. Yum! You can also buy coffee beans to enjoy back at your hotel or when you're home from your trip to Japan.

When I visited I commented on the gorgeous arrangement of flowers next to the La Marzocco espresso machine, and the owner told me his mum runs a florist and she brings in flowers for him. I love this divine family-style cafe in Fukuoka. I'm sure you'll spot a few beautiful arrangements to dreamily meditate on while you enjoy your coffee and cake.

7

7

8

9 COFFEE COUNTY
コーヒーカウンティ

w   coffeecounty.cc
A   1-21-21 Takasago, Chuo-ku, 810-0011
T   092-753-8321

CAFE/COFFEE | Coffee County, one of Fukuoka's most famous roasters, is located just around the corner from the Hightide flagship store (*see* p. 245). In fact, they actually make a special blend specifically for Hightide. It's absolutely delicious, and I recommend ordering it when you go to Hightide store. Then, double up your caffeine fix with another cup at Coffee County.

While the beans are roasted at their roastery in Kurume, this Fukuoka branch has a little indoor cafe area. You can pick up some beans here as a lovely keepsake, too. Choose from blends such as Yara AB Kenya, Finca La Parcelita Typica Colombia and The Ethiopian roast.

The owner of Coffee County spent three months in Central America working on a farm and studying coffee making, establishing such a love for the process and lifestyle of the farm, he opened up his own roastery in Kurume in 2013. If you visit their website, you can see some beautiful travel snaps from what looks like an incredibly rewarding and special time on the farm.

Be sure to get your caffeine fix at Coffee County!

10 KAI
回

w   facebook.com/kaicurry
A   3-13-20 Yakuin, Chuo-ku, 810-0022
T   092-525-4027

RESTAURANT/CURRY | One of the fantastic things about Japan is they do so many things incredibly well, and when it comes to non-Japanese cuisine you will often find yourself pleasantly surprised. The cute owners of Kai Curry travelled extensively within India to get inspiration for their Indian- and Japanese-style curries. Bringing back ideas of mixing spices and incorporating this knowledge with Japanese spices and ingredients, such as yuzu (a citrus fruit), shiso (a herb) and seasonal Japanese vegetables, means an amazing curry like you've never tried before.

You can order the curry of the day from your choice of meat or lentils and add on colourful pickled toppings, which they encourage you to mix into the curry after you have tasted the curry on its own. The ground floor is bench-counter seating, where you can watch the staff cook your curry as you wait. The interior is small, creating a buzzy atmosphere. You'll notice a range of small charming details, such as arrangements of dried flowers displayed around the restaurant. And the spice cupboard is impressive and decorative.

In addition to the colourful rainbow curries, the restaurant also makes its own spiced whisky, and a range of local and imported craft beers and organic wines are available.

It's a very popular curry shop, so don't be surprised if you find yourself having to wait for a seat, or you can phone ahead for a reservation in the upstairs dining area. If you take a peek at the bookstand at the front of the restaurant, you'll notice just how many Japanese magazines this restaurant has been featured in.

9

10

10

12

12

11 FUKUICHI RAMEN
福一ラーメん

A   Hilark bldg, 2–10–12 Hakata Ekimae,
Hakata-ku, 812-0011

RESTAURANT/RAMEN | This is one of my favourite ramen shops in Fukuoka, and I've visited on multiple occasions. Like most of Japan's best ramen places, Fukuichi Ramen is unpretentious. The shop fit-out is an L-shaped counter with seating for about a dozen patrons. You place your order directly with the staff, rather than using a ticket vending machine (as is the case in many other ramen restaurants). There isn't an English menu, but there are images of the ramen on the walls, and with a bit of pointing and smiling I'm sure you will have your ramen in no time.

The basic ramen in tonkotsu (pork) broth is delicious as it is, but I also love the ramen with wonton for ¥600. You can add extra ramen noodles for ¥200 if you're super hungry. Beer is by the bottle at ¥450, and a glass of sake will cost you ¥350.

I'd be lying if I didn't tell you the initial reason I visited was because of the cute pale blue ramen bowls with maroon text branding. But the thin ramen noodles are so good that I keep coming back.

12 THE BASKET
ザ バスケット

W   facebook.com/thebasketfuk
A   1-12-15 Yakuin, Chuo-ku, 810-0022
T   092-406-7939

RESTAURANT/BURGERS | After years of working in a burger store in Tokyo, the owner moved back to his hometown of Fukuoka and opened up The Basket, a popular corner cafe and burger shop with seating to accommodate 10 people, in what used to be his mother's basket store (*see* p. 242). He and I had been messaging about this book, and when I arrived to take photographs of the venue, they had just closed for a break, but he graciously offered to let me in to enjoy a burger in the closed store. 'We still have ingredients', he kindly said in Japanese. Naturally, I declined his offer, not wanting to impose, but I vowed to be back on another occasion.

Keeping my word, I returned to the shop a few days later – this time with two Australian friends and their gorgeous baby girl. My friend Ben and the owner struck up a lovely conversation, and the overall vibe was happiness, deliciousness and a sense that we were in Fukuoka's coolest spot. Mid burger, Ben proclaimed that it was one of the best burgers he's ever had in Japan – and he wasn't wrong.

You can order burgers or sandwiches with everything from double patties to avocado, and the burgers come with French fries. I recommend the cheeseburger. The menu also features a Mexican burger, a double cheeseburger and a barbecue cheeseburger. Drinks-wise, The Basket offers a range of American craft beer, such as Fantastic Haze IPA and Ponto Session IPA. It also has Japanese beer and – my favourite – Heartland!

Not only is the burger and vibe incredible, the music choice is on point. The shop is located on one corner of a five-way intersection, so if you find a seat by the window you can enjoy watching the world of Fukuoka pass by as you eat. The owner sent me off with his own copy of a local magazine of things to do, along with his must-see recommendations, such as Takohira Takoyaki (*see* p. 252). The community kindness and spirit doesn't get much better than this.

Pretty please pop in for one of Japan's best burgers, and say hello from Hello Sandwich.

13 TAKOHIRA TAKOYAKI
たこ平

A   1-12-17 Takasago, Chuo-ku, 810-0011
T   092-515-6213

RESTAURANT | Takohira Takoyaki is a little restaurant that was recommended to me by the owner of The Basket (*see* p. 251). They are so friendly in here, and Japan's famous takoyaki (fried octopus, originally food from the Kansai region) are so authentic and delicious.

You can pick up take-away takoyaki made in front of you at the window, or find a seat inside. You select from a range of different types of takoyaki, such as with sauce only, sauce and mayonnaise, shallot topping or shallot and sauce topping – to name a few. For take-away, eight balls will only cost ¥350! And the price go up to ¥590 for 18 balls! It's cheap and cheerful and oh-so delicious.

As the takoyaki is made right in front of you, you can enjoy watching the whole process, including the magnificent spin with the takoyaki spike. When it's done by a team as skilled as the owners of Takohira Takoyaki, you will be mesmerised.

Please take this as a warning, pretty please ... if you happen to get take-away, please promise to wait until they cool down before eating them. The insides of these fried octopus balls get incredibly hot. So no matter if you think they're safe to eat, tack on an extra 5-minute wait time. You'll thank me later.

14 SHOCHU BAR MOGURA
焼酎バ- 土竜

A   1-11-25 Shirogane, Chuo-ku, 810-0012
T   092-526-5791

BAR | Okay, so if you only go to one place in Fukuoka, Shochu Bar Mogura should be it. Like most good things in Japan, it's almost impossible to find, hidden in an alleyway, but the mission is well worth it. It's run by the sweetest couple who can understand a little English, and it's so chilled and comfortable that you'll want to snuggle into this bar for the night.

It has a giant menu full of options, including edamame, karaage (fried chicken), salads, tofu, hotpots – to name a few – and there are over 500 types of shochu (Japanese potato-based liquor) to try! In Japan, it's not uncommon to buy an entire bottle of shochu and leave it at the izakaya (small bar) and drink a little each time you visit. It's just one of the many charming Japanese customs.

The treasure trove of collected nostalgic items adorning the space includes retro signage, old televisions, a tiny yellow fridge, movie posters, kerosene heaters, peko-chan figurines and walls lined with Showa-era (1926–89) vinyl. There is a range of rooms available for all sorts of drinking meet-ups. Tables, couches, and even a private tatami room. When I visited, my friend was breastfeeding, and the owner closed off a room for her so that she was able to have privacy. So lovely.

And, perhaps I took advantage of the 500 types of shochu and ended up leaving my camera at the bar. Luckily, I had made the reservation for our group, so they had my phone number to call. I asked my taxi to go back to the bar, and when I arrived the owners had felt so bad for me that they gifted me some sweet bread and chocolate that they had gone out to get from the local convenience store. I love this country so much! You really shouldn't miss this bar – it's so divine and welcoming. Please say hello from Hello Sandwich when you visit!

14

13

14

15 NEO MEGUSTER STANDING BAR
ネオ メグスタ

A   1-10-16 Akasaka, Chuo-ku, 810-0042
T   050-5327-5333

BAR | Neo Meguster Standing Bar is one of my favourite bars in Fukuoka. It's casual and no frills – a buzzy standing bar where you can easily relax.

One of the things I have always loved about Fukuoka is that each train station has its own little logo that refers to the particular suburb it's in. For example, Ohori-koen station is famous for hanami (cherry blossom viewing) in Ohori Koen (*see* p. 240), so the logo of this station is a sakura (cherry blossom). It's so sweet and unique to this city. In reference to that, at this standing bar you're given a train station card and that becomes your 'table number'.

The food and drinks here are cheap and cheerful, and an English menu is available. A glass of sparkling wine will cost ¥500, sake and shochu (Japanese potato-based liquor) are ¥400, and if you like sweeter drinks, you might like the umeshu (plum wine) for ¥500. Umeshu can be enjoyed on the rocks, but it's also delicious mixed with sparkling water. You will find both Japanese and Western food here, such as karaage (fried chicken), mackerel with sesame, an assorted ham platter and a beef shoulder steak. You'll also find yuzu-pepper flavoured tabasco sauce on the counters, which is so delicious on so many of their dishes!

I last visited during the afternoon and there were standing spots available, but this bar gets very busy at night with a fun and bustling vibe. Oh, and the staff love putting images of their guests on the bar's Instagram, so be sure to be portrait ready! Don't worry about them sneaking a snap of you, as they will ask your permission before posting.

16 MORRIS RED FOX
モーリス レッドフォックス

W   morris-pub.com
A   7F, 2-1-4 Daimyo, Chuo-ku, 810-0041
T   092-771-4774

BAR | Okay, so I hear you asking: 'why would I go to a British pub while I'm in Japan?', and I hear you! But, with rooftop terrace bars being uncommon in Japan, it's one of the places I like to go to chill out each time I visit Fukuoka. Morris has four branches in Fukuoka, but I have only visited Red Fox for its terrace and views overlooking the city.

Take the elevator up to the 7th floor, turn right and head to the bar to order snacks and a drink. The rooftop terrace has simple outdoor pub-style furniture with timber chairs and tables. During the colder months, they bring you a blanket and outdoor heaters to keep you warm as you enjoy the view with your drink. The terrace is located on the same floor as the bar, just to the left of the elevator, so it's easy to carry your drinks out there.

They feature 11 types of draft beer from all around the world, if you happen to be a little homesick, but also serve a range of Japanese craft beers. If you're really, really homesick, this is the place to come for all sorts of pub food, like fish and chips, bangers and mash, pizza or nachos. For those of you who fancy saving some yen, happy hour is between 5pm and 7pm for half-price cocktails.

Red Fox's location right in the centre of the city makes it an easy spot to pop in and rest your feet after a day of exploring.

16

15

15

BEPPU

**THE SPOT TO
GO IF YOU LOVE
ONSEN (HOT
SPRINGS)**

**33.279° N
131.500° E**

13

別府

Our perspectives and impressions of cities are often based on personal experiences, and although I travelled to Beppu on Kyushu Island by myself, I left with such a warm heart and many new friends. If you manage to find charming locals like I was lucky enough to, your impression of this city will no doubt be one of the most cherished memories of your Japan travels. From the hotel shuttle bus driver who kissed my business card and then later phoned to invite me to lunch, to the owner of Beppu Sake Stand Jun (*see* p. 280) who closed her shop to tour guide me around, the local people of Beppu are incredibly kind-hearted and extremely generous.

Beppu is well known for its onsen (hot springs), boasting 2,850 of them, so a visit to one is essential. You'll want to start at Ekimae Koutou Onsen (*see* p. 258) or Takegawara Onsen (*see* p. 260), two of the city's most famous onsen. For more local Beppu culture, I recommend that you try tori-ten (famous Beppu chicken tempura) at Toyoken (*see* p. 280). Creativity can be found at gems like Spica (*see* p.274), Punto Precog (*see* p. 258) and Kiyoshima Apartment (*see* p. 260).

Instead of neon lights, shopping malls and suburbs filled with busy city life, you'll enjoy Beppu if you love exploring small towns and aged Showa-era (1926–89) architecture.

1 EKIMAE KOUTOU ONSEN

駅前高等温泉

A   13-14 Beppushi Ekimaechou, Oita
T   097-7210-541

ATTRACTION/ONSEN | This is one of Beppu's most famous public onsens (hot spring bathhouses) and was built during the Showa era (1926–89) some 80 years ago. It is designed in the Taisho–Roman architectural style with a green tongari roof that sits above a white façade and has German-style decorative timber finishes. Inside, there are the most incredible pink-, blue- and yellow-coloured glass windows that create the dreamiest light.

When you enter the onsen, you'll be greeted by receptionists, and the ticket vending machines are just to your right. There are two options of baths. An Atsuyu (very hot water bath) and a Nuruyu (normal hot temperature). I recommend selecting the Nuruyu as the Atsuyu is quite hot, even for Japanese people who are used to these natural hot springs. A ticket costs just ¥200 for the Nuruyu bath. You can also rent a bath towel for ¥50 and a hairdryer for ¥10, and items for purchase include soap, shampoo, conditioner, razors, toothbrushes and so on. It's not uncommon in Japan to see people walking around the streets with bath baskets with these kinds of items (if they bring their own). If you don't fancy popping into the bathhouse, you can wash your hands from the hot spring hand bath just outside of the main building.

This special and historic onsen features a bath beautifully stained in a way that only 80 years of use can create. The water is slightly reddish-brown in colour and contains a lot of sodium and bicarbonate ions that will make your skin feel so beautiful and smooth afterwards.

It's only a minute's walk from Beppu train station. Enjoy relaxing in this onsen!

2 PUNTO PRECOG

プント プレコグ

W   puntoprecog.jp
A   3-5 Motomachi, Oita, 874-0944
T   03-6825-1223

ATTRACTION/CREATIVE SPACE | Punto Precog is a 'free space', in other words an always changing creative space that people can rent to host exhibitions and lectures, have pop-up cafes or pop-up markets and so on. There is a strong focus on the arts and cultural crossover here. At the time of my visit, they were running a cute Sichuan hotpot event for a few months. Perfect for steamy cosy nights!

The word punto means 'base' in Spanish, while precog is short for precognition – a prophet of the future – which is taken from the character in the film *Minority Report*. Since punto precog is produced by Asa Nakano, who lived and worked in Spain, and by Akane Nakamura, who runs a cooperation called precog, these two words represent this collective perfectly.

I definitely recommend a visit to check out what amazing pop-up event is taking place at the time of your holiday. Keep in mind that opening hours vary, so be sure to check on the website before you visit.

It's a 5-minute walk from Beppu station. From Saihoji-street, enter Shingu-street, and it's on your right, in front of Osako store. You can't miss it!

3 KIYOSHIMA APARTMENT
清島アパート

W   beppuproject.com
A   2-27 Suehiro-cho, Oita
T   0977-22-3560

ATTRACTION/GALLERY | Creative types won't want to miss a visit to Kiyoshima Apartment, an initiative of the non-profit organisation Beppu Project, where an old traditional apartment building has been turned into an artist's residency, galleries and exhibition space.

It's a fantastic space for local people to interact, collaborate and inspire each other and an inspirational spot for anyone interested in the arts and crafts to visit. Be sure to check the website before you visit to see if it is open to the public with an event or exhibition on.

The 2nd floor is the residential space for artists in residence, so it's definitely out of bounds, but on the 1st floor, when open for an exhibition, you will be able to see artist's studios and a gorgeous tatami floor exhibition space to your right just upon entry. Be sure not to walk on the tatami with shoes on. And a pro-tip that I only learned after years of living in Japan: you should never walk on the joins of tatami mats, but rather on the rice straw sections only.

The apartments are open to the public twice a year to introduce Kiyoshima Apartments to local residents. Usually this is in February and July, but be sure to check online.

I loved my visit here and found that seeing the work of locals and the studio set up reminded me of my days studying Fine Art at the University of New South Wales COFA. Enjoy!

4 TAKEGAWARA ONSEN
竹瓦温泉

A   16-23 Motomachi, Oita
T   0977-23-1585

ATTRACTION/ONSEN | Takegawara is one of Beppu's most famous and oldest onsen (hot springs). It was constructed in 1938 and has a Chinese-inspired gabled tiled roof, but an older building was on the site as early as 1879, built with a bamboo roof. It's conveniently located in the middle of Beppu city.

While I was in Beppu, a kind taxi driver and I got chatting about the city and this book you now have in your hands, and he stopped the meter at the location I wanted to go to, and then drove me 'service de' (complimentary extra trip) to this onsen because he wanted to show me the exquisite building. He asked me to get out of the taxi and take some photos for the book! How divine! According to the world's sweetest taxi driver, this is one onsen not to be missed. From where I took photographs, I could hear the sound of people pouring buckets of hot spring water over themselves and chatting away in a relaxed manner.

Takegawara Onsen features a Showa-era style (1926–89) high-ceiling lobby where you can sit and relax after your bath. The women's bath is made of a mix of sodium-hydrogen carbonated spring water, and the men's is sodium, calcium, magnesium-chloride and hydrogen carbonated spring water. Both of these baths are incredible for chronic pain, stiffness in muscles and joints and high blood pressure – among other things.

Even if you don't fancy taking a bath, it's worth visiting this onsen just for the incredible architecture, which can be viewed from the outside. A regular onsen costs ¥100 and a 'sand' bath costs ¥1,050

4

3

A   6 kumi Horita, Oita

T   0977-25-1126

A   Furo hon, Oita, 874-0044

T   0977-67-3880

ATTRACTION/ONSEN | You can't come to Beppu, a town famed for its hot springs, and not visit an onsen (hot springs bathhouse). This family-run gem is hidden in the middle of the mountains and set deep in a forest, and is such a dreamy retreat and my pick of the mix.

It can only be accessed by car or taxi and is about a 20-minute taxi ride from the city centre. As you weave through the windy mountain roads further and further into the Horita area, you get the sense that you're about to enter something very special. In fact, my taxi driver was very surprised that I even knew about this hidden-away place, as, although he was local, he wasn't aware of it.

Whilst Mugen No Sato has public baths, it also has private baths, which might be handy for couples, families or for those with tattoos (tattoos aren't usually allowed in onsen). Or perhaps even for those who might be a little bit shy about being naked in public. A shared bath costs ¥700, a private/family bath starts at ¥2,500 for one hour. The most popular private bath is the Taki (waterfall) one that looks out onto two incredible waterfalls. A dip in it will cost you ¥3,000 for one hour and is probably the best money you will ever spend in Japan. My skin felt incredible after this dip, and I can't recommend it enough!

You can't make a reservation for the private baths, so pack a book to read just in case you find yourself having to wait a while. Better still, pack a sketchbook and enjoy sitting outdoors and draw the gorgeous forest. I promise you that the wait will be well worth it, and the waiting itself is, in fact, a beautiful meditation.

Here is a little pro-tip for you: phone in advance to check if the onsen is open, as in bad weather the onsen water conditions change and it will close.

ATTRACTION | Ashi mushi, which literally translates as 'foot steam', is exactly what the name suggests: a foot steam bath housed in a wall-less timber hut and offered for free by the city of Beppu, used by travellers and locals alike. The foot steam bath is manned by helpful staff who will assist you if you're unsure of anything, but there are also signs posted in many languages.

To use the steam bath, you open the lid of the timber box in front of the seats and slide your feet into the leg holes. You'll immediately feel relaxed. Be sure not to put your feet too far forward as that is where the steam comes out and it can be rather hot. Instead, keep your feet close to your body and you will find this an incredible way to relax after a day of wandering around the streets of Beppu.

Alongside the free foot steam bath there is also a free foot bath, so you might like to wash your feet in the foot bath beforehand and then use the steam section afterwards.

It is open daily 9.30am to 7.30pm and is a relaxing and invigorating experience.

7 JIGOKU MUSHI KOBO KANNAWA

A   Kitanaka, Oita, 874-0845

ATTRACTION | The people of Beppu have been using the onsen (hot springs) for centuries, not only for baths but also for cooking food in the hot steam. With no need to add any oil, this clean type of 'hell steam cooking' is an incredibly healthy and fun way to enjoy your food. Beppu locals also say that the minerals in the steam bring out the natural flavours of the food.

The Jigoku Mushi Kobo Kannawa (Steam Cooking Center) is run by a team of volunteers and is somewhat a mix between a community kitchen and a restaurant. You can either bring your own food or purchase it at the centre. The steam chambers can be rented for ¥340 to ¥550, depending on the size you would like to use. Some of the popular items to steam include vegetables, seafood, meat and eggs. Everything that you need to cook your food with, such as gloves and steam nets, is provided. The staff will assist you, so there's no need to worry about getting the timing right, and there's a dining area where you can enjoy your fresh and healthy steam-cooked meal.

Jigoku Mushi Kobo is a few steps from the Kannawa bus terminal, which is about 15 minutes by frequently departing buses from JR Beppu station. Buses number 5, 7 and 9 are the fastest.

8 UMI JIGOKU 'HELLS'

W   umijigoku.co.jp
A   559-1 Kannawa, Oita
T   0977-66-0121

ATTRACTION | Umi Jigoku, which translates as 'sea hell', is perhaps the most beautiful of Beppu's 8 'hells' (so hot that you cannot enter). The water is scorching at approximately 98°C (208°F), so while these hot springs are not for soaking in, they make for an incredible sightseeing experience. Umi Jigoku, although only the size of a small swimming pool, features cobalt blue water that looks more like something created from a bath bomb as opposed to the explosion of Mt Tsurumi, 1200 years ago. The depth of the water is said to be 200 metres (656 feet), and the steady steam rising from Umi Jigoku creates such a surreal and magical viewing experience.

In addition to this 'hell', there's also a small red-coloured 'hell' in the area next to the large pond. The eerie red water looks like something better suited to a set of *Jurassic Park*, and it's hard to believe it is, in fact, real. Near the small red 'hell' is a greenhouse featuring giant lily pads, which you should check out if you have time.

There is a reasonably large gift shop selling a wide range of onsen towels and bath salts, and if you are hungry, pop into the cafe for dishes such as chanpon and tori-ten (famous Beppu chicken tempura). I wouldn't exactly come here for the food but it also sells a range of ice-creams and drinks, and if you can get a seat at the counter that overlooks the 'hell', you can enjoy a snack and watch the view at the same time. Entry to Umi Jigoku costs ¥400.

8

SAKE

Sake (pronounded sa-keh, not sa-ki), often referred to as nihonshu, is an alcoholic drink made from fermented rice. The fermentation process takes about six weeks, during which time the fermentation of the sugar and the rice occurs simultaneously.

If you're new to sake and want to try one that's not too sweet, I recommend Dassai sake; one of my favourite sakes, the taste is smooth, yet crisp and not too sweet. You will find it on the menu at some izakaya (small bars) and also at liquor shops – if you would like to bring one back in your suitcase.

ISSHIN RICE HOUSE DAIKANYAMA

A Twin bldg Daikanyama A ridge, B1, 30-3, Sarugaku-cho, Shibuya-ku, Tokyo
T 03-6455-1614

JAPAN SAKE AND SHOCHU MAKERS ASSOCIATION

W japansake.or.jp/sake/english
A 1-6-15 Nishishinbashi, Minato-ku, Tokyo 105-0003
T 03-3519-2091

SHOCHU BAR MOGURA

A 1-11-25 Shirogane, Chuo-ku, Fukuoka, 810-0012
T 092-526-5791

TAKAS HIMIZU SAKE BREWERY

W takashimizu.com
A 4-12 Kawamoto Mutsumi-machi, Akita, 010-0934
T 018-864-7331

Sake is best enjoyed cold to allow you to fully enjoy the flavours. However, in winter and at early spring festivals, it's wonderful to enjoy some hot sake to warm yourself up and keep cosy!

At many izakaya you can order sake by the glass or in a tokkuri (a small carafe) with ochoko (or choko for the informal version) cups. The etiquette is to pour for others and have them pour for you – never pour for yourself. It's polite for the receiver to hold their ochoko with both hands and tilt it slightly towards the sake tokkuri being poured from. Once their cup is filled with sake, it's custom for them to then pick up the sake tokkuri and return the favour. This technique and etiquette is the same for pouring beer and wine.

There are various other vessels for sake, such as masu (timber boxes). These are often used for ceremonial purposes, such as hatsumode (the first trip to the shrine each year). I adore sakazuki, which is a wide-mouthed, flat, older-style vessel used for special ceremonial occasions, such as weddings. They are extremely beautiful but also extremely difficult to sip from. Cold and sparkling sake can be enjoyed from a wine glass, which is quite a new trend adopted by restaurants and sake breweries so that you can enjoy the aroma and colour of the sake, as well as the taste.

You can find sake ochoko at second-hand stores and markets, and it's acceptable to mix and match. Collecting a few sake ochoko during your trip to Japan might be a lovely keepsake. At some restaurants, such as Isshin rice house in Tokyo's Daikanyama, they bring out a tray of ochoko and you can select your own.

Another endearing sake and shochu (Japanese potato-based liquor) experience, if you plan on spending longer in Japan, is that many izakaya will let you buy a large bottle of sake and they write your name on it and store it behind the bar, and each time you visit you can drink from your own bottle. Like a mini home away from home! Shochu Bar Mogura (see p. 258) in Fukuoka is one such place. This concept is so sweet and so, so Japanese. The trust in this country is unbelievable.

The Japan Sake and Shochu Makers Association in Tokyo's Minato-ku has over 50 types of sake, shochu and awamori (Okinawan sake, which is distilled rather than fermented). I recommend the seasonal tasting flight, which includes a range of sake, both sparkling and flavoured. It's a fantastic place to start your sake journey.

If you're in Akita book a tour of historic Takashimzu Sake Brewery (see p. 202) for tastings and shopping, or have dinner and try the local specialty awamori at Shirakachi in Okinawa (see p. 308).

9 KANNAWA TOWN

_A Kannawa, Oita, 874-0043
_T 097-7242-828

ATTRACTION/TOWN | At the top of the mountains in Beppu, in the town of Kannawa, it's not uncommon to see hot steam rising from the small openings covered with metal grates in the pavement. It makes for the dreamiest sight. If you stand on top of the grates on a cold day, you can let the steam warm you up! But be sure to be careful as it's extremely hot, and breathing in the steam can be overwhelming.

Wandering around the stone-paved roads of this little town is a lovely way to really grasp just how incredible the onsen (hot spring) landscape is here. These streets are mostly lined with ryokan (traditional Japanese inns), onsen, small temples and some small eateries. It can feel a little touristy near the steam-food places, but the steam streets are undeniably authentic.

The most famous onsen in this area is Kannawa, which started in the 13th century and is the hottest onsen in Beppu. Because the hot-spring water runs very close to the ground in this area, it used to be a particularly dangerous place to walk around but has since been developed to create one of Beppu's most famous onsen. Entry to this historic onsen is only ¥100. It makes for a lovely morning or afternoon and is best accessed by taxi.

Should you like to stay overnight, there are a number of onsen in the area that offer accommodation.

10 HACHIMAN ASAMI SHRINE

_W asami.or.jp
_A 2-15-19 Asami, Oita, 874-0812
_T 0977-23-1408

ATTRACTION/SHRINE | Hachiman Asami is one of Beppu's most famous shrines. It was founded by Noh Naoto Otomo in 1196 and is not only famous for its purified, sacred water and the Onsen Shrine Mikoshi Festival, but also for its impressive shrine and surrounding grounds. It features an enchanting Japanese garden with ponds and winding stairs that take you through the garden.

At the main entrance you are greeted by a beautiful staircase set inside a red torii (gate) that leads up to the main shrine. Before you walk up the stairs, wash your hands in the purifying, sacred water to the right of the entrance. There is a special technique to washing your hands at shrines, so follow what others do or read the instructional diagrams. Beppu is famous for its natural onsen (hot springs) and this special purified water can actually be consumed, so you might see people filling up their water bottles using filters here. Once you reach the top of the stairs you can make a wish at the shrine using a ¥5 coin. Again, follow the rules for the way to pray and wish in terms of when to bow and clap.

Set in the beautiful garden, you will see the famous ancient tree just to the left of the shrine, so allow enough time to explore the small garden down the winding stairs. You will come across a stone torii, and legend has it that if you throw a stone and it lands on the top ledge of the gate, your wish will come true!

The shrine is located quite high up, so you can peek at some lovely views over Beppu city.

10

10

9

11

12

12

11 RAKUTENCHI AMUSEMENT PARK

w   rakutenchi.jp
A   18 Nagarekawa-dori, Oita, 874-0821
T   0977-22-1301

ATTRACTION/THEME PARK | We all know that Hello Sandwich loves a retro amusement park, not just because of the faded pastels and style but also for the nostalgic vibe. The playful signage, the candy fairy floss, the sounds of kids on rides – all mixed together creates such a sweet fantasy land. And when you match a fantasy land with Japan, you're in for a treat.

Rides at Rakutenchi include a rollercoaster, a spinning space ship and a ferris wheel. In summer there's even a water slippery slide. As well as all these wonderful things, this park is also set in the most incredible location quite high up of one of Beppu's many mountains, so travelling up there, through the winding roads (best by taxi) or via the cable car, is an experience in itself.

The park has an incredible suspension bridge for the brave who would like one of the best views over Beppu city. When I walked over it, I was just recovering from a badly broken ankle, and actually it was terrifying – I vowed never to go on a suspension bridge in an earthquake-prone country ever again, but we all know that I will do almost anything to 'get the shot'. Honestly, the middle of this bridge has the most spectacular views over Beppu city and shows you its size and layout.

Although I don't go on the rides at amusement parks, I always wander around taking photos and drawing and relaxing in the cafes. This amusement park was one of my favourite things to do in Beppu!

12 BEPPU STATION MARKET

w   ekimachi1.com/beppu/ichiba
A   6-22 Chuomachi, Oita, 874-0936
T   0977-22-1686

SHOP/MARKET | Beppu Station Market is a super-cute market with a retro vibe, located in a street underneath the train tracks of Beppu train station, much like a shotengai (undercover shopping street). Although this market is just a few blocks long, its nostalgic style is a fantastic way to check out the local foods of Beppu. To access the market, head under the tracks heading towards Oita, and you will find the open fruit and vegetable store that marks the entrance. I absolutely recommend visiting, especially with its easy-to-access central location.

I bought some tori-ten (famous Beppu chicken tempura) here, and because I had already eaten beforehand (but still wanted to try something from this local store), the kind store owner said that he could give me just a few pieces, and much to my surprise the price was only ¥100! It was the most delicious chicken tempura I've had in my life.

Food shops at the market include tori-ten, a range of fresh fruit and vegetable stores, and fishmongers. You can also find a pet shop and a clothing store. There are small 'dining' areas with plastic chairs and tables where you can enjoy your take-away snacks. And at Beppu Station Market, you'll find some of the friendliest local shopkeepers!

13 SELECT BEPPU

W   selectbeppu.thebase.in;
    beppuproject.com/work/541
A   9-34 Chuo-cho, Oita, 874-0939
T   0977-80-7226

SHOP/HOMEWARES/ART | Select
Beppu is a hub of creativity and the best place
in Beppu to get handcrafted items made.
This beautiful 2-storey traditional Japanese
house has been converted into a shop on the
ground floor and a gallery space on the 2nd
floor. In the shop you will find items made
by local artisans, such as woven baskets,
ceramics, zines, garments and furoshiki, a
small lightweight all-purpose towel used for
everything from wrapping gifts and bento to
drying dishes and hands and even wetting
and wrapping around your head or shoulders
to cool down in summer.

Beppu is known for its locally woven
baskets, so if you're looking for a beautiful
traditional gift, a basket from this store is a
beautiful option. Due to the high level of skill
and curation, the baskets are priced at around
¥10,000 to ¥20,000 but are so divine it's not
hard to justify purchasing this keepsake.

If you head up to the 2nd floor, you will
find a beautiful, colourful floral mural on
the traditional sliding doors. Before heading
upstairs, take your shoes off and leave them
facing outwards at the bottom of the stairs, as
a sign of good manners.

The staff also run a website promoting
Beppu creative life. They recommended
areas for me to visit, taking time to pin the
places on my iPhone, and sent me off to their
favourite cafe for lunch around the corner,
Mumumu (*see* p. 276). After I finished my
lunch, one staff member was heading off to
her own lunch and offered to show me one
of her favourite shops! I'm not sure if it's
the small-town style or if Beppu Select staff
are just so incredibly generous, I suspect a
combination of both. Please pop in here and
say hello from Hello Sandwich!

14 SPICA
京都府立植物園

W   spica-beppu.com
A   1-34 Tatemachi, Oita, 874-0936
T   090-9476-0656

SHOP/HOMEWARES/GALLERY |
Spica is a well-known Beppu store with both
an elegant and relaxed shop fit-out, and
super-cute staff. It sells a gorgeous range
of homewares, locally handmade items,
garments and interior items. Stop here for
beautiful copper vessels, and, if you're lucky,
you can pick up some artists' zines. One of
my favourite things that I bought here was
a photography zine made by a Beppu-based
illustrator and photographer.

I adore the Ogada ware ceramic items,
especially the teapot and mug. They are
such beautiful take-home pieces, and every
time you pour yourself a tea or coffee back
home you will remember your divine trip to
Beppu! If accessories are more your souvenir
of choice, I recommend taking a peek at the
Naoto Uchiyama earrings. These pierced,
pressed brass circle earrings are so fine and
beautiful. You instantly get the sense that
this is a well-curated collection of the best
of the best from not only Beppu, but also
internationally, with some divine woven
bags from South Africa.

Spica features a gallery to the left of the
entrance, which hosts exhibitions ranging
from indigo garments to photography.
Spica also stocks local coffee beans, local
handmade lemon pickled honey and
cocoa spread.

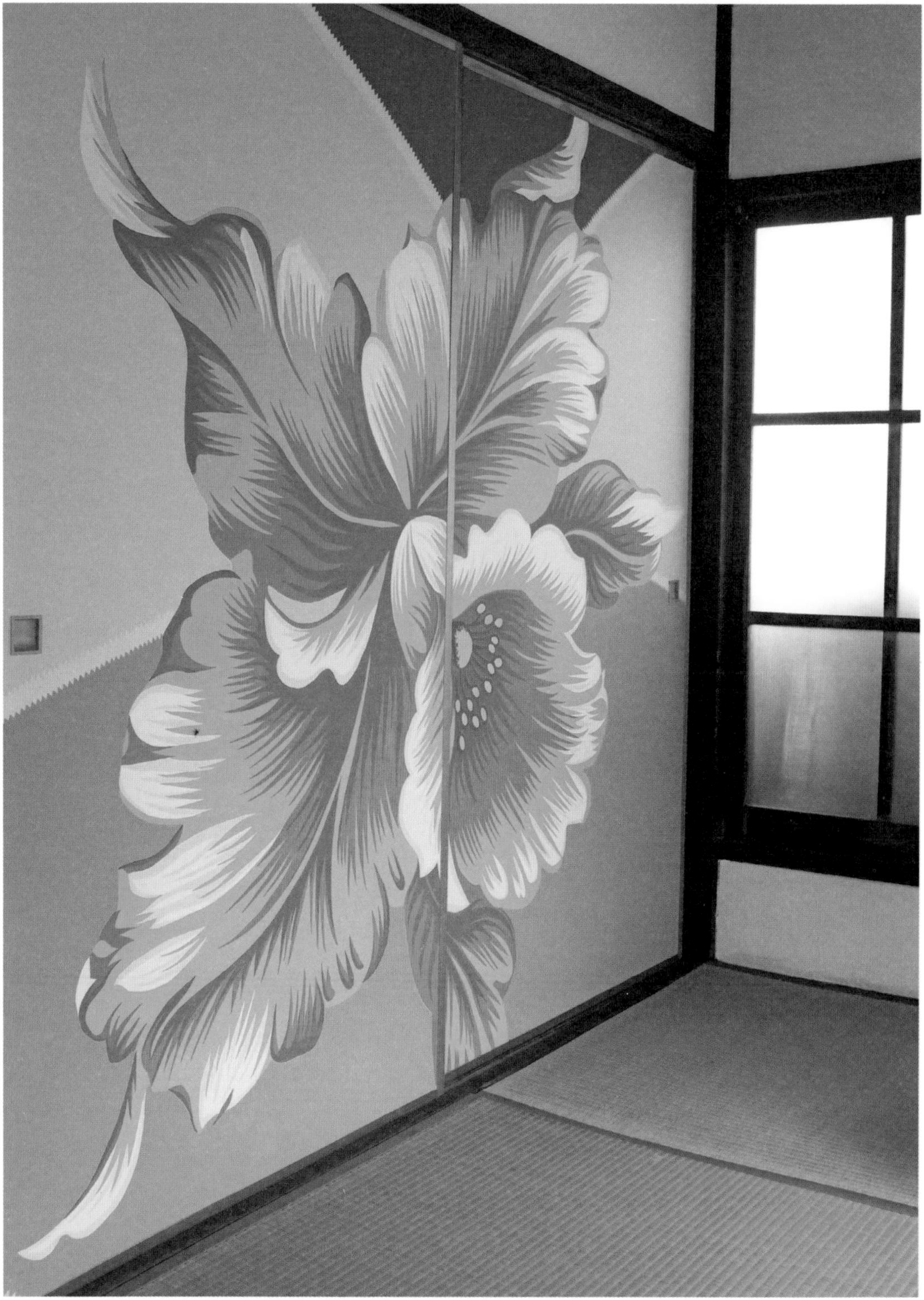

15 MUMUMU
喫茶ムムム

A   1-27 center-cho, Oita, 874-0936
T   080-3119-5261

CAFE | Around the corner from Select Beppu (*see* p. 274) is this cute little cosy cafe with a nostalgic Showa-era (1926–89) interior, featuring timber furnishings and dim lighting that will take you back in time and instantly relax you. But it's not only about the interior here ... the first thing you'll notice is the smell of the delicious coffee roasting. The pour-over coffee is made with such skill and care, and the soft jazz music is often broken with the sound of coffee beans being freshly ground for each coffee order. It doesn't get much fresher than that!

For breakfast, they serve a morning set for ¥700 that consists of buttered toast, scrambled egg, wiener sausage, salad and a drink of your choice (coffee, tea or juice). From 11am you can order items such as grilled sandwiches and pasta set lunches (with salad), but I must insist that you try the omurice. It's a popular Japanese dish that consists of chicken rice with ketchup covered with a fluffy omelette. The store even writes its name in Katakana (one of the three Japanese alphabets) in ketchup on top of the omelette. You can also order from a range of sweet cakes. The Select Beppu staff are often seen eating here – always a sure sign of something good when the locals dine at a restaurant!

At the back of the cafe, they have a little selection of books and magazines about the Beppu area, and although these are in Japanese, the images, websites and maps listed in the magazines might inspire you with ideas about places to visit.

16 BASARA HOUSE
バサラ ハウス

A   3-2-2 Kitahama, Oita, 874-0920
T   070-2304-5195

CAFE | As you walk up to Basara House you'll feel as though you've stumbled across a hidden secret cafe in a local location. It is a cute place for lunch or sweets and a coffee, and you can walk to it from Beppu station.

The charm is the old, renovated Japanese traditional house with exposed original beams. Dotted with plants and lots of cosy seating options, the space is comforting and relaxing. Snuggle into the couch if your feet and back need a good rest after exploring Beppu, or sit at the bench table if you're just popping in for a quick coffee or drink. I adore the exposed wall with pink paint details, colourful patterned tablecloths and hanging fairy lights.

For lunch, Basara House offers a range of curries and Asian-fusion dishes, as well as hamburgers. If you're hungry, try the chicken curry, the bean curry or the minced pork curry for ¥800. You can accompany your meal with a fruit soda, iced-chai or hot tea. In summer, you can find kakigori on the menu, a refreshing Japanese shaved-ice dessert served with your choice of flavoured syrup.

Basara House hosts live music nights from time to time, so you might be lucky and catch something very special! Note that opening hours are irregular here, so it's good to check ahead of your visit.

16

15

15

18

18

19

17 COFFEE STAND STAIRS
コーヒー スタンド ステアーズ

A   3-6 Motomachi, Oita, 874-0944

CAFE/COFFEE | Coffee Stand Stairs, which opened in 2016, is a sweet little cafe in a hip area and perfect for that much-needed caffeine hit. You won't miss it, with the exterior featuring graphic black and white hand typography signage and a sandwich board sign that you'll see as you're walking along the street. There are a few plastic chairs out the front and a little standing counter around the corner that make for a fun atmosphere.

It serves espresso, pour-over and iced-coffee, and you can also order a soothing hot chocolate. It's a good spot to mingle with the locals, or relax in between exploring Beppu.

18 TOMONAGA PANYA

A   2-29 Chiyo, Oita, 874-0942
T   0977-23-0969

CAFE/BAKERY | Tomonaga is Beppu's oldest and most famous bakery. Located in an almost completely residential area, it's often recommended by locals – always a fantastic sign! You'll experience the sweet smell of the raisin and chocolate-filled breads upon entering the store. There is almost always a queue, and you need to take a number when you enter through the rattling sliding glass doors. An English menu is available.

Tomonaga is also home to Beppu's cutest breads! Don't miss the dog-shaped bread with cream filling. All of the breads are baked onsite, and the most popular types of bread sell out quickly.

Be sure to visit early in the morning to avoid the disappointment of missing out! It's is only a 10-minute walk from Beppu station.

19 OKAMOTOYA

W   jigoku-prin.com/en
A   3Kumi, Myoban, 874-0843 (Myoban Hot spring Okamotoya Shop), Oita, 874-0843
T   0977-66-3228 (Myoban Hot spring Okamotoya Shop)

CAFE | Okamotoya is famed as the original and the best for serving jigoku-mushi (hell-steamed) pudding. This hell-steaming cooking method has remained unchanged since 1988! The puddings here are a must-try, with just the perfect amount of bitterness to the caramel on top of the sweet steamed pudding. I tried the custard flavour, but they also have flavours such as banana, strawberry, potato, coffee and green tea – some of which are seasonal.

If you happen to feel like something a little savoury before your pudding, you can try other popular items, such as their famous soft-boiled egg topped with rice, curry rice or delicious udon noodles. Naturally, you can also find tori-ten (famous Beppu chicken tempura) here. There is seating both inside and out, but, if you can, try and sit at the very far end of the restaurant on the tatami-covered seats next to the giant windows overlooking the city. Between the taste of the pudding and such a gorgeous view, I almost cried with how perfect it is!

I would also recommend buying one or two of the onigiris (rice balls) on display in baskets near the cash register. They're wrapped in saran wrap and look so incredibly handmade. Once you've taken just one bite of these onigiri, you will find it hard to ever go back to onigiri from convenience stores.

After your visit, pop outside to the carpark where you'll get a great view over the city and lovely photos of the Beppu bridge.

20 TOYOKEN
東洋軒

W toyoken-beppu.co.jp
A 7-8-22 Ishigaki Higashi, Oita, 874-0907
T 0977-23-3333

RESTAURANT/TEMPURA | Beppu is famous for tori-ten (chicken tempura: 'tori' is the word for chicken and 'ten' is short for tempura). Ask any taxi driver what you should do while you're in Beppu, and besides visiting the hot springs, eating tori-ten is always one of their musts. Toyoken, a short taxi ride from Beppu train station, is Beppu's most famous spot to enjoy this local delicacy. You can expect to queue for an hour or more, so you might like to pack a book.

The tori-ten comes with a citrus to squeeze over the tempura and a light ponzu-like dipping sauce with a dash of mustard. You can mix the mustard into the sauce with your chopsticks, if that's your taste preference. The tori-ten plates cost between ¥800 and ¥1,250.

The lunch menu is also very reasonable and includes various Chinese food sets priced from ¥750 to ¥1,020. Options include marbo tofu and fried rice. For dinner the courses range from ¥6,500 to ¥15,000. You can also order personalised set dinner meals, including a tori-ten with miso, rice and pickles.

Toyoken also has a range of self-branded products, such as sauces and spices, available for purchase that might be an excellent take-home.

If you are a group of more than four people, you are able to make a reservation at dinner time from 5pm.

21 BEPPU SAKE STAND JUN
別府 酒スタンド 巡

A 1-1-1 Kitahama, Oita, 874-0920
T 080-9291-6714

BAR/SAKE | This is hands-down Beppu's best bar. Opened in 2019, this standing sake bar is the sister store of a sake shop, also in Oita, and it has an incredible selection of local sake. It has a pay-as-you go system, where you put the amount for your drink inside a timber sake cup.

From the outside, the modern light timber façade will immediately take your fancy. Peek through the large open windows and spot all the locals laughing, and it's hard to not want to go in.

While the menu is in Japanese, you can always ask for the osusume (recommended) sake, and the staff will help you. Soni-chan, the bar manager, has a Korean background and mixes Japanese, French and Italian cooking with Korean food. I recommend the seasonal kimchi (made with pear during my visit), and the pâté served on toasted bread with figs and prosciutto. You can also order pickles and other vegetables, and seasonal fried dishes.

Although I visited the bar alone, I found myself chatting not only to the other patrons but also to the super friendly staff. When I mentioned this book to Soni-chan, she offered so many lovely recommendations and we decided to visit a few places before the bar opened at 12pm. It was incredibly kind as she had put her child in daycare early, had borrowed the car from the owner of the sake shop and had closed the shop until the afternoon just to take me around! This was so generous and showcased the nature of the local inaka (countryside) people.

Pretty please visit this bar. And send Soni-chan my love! It's on the corner of the Kitahama area, about a 5-minute walk from Beppu station.

21

21

21

KISSA
–TEN

Kissaten (often shortened to kissa) are retro-style coffee houses, inspired by European cafes that peaked in Japan during the '70s. People would frequent these cafes to try coffee made from fancy coffee machines and listen to their favourite music on often hard-to-find vinyl.

Kissaten serve drip coffee and food, such as simple Japanese sandwiches (often a 'mixed sandwich' like ham and lettuce or egg and mayonnaise), and soda float drinks, which are usually blue or green with a scoop of ice-cream and a maraschino cherry on top. Aside from these basics, you can also find some menu variety, depending on the kissaten, including curries, katsu (cutlet served with rice and shredded cabbage), omuraisu (omelette rice), spaghetti and a range of cakes. Kissaten are usually very cheap and cheerful and you can easily find a lunch or breakfast set with a main dish and a drink for under ¥1000.

Kissaten interiors are often retro in style with a '70s colour theme. Think mustard or brown leather couches and a range of indoor plants or quirky ornaments loved by the owner. This is part of the appeal of kissaten, they contain individual charm. And, often a thin napkin (serviette) is wrapped and twisted around your spoon. I just adore this retro-style presentation because of its nostalgia.

Kissaten are frequented by solo diners who want some time out and a snack, which means they are often quiet and peaceful. Before April 2020, you could smoke inside almost all kissaten, which, although I don't smoke myself, I adored as part of the nostalgic vibe, but slowly this is starting to fade out with new non-smoking restrictions. Many retro kissaten from the Showa era (1926–89) in Tokyo's Ginza area even feature ashtrays built into a hole in the middle of the round tables. Kissaten are so popular in Japan that you can find magazines and books dedicated solely to them.

One of Tokyo Shibuya's most famous kissaten, Meikyoku Kissa Lion, which has been standing for almost 100 years (since 1926), has a focus on classical music, and chatting is strictly prohibited. If you visit it, you will find yourself sitting on church pew-like seating set up all facing one direction. Because of the no speaking rule, it's extremely special, and you might feel as though you've stepped back in time to a scene from a black and white film.

Some of my absolute all-time favourite kissaten are Pine Tree in Atami (*see* p. 61), Bon Bon in Nagoya (*see* p. 150) and Madura Kissaten in Osaka (*see* p. 128). If you're in Tokyo, you can usually find kissaten in any local area, such as Koenji, Asagaya, Hatagaya and Kichijoji, but Coffee Shop Ace in Kanda (*see* p. 33) is a special nostalgic option.

OKINAW

THIS BEACHY ISLAND
IS SO DIVINE IT'S
ALMOST SURREAL

26.358° N
127.806° E

14

A 沖縄

Based on the places I've travelled to, Okinawa makes me think of an exciting and eclectic mix of aspects of Japan, America, Australia and even Hong Kong. The beaches, such as Manza Beach (*see* p. 284), are dreamy and the sea is as clear as any I've seen in Australia. The locals are so friendly and cheerful, and the mood a slow island pace. The island is exposed to many typhoons, and you definitely need a car or taxi to get there, but if you're interested in a mix of Japanese and Western culture, then you should definitely book a trip to this dreamy place.

The cuisine, with its American influence and local delicacies, is some of the most delicious food I've tried in Japan. The range of Japanese-meets-American foods at the beachside restaurants in the American Village (*see* p. 289) and Okinawan specialties at Mashiki Market's (*see* p. 289) are Hello Sandwich recommendations. The best soba I've ever had was at Okinawan Soba Eibun (*see* p. 298), and you can't visit Okinawa without trying spam musubi at Pork Tamago Onigiri (*see* p. 300).

Okinawa is also a feast for the eyes. The pastel eyes, specifically. The light is different to the rest of Japan, and the building colours and styles are so cute that you will want to pull your taxi over everywhere to take photos! The town of Kin (*see* p. 290) is a great place to do this. Even the bus stops and taxis are ridiculously cute! The taxis are often blue and feature tropical-style illustrations or motifs. If you're familiar with the style of Tokyo taxi drivers, you'll notice a somewhat laid-back approach of the drivers in Okinawa. In a fantasy life, I might dream about relocating from Tokyo to Okinawa. Or maybe a holiday house there would be lovely.

1 MANZA BEACH
万座ビーチ

W   an–aintercontinental-manza.jp
A   2260 Serakaki, Onna, Kunigami,
      904-0404
T   098-966-1211

ATTRACTION/BEACH | Coming from Australia, with it's incredibly beautiful beaches, I'm not easily impressed by beaches when I travel, but I would go so far as to say that the beaches in Okinawa are some of the most beautiful that I've ever seen. Just a few minutes drive from Cape Manzamo (*see* p. 286), you will find yourself at Manza Beach. It is easily accessed from a nearby carpark, making it the most convenient beach stopover ever. Manza is one of my most favourite beaches on Okinawa's main island. And I don't think I'm alone, as it's the backdrop for many a wedding photo shoot.

I love that here you see not only the beautiful clear water and white sands but also amazing rock formations in the water. The ocean is so still and turquoise, it's just incredible. I recommend buying an ice-block or ice-cream and enjoying it under the shade of the palm trees, and relaxing on the sand, reading your favourite book or meditating.

You might enjoy taking some photos here with the tropical palm trees and rock formations in the ocean as a graphic photographic element.

2 BUSENA BEACH

A   1808 Kise, Nago, 905-0026
T   0980-51-1333

ATTRACTION/BEACH | Busena Beach is one of Okinawa's many beautiful beaches. The water is crystal-clear aquamarine and the sand is as white as can be. With the beach hidden and protected behind a row of trees, the suspense will build as you walk from the carpark towards the sand. You'll likely catch a glimpse of the yellow flag before you spot the white deck chairs placed under white umbrellas, which give it the most amazing resort-like vibe. This is set off by a lifesaver's high seat that could be something out of a scene from a retro American film.

To the right of the path, you will find a range of brightly coloured foot-peddle paddle boats and some surfboards. Perfect for families, this beach also has a safety net to keep out any unwanted sea life.

Spend an afternoon walking along this gorgeous beach and taking photos, or bring a journal and enjoy a relaxing time writing about your travels with the sea breeze on you.

Before your trip, you might like to download some traditional Okinawan music. Trust me, it will really set the mood! It's best to get a taxi here. Note that this beach is managed by a hotel called Busena Terrace, so you have to pay a fee to use the beach. You might like to pop into a restaurant or buy a bento box from a supermarket en route for a picnic on the beach.

1

2

2

3 SESOKO BEACH
瀬底ビーチ

W   okinawatraveler.net/en
A   5583-1 Sesoko, Motobu, Kunigami, 905-0227

ATTRACTION/BEACH | Sesoko Beach is another of the most beautiful and also one of the most popular beaches in Okinawa. It's situated on Sesoko Island, accessible by crossing a short bridge in the Motobu area. It's best to get a taxi here or you can pay to park your rental car, if you happen to have one.

Sesoko's sand is incredibly white and the still, crystal-clear water is so peaceful. The shoreline is covered with millions of washed-up coral and shells, so you can spend a happy little while admiring these treasures. The beach is also surrounded with rock-shelters, perfect for protection from wind and sun.

Like most of the beaches in Okinawa, you can park at the paid parking station a short walk from the beach, and on the walk you'll find a little shop where you can pick up beach essentials like float rings. It's quite common for people in Japan to enjoy the ocean on colourful floats.

In addition to this beach being rather touristy, it's also under a flight path, so your tranquillity might be interrupted at times with a jet passing overhead. For a short stay, however, I found the novelty of this rather interesting and felt somewhat like I was in a film!

Be sure to pack your camera and a book, as you could spend hours relaxing here.

4 CAPE MANZAMO
万座毛

A   Onna, Kunigami, 904-0411
T   098-966-1280

ATTRACTION/WALK | This sea-cliff walk will impress even those familiar with Sydney's famous Bondi to Bronte beach walk. Everything from the refreshing ocean breeze and the beautiful view to the peaceful walking track will leave you feeling refreshed.

The short walking track from the carpark follows a winding path that gives unobstructed views over the Manzamo rocks, which some say resemble an elephant's trunk. Look out over the limestone cliffs and spend a meditative moment watching the waves crash onto these majestic rocks. Continue along the track and you will find yourself overlooking Manzamo Beach, with its large and small Shinto shrine rocks not far from shore. They are connected by a traditional rope that symbolises the marriage of the deities, Izanagi (male) and Izanami (female).

Make sure you have your camera ready to capture this stunning scenery. Although windy at times, it is a lovely spot to have your portrait taken, and the polite locals will no doubt be more than willing to assist.

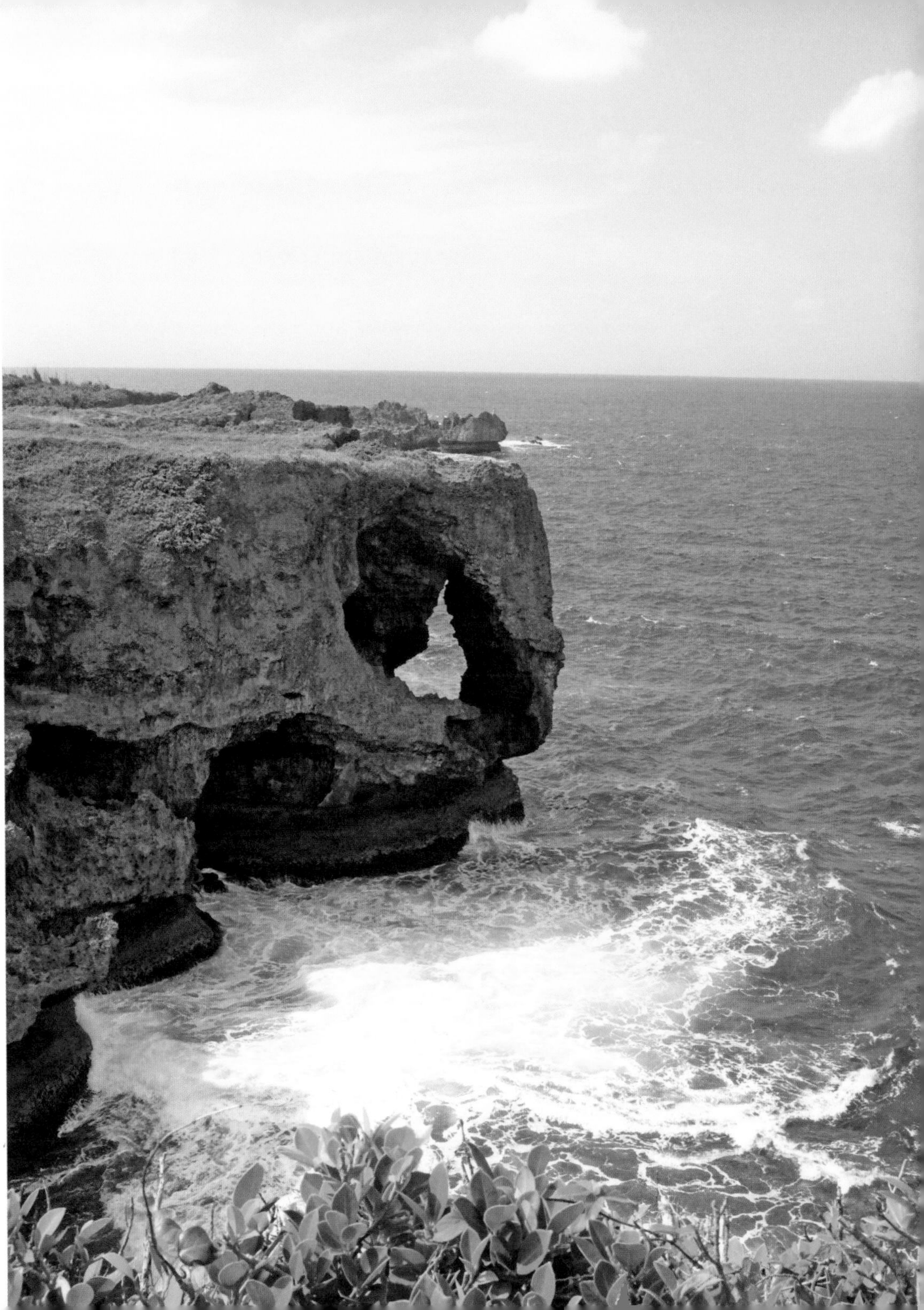

5 AMERICAN VILLAGE
アメリカンビレッジ

W okinawa-americanvillage.com
A 9-1 Mihama, Chatan, Nakagami, 904-0115
T 098-926-4455

**ATTRACTION/BEACH/SHOPS/
CAFES** | The American Village in Okinawa
is a quirky American-themed village built
for the US military and definitely not
to be missed. When we drove up to it at
night, I was completely shocked as it was
illuminated like a suburban Christmas lights
competition, or what I imagine Las Vegas
is like. It seems like it's Christmas here
every single day of the year (although only
one shop is actually Christmas-themed).
With an almost LA-like movie-set vibe, the
American Village is a place where you can
shop (*see* Aeon, p. 297), eat, see a movie and
relax. You might want to spend half a day
and have dinner here, too.

Set right on the beach, the American
Village's architecture is colourful and dotted
with bridges over small rivers, and you
feel a little as though you're in *The Truman
Show*. It also has a street of beachside
restaurants where you can enjoy food such as
hamburgers, taco rice and even spam musubi.
You can also find nice coffee shops and fun
izakaya (small bars), just look out for the
red hanging lanterns. You can either dine
in and look over the water or get take-away
and sit right on the beach to enjoy your food
or coffee.

If you have time, you might like to
catch a film at the retro '80s-style cinema,
which looks like a set from *Stranger Things*
with its neon lights. You could also enjoy a
hamburger and beer at one of the outdoor
cafes by the river. Be sure to take a peek at
the illuminated ferris wheel.

6 MINATOGAWA STATESIDE TOWN
港川ステイツサイドタウン

A 2-18-3 Minatogawa, Urasoe, 901-2134
T 098-941-3939

**ATTRACTION/TOWN/SHOPS/
CAFES** | This little town was originally built
to function as military housing but now is
a collection of super-cute cafes and unique
shops. The area of Urasoe has been urban-
planned and the ten streets are arranged
in a grid and named after American states,
such as Arizona, Florida, Texas and Nevada.
The architectural style reminds me a little of
the fibro beach houses in New South Wales
(NSW) South Coast – towns like Culburra,
Gerroa and Gerringong. This area has the
same nostalgic feel with an added cute
Japanese-meets-American flavour.

Here you will find Japanese food, curry,
ice-cream, coffee, soba and an array of
homeware and vintage stores. Some of my
favourite not-to-miss places are Okinawa
Cerrado Coffee and Ippe Coppe (*see* p. 297)
for amazing baked goods, of which a portion
of the profits are sent to disaster relief in
Tohoku. Portriver Market is a must-stop for
the cutest homewares and divine pottery. It
also sells vegetables and shop-branded tote
bags. The shop is the embodiment of the
chilled Okinawa style and lifestyle, and its
motto is: 'We need Good Style & Happy Life'.
Now that's a slogan I can live by!

Minatogawa is an easy and essential
morning or afternoon stop for those who
love charming little retro villages.

7 KIN
金

w   visitkintown.jp/en

ATTRACTION/TOWN | Undeniably one of my favourite parts of Okinawa, Kin is a small town set just across the road from one of the many US Army bases in Okinawa, built to serve the American soldiers on the base. The border and gate are still there, but back in the day the town of Kin was full of buzzy bars and restaurants for the Americans to come and frequent. Although Kin is now well past its heyday, with only a few spots open, the area has such a charming vibe and makes for a beautiful opportunity to explore the fading façades and imagine the life that once was. It almost feels like a movie set, and it's hard to believe that this is Japan. You will notice that many of the faded signs are written with prices displayed in dollars, not yen. I absolutely adore the retro and semi-abandoned feeling of this town.

Kin is also famous for its two awamori (Okinawan sake) breweries that take advantage of Kin's abundant water supply from the bottom of Mt Onna. The horizontal water wells of Ukkaga and Kintaga are popular canoeing and birdwatching areas, if that's your cup of tea. Personally, I'd prefer a cup of awamori and to continue exploring Kin.

There are many photo ops in Kin! This area has the most amazing collection of faded tiles. Just make sure you look down every now and then, and I'm certain you won't be disappointed by these small artwork-like creations! Keep your eyes peeled also for some beautiful vibrant walls in colours like red and hot pink that look more like Mexico than Japan. Speaking of Mexican, King Tacos (*see* p. 303) is also here.

8 MOTOBU TOWN MARKET
もとぶ町営市場と中曽根

w   motobu.main.jp
A   4 Toguchi, Motobu, Kunigami, 905-0214

SHOP/MARKET | Motobu Town Market in the Nakasone area has a very relaxed, retro feel – not unlike the markets in Hong Kong. This lovely little town market set on the waterside is full of charming local Okinawan shopkeepers. As you walk around, take joy in the faded pastel signs, rusting rooves and all of the other beautiful textures that can only be created with age.

It's a small market, but what it lacks in size it makes up for in charm. You can expect to find a fish shop, coffee shop, tea house, dressmaker and fruit and vegetable vendors. When I visited, some of the shops weren't open and when I asked if it was closed, the reply was, 'Oh no, they just open whenever they like'. It's such Okinawa style!

You could easily spend two hours here if you pop into the nearby and famous Kishimoto Honten soba shop. This restaurant was established in 1905 and is known to have the best soba in Okinawa! At lunchtime, you can expect to wait between 30 and 60 minutes to enter. A dish of soba will cost ¥650. You can also get kagikori (shaved-ice dessert) from famed Aragaki Zenzai (*see* p. 298), also only a short walk away.

On the third Sunday of every month it hosts the Motobu Handmade Market, where local creators sell handmade items, such as yachimun (pottery), woodwork and apparel. The event is lively, with street performances and festival-like food stalls selling deep-fried fish. If you're tossing up which day to head to Motobu Old Market, my money is on Sunday.

To get here, take the Yanbaru Express bus and jump off at the high school entrance outside the market area. It's open seven days a week.

7

9 MASHIKI MARKET
牧志公設市場

W kosetsu-ichiba.com
A 2-7-10 Matsuo, Naha, 900-0014
T 098-867-6560

SHOP/MARKET | Mashiki Market is one of the oldest food markets in Okinawa's capital city, Naha. It has been running since 1950 and is housed in a lovely retro shotengai (undercover shopping street). Although touristy, its retro vibe and offerings of Okinawan local food make it a fun attraction.

Food on offer includes seafood from Okinawa's coast, beef, pork, tropical fruits, vegetables, sweets, sponge cakes, tofu and local Okinawan spices. You can even purchase food from the 1st floor, cook it onsite and eat it at the market's 2nd floor dining area in a style called mochiage.

There is a coffee stand that sells hiyashi (chilled) lemon, which is actually made of shikuwasa (an Okinawan lime-like citrus fruit) and is so refreshing.

Be sure to bring cash, as there are no ATMs/cash machines. The market is a 9-minute walk from Mashiki monorail station and is open seven days a week, except the fourth Sunday of each month.

10 NAKASONE STORE
仲宗根ストアー

A 6 Toguchi, Motobu, Kunigami, 905-0214
T 0980-47-2023

SHOP/SUPERMARKET | I adore finding little general stores when I travel, especially ones that look like they haven't changed decor for many years. If you love a little charm while you shop at a supermarket, come to Nakasone – the most divine tiny general store. The nostalgia here embodies the overall charm of Okinawa, and if you love food packaging and retro style, this is one shop you won't want to miss.

As you walk in, on your right you'll find a bread stand filled with bread in the cutest packaging. Think polka dots, cartoon characters and gingham prints. Squeeze through the tiny aisles and you'll find retro packaging on sake, pastel coloured dish cloths and unique bento with hand-drawn signs. So adorable!

I recommend buying some bread, obviously, but also picking up some local sake as a cute Okinawan omiyage (souvenir). I bought a retro packaged awamori (Okinawan sake) for a mere ¥370. Outside the store, you can find a row of flip-flops, or beach sandals as they call them in Japan.

11

12

12

11 AEON
イオン

W aeon-ryukyu.jp/store/aeon/chatan
A 8-3 Mihama, Chatan, Nakagami, 904-0115
T 098-982-7575

SHOP/SUPERMARKET | A trip to any supermarket in Okinawa is fun because you can really get an idea of the culture, and a lot of the larger supermarkets, like Aeon, have aisles and aisles dedicated to local specialities.

Things to look out for are: Okinawan soba, spicy oil for soba, shikuwasa (an Okinawan lime-like citrus fruit) syrup, goya champaru packet recipe starters and, you guessed it, so much spam. They make special spam rice musubi (wraps, *see* p. 300) in Okinawa, which are a must-try!

Because taco rice originated in Okinawa (*see* p. 303), you can also find taco rice bento in the supermarket's bento section. If that's not enough to make you want to move to Okinawa immediately, I'm not sure what is. You can also find special chu-hi (alcoholic canned drinks) in almost every fruit flavour you can imagine.

Aeon, part of an American company, is actually also a large department store, selling everything from clothes and shoes to toiletries and a wide range of Okinawan omiyage (souvenirs). It could be your one-stop shop if you're after chopsticks, towels, fans and other Japanese essentials. Aeon is located in the American Village (*see* p. 289).

12 IPPE COPPE
イッペコッペ

W ippe-coppe.com
A 2-16-1 Minatogawa, Urasoe, 901-2134
T 098-877-6189

CAFE | Established in 2008, this lovely little outdoor courtyard cafe has a unique range of kakigori (shaved-ice dessert). With flavour combinations such as red shiso and lemon, and shikuwasa (an Okinawan lime-like citrus fruit) with lime, the kakigori here is some of the finest I've ever had.

Order your kakigori from the little window on the right side of the entrance, and you'll be given a number for your table that will be called when your kakigori is ready. Ippe Coppee is also well known for its delicious bread and coffee, and be sure to try one of its famous scones, which have a crispy outside and rich, moist inside.

The garden is a beautiful place to sit, and to the back of the garden, there is a lovely little washitsu (traditional Japanese floor seating area), where you take your shoes off and step up to a picnic mat and small table (like tatami seating–style). Next to this area, you'll hear a lovely little summer bell ringing in the garden, which further adds to Okinawa's overall summer vibe.

As you can imagine, it gets incredibly hot in Okinawa, but the staff at Ippe Coppe have placed a basket of fans made from giant folded leaves to help keep you cool against the heat.

Ippe Coppee's bread can be shipped within Japan, too. So even if you run out of bread, fear not – if you live in Japan, you can pop online and order some more!

13 ARAGAKI ZENZAI
新垣ぜんざい

A 11-2 Toguchi, Motobu, Kunigami,
   905-0214
T 098-048-4731

CAFE | If you're at Motobu Town Market (*see* p. 290), you must go to famous Aragaki Zenzai. It has been running since 1948, and the menu hasn't changed in all of that time. The kakigori (shaved-ice dessert) served here has boiled, then sweetened adzuki (red sweet beans) added to the bottom of the bowl and is then covered with shaved ice. It's the perfect refreshing treat for the hot Okinawa climate. Many adzuki kakigori across Japan are served with the red bean on top of the shaved ice, however here the red bean is hidden at the bottom of the dish, so your kakigori comes out looking like a cute snow cone with hidden treasures!

You order through a vending machine and there's even a button for ordering 20 servings of kakigori! Kakigori party, anyone? Although the vending machine is only in Japanese, it's clearly numbered, so when you see the blue button with the number 1 (and a price of ¥250) your ticket will be for one bowl of kakigori. You can then pass this to the shop owner who will bring your kakigori to your seat for you. When I visited with a friend, we only ordered one but the lady brought two bowls so we could share – without us even asking! So sweet, so Okinawa!

14 OKINAWAN SOBA EIBUN
オキナワ ソバ エイブン

W sobaeibun.okinawa
A 1-5-14 Tsuboya, Naha, 902-0065
T 098-914-3882

RESTAURANT/SOBA | Okay, I think this is the best soba I've ever had. English menu, friendly staff, delicious and cheap soba in a lovely modern setting with timber counter tables and modern tiles – what more could you ask for?

The owner travelled all around Okinawa's islands and tried various types of soba to research his original Okinawan Soba Eibun signature flavour. Take one look at this restaurant's Instagram, and you'll be craving Okinawan Soba Eibun in no time.

The soba is made from a pork stock that has been slowly boiled for eight hours with additions of bonito and kelp, and the toppings list is endless. The homemade koregoosu pepper is made from awamori (Okinawan sake) pickled island peppers. It also offers the regular spices, such as yuzu pepper and Japanese pepper, and they even have a garam masala pepper. When you select your soba, you can also select from toppings such as onsen tamago, hard-boiled egg, pork, extra noodles and their recommended topping, coriander. They are not wrong – the flavour pairing is amazing! In fact, they love coriander here so much that they also sell a coriander paste, which tastes incredible.

In addition to the unique flavour, the dishes are also visually appealing. Each one is presented on a beautiful timber tray with colourful toppings and trademark red-paint dipped Okinawan chopsticks.

It also sells branded merch, such as tote bags and baby bibs for those mini-me soba lovers! You can also pick up a box of handmade soba, which comes in the cutest blue and white graphically designed box.

14

13

14

15 ISHIGUFU RAMEN
いしぐふー らーめん

W ishigufu.jp/shop/torisobaya
A Kansas Street no. 40, 2-13-6 Minatogawa,
   Urasoe, 901-2134
T 098-879-7517

RESTAURANT/SOBA | Ishigufu restaurant has seven branches all over Okinawa but this one definitely has the cutest eye-catching entrance, with a white concrete wall, red sign and façade dotted with three orange waiting chairs. My Okinawan friends confirm that this is their number one soba in Okinawa. So this is absolutely not to be missed!

Although called 'soba', Okinawan soba is in fact made from wheat and kansui (a type of lye water). These ingredients give the soba a ramen-like texture, which is yellow in colour and somewhat springy in texture. The specialty broth at Ishigufu is made with a chicken stock, and it's a delicious and unique flavour.

I highly recommend ordering Ishigufu's 'specialty handmade soba', which comes with locally sourced chicken and two types of toppings for ¥800. If you're more than a little peckish, you might like to order the steamed or grilled dumplings as a side with your soba. Depending on the set you order, you can also help yourself to the delicious and healthy salad bar, which is just to your right as you enter the restaurant.

A little trivia is that because Okinawan soba is similar to ramen and contains less than 30 per cent soba powder, the fairtrade organisations didn't want to recognise it. But in 1978 (six years after Okinawa was returned to Japan), 17 October became known as Okinawan Soba Day in Japan. It celebrates the anniversary of the day this unique soba was officially recognised by the Japanese government.

16 PORK TAMAGO ONIGIRI
ポークたまごおにぎり

W porktamago.com
A 2-8-35 Yubinbango, Naha, Matsuo,
   900-0014
T 098-867-9550

RESTAURANT/ONIGIRI | A fusion of American and Japanese food, spam and egg onigiri (rice balls) are perhaps the most quintessential Okinawan cuisine. After World War II, when there was an over-abundance of spam stocks from the US military, it became available to civilians, and the Japanese locals came up with the idea of popping spam and egg inside rice and seaweed to form what is known today as spam musubi (another name for onigiri). The word musubi translates as wrap, so it's literally translated as 'to wrap spam and egg in rice and seaweed'. Before the spam goes into the musubi, it's usually marinated with a teriyaki sauce.

To try one of these Okinawan classics, head to the Matsuo branch of the Pork Tamago Onigiri stores. It's a take-away store, but there is a dining hall area diagonally opposite. The classic dish is the pork and egg, but you can select from a wide range of musubi off the English menu. I selected pork and egg with tempura goya (a bitter Okinawan vegetable). Another recommended option is yuzu, where yuzu pepper is added to the classic spam and egg musubi. You can enjoy an Okinawan Orion beer or an iced Jasmine tea with shikuwasa (an Okinawan lime-like citrus fruit).

Next door to the Matsuo branch is a cute little supermarket selling seafood and vegetable tempura from a paper towel–lined cardboard box. When I visited, the only other customer patted me on the shoulder and said, 'It's so delicious! Enjoy it!' So utterly sweet! The supermarket also sells pork and egg musubi, and I absolutely adore its food photography advertising the various types of musubi wraps pinned onto the entrance doors.

15

15

16

17

17 KING TACOS
キングタコス

W   facebook.com/kingtacos
A   4244-4 Kin, Kunigami,
    904-1201
T   090-1947-1684

RESTAURANT | King Tacos is the birthplace of taco rice! This restaurant in Kin town (*see* p. 290) is not to be missed. Let me explain ... while tacos in shells were introduced to Okinawa in 1956, taco rice was created in 1984 by Matsuzo Gibo at his first store called Parlor Senri. He wanted to create a dish to give young American soldiers a cheap and satisfying meal. Taco rice consists of rice topped with the beef mince meat that you would find inside a regular taco, then it's topped with tomato, cheese and lettuce. Unfortunately, Gibo's original store closed its doors in 2015. However, this sister store, King Tacos, has inherited the same flavours, and this branch was the first of many in Okinawa.

As you enter the store, you'll find a vending machine to the left. Select the taco rice and whatever drink you like, or you can get water from dispensing machines. Once you've got your meal ticket, you pass it to the staff behind the counter, who will prepare your meal while you wait.

I recommend popping to the upstairs seating area and sitting by the window if you can. I sat here and overlooked the suburbs of Okinawa whilst eating taco rice. It was definitely one of my favourite meals and areas because of the American military history and the incredible fusion of American/Mexican/Okinawan food.

King Tacos is popular with both locals and travellers, and it's not uncommon to see a crowd of customers waiting for their take-away outside the store. It's so cheap and cheerful, so be sure not to miss this experience!

18 SEA SIDE DRIVE-IN
シーサイドドライブイン

W   seaside-drivein.com
A   885 Nakadomari, Onna, Kunigami,
    904-0415
T   098-964-2272

RESTAURANT | If you fancy having a meal with a view of a beach sunset, then this super-cute retro drive-in restaurant is for you. It began in 1967, and the founder was inspired by American fast-food culture. It was the first restaurant in Okinawa where all of the dishes could be taken out. Although you can't actually 'drive through', the key feature here is the roadside system where you can park and order at the outdoor take-away counter. Then you can sit on the ledge near your parking spot and look out over the sea as you enjoy your meal, ice-cream or drink.

The take-away counter is open 24-hours, and the restaurant dine-in area closes at 11pm. The menu includes Western, Japanese and Chinese dishes, as well as super-cute float sodas, espresso and local beer. There are lunch and dinner options, like steak, fried chicken and fried rice, or you might want to try a Japanese teishoku (meal set), such as fried prawn with rice and side dishes. Personally, I like the retro American style of plating Western meals and recommend ordering this over a teishoku.

For breakfast you can order an omelette, which, in true American form, comes with a side of French fries. I love the look of the bacon and eggs served with a side of fries and a frozen vegetable melody that looks super fun and retro! You can select rice or toast to accompany your meal.

It's a fun and historical dining option in Okinawa, or you could even just drive up, pick up an ice-cream from the drive-up counter, and sit on the ledges overlooking the water and enjoy the Okinawan sea breeze.

19 SHIRAKACHI

シラカチ

w   hyatt.com/en-US/hotel/japan/
hyattregency-seragaki-island-okinawa/
okaro
A   1108 Seragaki, Onnason, 904-0404
T   989-604-321

RESTAURANT | Eating dinner at Shirakachi restaurant in the Hyatt Regency Seragaki Island resort is the best way to tick off all of the Okinawan local dishes and specialties in one night, even if you're not staying at the resort. The kaiseki ryori (Japanese cuisine courses) is the perfect introduction to all of Okinawan cuisine, such as Goya chanpuru (a bitter melon and egg stir fried dish), rafute (braised pork) and Okinawa soba.

In this relaxed and elegant dining space, you can enjoy the vibrant energy of watching the chefs prepare the food for you at the teppan (iron griddle) from the counter seating. Or sit at one of the tables by the huge windows and look outside over the beautiful resort palm trees and pools.

Not only is the food divine, but the ceramic dishes, sake glasses and oshibori (wet hand towels) are gorgeous. I actually ended up finding the same wet towels in a nearby Aeon department store in the American Village (*see* p. 289) to take home. You will also be presented with what looks like a napkin on first glance but is actually a cute tie-wrap bib to wear. This kind of thing is quite common in Japan, so there's no need to feel embarrassed.

My pro-tip is either have a drink at sunset before dinner at the adjacent bar or finish off your dinner with a nightcap. You can also try awamori (Okinawan sake) from the extensive selection. Although awamori is made from long-grain rice, it's not a product of brewing like sake, but actually of distillation like shochu (Japanese potato-based liquor).

I highly recommend dining in this gorgeous restaurant. An English menu and English-speaking staff are on hand.

20 HYATT REGENCY SERAGAKI ISLAND

ハイアット リージェンシー 瀬良垣アイランド

w   hyatt.com/en-US/hotel/japan/hyatt-
regency-seragaki-island-okinawa/okaro
A   1108 Serakaki, Onnason, 904-0404
T   098-960-4321

STAY/RESORT | When I travel, I usually stay as close as I can to the bustle of a city and spend all of my time exploring it, but there is a time and place for resort-style holidays, and this is 100 per cent one of those. I can't recommend the Hyatt Regency Seragaki Island highly enough. Although about a one-hour drive from Naha, Okinawa's capital city, this northern part of Okinawa has so many beautiful beaches, and the resort is just so divine that it's hard to leave. It's set on its own tiny island, accessible by a small bridge that you can drive over.

You could easily spend days just relaxing by the many pools, spas, private beaches, bars and restaurants. Float up to the infinity pool, relax on one of the beach canopy beds, order a tropical Mai Tai from the pool bar or have a pedicure poolside. A charming tuktuk is only a phone call away to drive you around the resort. It's the perfect way to relax in a little bit of luxury after days exploring Okinawa.

The rates are surprisingly reasonable, and the rooms either overlook the beach or the pools and ocean. As it's on an island, it's completely pitch-black at night, so if you would like to have a beautiful evening view once the sun sets, I suggest requesting a pool-side room so you can overlook the twinkling lights over the many tiered pools.

The buffet breakfast has all of your favourite dishes from Western and Japanese cuisines, but there's a wide range of Okinawan cuisine for adventurous types. Think goya, pickled carrot and beetroot. I could easily stay a week here and never leave the resort once.

THE ESSENTIALS

LANGUAGE

The Japanese are such polite-natured people that although there may be quite a large language barrier with English speakers, they will do their utmost to try to understand and communicate with you – even if this means they bring out a translation app or device.

Over the last ten years, since I moved to Japan, there has been an enormous amount of English added to the country, and, to my surprise, when I travel with foreign friends, I've noticed that more places than I had expected speak English or have English menus that seem to be nowhere in sight when I visit by myself.

Having said that, don't expect every cafe to have an English menu – in fact, if you find yourself in a venue without an English menu you've picked a goodie! Not only is it likely to be authentic, it's also a great chance to communicate with the owners.

If you travel to touristy destinations, such as the ski fields in Hokkaido or temples in Kyoto, I am sure you can get by with English easily. But expect a little to be lost in translation when you're travelling around the smaller cities.

Here is a list of helpful words and phrases, and, as with most countries, a little effort with the local language goes a long way.

Hello	Konnichiwa
Thank you	Arigatou
Excuse me (also sorry)	Sumimasen
Sorry	Gomen nasai
What is this?	Kore wa nan desu ka?
How much is this?	Kore wa ikura desu ka?
Where is...?	... wa doko desu ka?
Where is the station?	Eki wa doko desu ka?
This is delicious!	Oishii!
That was delicious! (Thank you for the meal)	Gochisousamadeshita
Please	Onegaishimasu (or) Kudasai
One coffee please	Kohi o hitotsu onegaishimasu
Two miso ramens please	Miso ramen futatsu onegaishimasu
Cute!	Kawaii!
Great!	Sugoii!
I'm excited/ looking forward to it!	Tanoshimi!
English	Eigo
Japanese language	Nihongo
I don't understand	Wakarimasen
One moment please	Chotto matte kudasai
Bill please	Okaikei onegaishimasu
Cheers!	Kanpai!
Tap Beer	Nama bi-ru

GETTING TO & FROM AIRPORTS

Most international travellers fly in and out of Tokyo Narita (narita-airport.jp/en) or Tokyo Haneda (haneda-airport.jp/inter/en) airports. It's easy to arrange public transport as soon as you land in Japan, but if you prefer a fancy car, such as Blacklane, you can arrange for one online before your trip.

Haneda is a modern airport with excellent transport links (haneda-tokyo-access.com/en/transport) into Tokyo. The Keikyu line gets you into Tokyo in between 11 and 30 minutes and costs ¥410 to ¥610. There is also the Keikyu limousine bus that takes 30 to 60 minutes and costs ¥580 to ¥1,030, and the Tokyo monorail (tokyo-monorail.co.jp/english/haneda) that takes 25 to 40 minutes, and the price starts at ¥490.

Many of the low-cost carriers fly in and out of Tokyo Narita, which can cost an additional ¥4,000 via the JR Narita Express train into Tokyo (cheaper on buses or various trains), so be sure to factor this into your costing if you're on a budget. The JR Narita Express takes 60 to 90 minutes to Tokyo station. You can also get the limousine bus (limousinebus.co.jp/en/bus_services/narita/index), which takes 85 to 115 minutes and costs ¥3,100. Or you can catch the Keisei Skyliner into Tokyo, which takes 35 to 65 minutes and costs ¥2,200 to ¥2,470.

OTHER AIRPORTS

While many of the venues in this book are accessible via shinkansen (bullet train) from Tokyo, some cities do have their own airports should you decide to fly direct. Kyoto doesn't have it's own commercial airport but is accessible via Osaka airport.
Osaka: osaka-airport.co.jp
Fukuoka: fukuoka-airport.jp
Akita: akita-airport.com
Sapporo: new-chitose-airport.jp
Okinawa: naha-airport.co.jp
   All other venues in this book are best accessible via shinkansen.

GETTING AROUND ON PUBLIC TRANSPORT

PASMO & SUICA CARDS

I can highly recommend getting a prepaid IC travel card, if you plan on using public transport in many cities across Japan. There are many to choose from, but Pasmo and Suica are two of the most widely used. You buy them and top them up at ticket booths or ticket vending machines at train stations. Both Pasmo and Suica cards require a ¥500 deposit. You can add ¥1,000 or even ¥10,000, depending on how much you intend to use your card.

   You simply swipe your IC card through ticket gates on both Japan Railway (JR) and metro trains, and on most buses. Pro-tip: you can have these cards personalised at the train station ticket vending machines so your card has your name written on it – it's a lovely keepsake. Or, you can return your card at the airport when you are leaving Japan and redeem your ¥500 deposit and any unused money.

   The cards can be used not only on transport but can also be used to pay in various stores, such as convenience stores and some vending machines, as well as at various restaurants and cafes.

TRAINS

Trains are, in my opinion, the best option for travel around Japan. They are easy enough to navigate these days, with the recent addition of English to most train stations and trains. You can use Google Maps to type in your destination and work out where you need to transfer and also, helpfully, which train and which platform to take.

   If you intend to travel around Japan, such as between Tokyo, Kyoto and Osaka, it might be cost-efficient for you to purchase a

Japan Railway (JR) Pass, which can only be purchased in your country of origin before entering Japan. You can validate this either at the airport on arrival or when you intend to use your first shinkansen (bullet train). Be sure to only validate this before your first shinkansen trip to maximise your bullet train usage. If you're mainly in Tokyo but want to take a trip to Okinawa or Sapporo, for example, you might find it more economical and efficient time-wise to use a Pasmo or Suica (*see* p. 310) for train travel in Tokyo and then pay for a flight.

If you travel with the JR Pass, this only works on Japan Rail (JR) trains. So any trips taken on privately owned train lines will need to be paid for additionally.

Once you step foot in a train you will notice just how quiet public transport is in Japan. If you need to talk, you should definitely whisper. And answering phones or playing loud music on headphones are both giant no-nos. If it's essential to take a call, simply answer your phone in a whisper and say that you're on a train and you'll call back as soon as possible. Turn your phone onto silent as soon as you step foot onto public transport. Shinkansen (bullet trains) offer designated phone use areas.

BUSES

Buses are a little challenging as many have minimal (or no) English, but once you manage to work out which one to get they can be rather handy servicing some tricky-to-get-to locations.

Buses around metropolitan areas in Tokyo are usually ¥200 regardless of whether you go one stop or the full journey. You enter through the front door and pay ¥200 either in correct change or by touching on your Pasmo or Suica card. To exit at your stop, press the stop button located in various locations around the bus and exit through the back door. A simple nod or bow will suffice to thank your driver politely.

One of my favourite bus services is Tokyo's Shibuya Community Hachiko ¥100 dog bus that travels between Shibuya, Daikanyama and Harajuku. It's incredibly cheap and it's the cutest little dog-shaped bus! Jump on if you see it and simply put ¥100 into the slot upon entry.

TAXIS & RIDE-SHARING

Although Uber Black has recently come to Japan, it's mostly taxis that are used. Taxis can be hailed by putting your arm out. Once the taxi stops, you should sit in the back seat, but wait for the driver to open the back door for you. The driver will also open the door for you automatically at your destination, so there is no need to open the door yourself. You should not tip the driver, as there is no tipping in Japan (*see* p. 315).

During the day, most taxis (depending on the city) will charge ¥430 upon entry. In the evenings, there is a slight increase and there's an additional night surcharge. If you book your taxi, you will also be charged a small fee depending on the company and time. Taxi drivers will also politely and patiently wait for you to find the correct change, so you don't have to rush. They are generally happy if you give them small change.

I generally ask taxi drivers in more rural areas if it's okay to pay with a credit card as soon as I start the fare, but having some cash on you in Japan never hurts as it's a widely cash-only country (*see* p. 312). This, however, is slowly changing, but better to be safe than sorry.

If you have the address of your hotel or destination on a card, or the address in Japanese on Google Maps, it is useful to show the driver this. For ease, screenshot the Japanese address and show the driver the enlarged photo. You can also print out addresses in Japanese to show the driver; you can say 'koko made onegaishimasu' or 'koko made kudasai', which translates to 'please take me to this address'.

Some drivers (for example in Kyoto) like to use their GPS to find the location via the phone number, so if you feel like being super safe and prepared you can also give the driver the phone number.

Taxis in each city in Japan or perhaps on each island have variations in their taxi design. I've seen peach-shaped lights in Fukuoka and love-heart shapes in Kyoto. It's the luck of the draw.

Taxis in Okinawa often feature tropical designs, and they are also known to be cheaper than on mainland Japan.

BIKE RIDING

Fancy getting around like a local? Then renting a bike is the transport for you! Pop on your little mamachari (mama-style bike complete with shopping basket and chain guard) and ride around like the rest of the cool locals! It's such a brilliant way to see a city, wandering in and out of backstreets where the best things are found.

You can ride on both the footpath and the road, and helmets are not required by law. It's a very calm experience, with traffic, pedestrians and cyclists all being equally kind and patient to each other. If you are walking on a footpath you may hear the sound of a bike bell, and this means that a bike wishes to pass and that you should stand to the left of the footpath to allow it. Having said that, many cyclists will try their hardest not to inconvenience anyone, so you will often hear a cyclist back-peddling to let pedestrians know they're there, instead of using their bell. It's incredibly kind.

In Tokyo, you can rent a bike from Tokyo Bike (tokyobike.com) for ¥1,000 per day. You won't regret it! I can't recommend bike riding in Tokyo enough. It's my favourite hobby!

PRACTICALITIES

OPENING HOURS

Japan generally opens later and stays open later than in Western countries. It's perfect for those who like to have a few drinks and go to karaoke at night, then sleep in a little!

Most shops open at either 10am or 11am and close anywhere from 7pm to 9pm. There is no one opening hour–style that fits all in Japan, so be sure to check venues in advance.

CASH

Japan is still quite a cash country. Many restaurants and bars won't accept credit cards so it's best to have some yen on you at all times.

Not all cash machines/ATMs in Japan accept foreign cards, so I find the best place to withdraw cash is from ATMs at selected convenience store (try the larger ones like 7-Eleven, Lawson and Family Mart) or a Japan Post Office.

Another good tip is to top up your Pasmo or Suica (transport cards, *see* p. 310), as these can be used in a number of supermarkets, convenience stores and vending machines.

When paying with cash, you can take your time to get the correct change. People are more than happy to wait for you to get everything right to that last one yen coin. One thing to do if you can, is to try and place the notes all in the same side and direction, and then the coins grouped as neatly as you can.

Some lunch venues, such as cafes, but not izakaya (small bars, *see* p. 314), will kindly split the bill for you, ask 'okaike betsubetsu onegaishimasu', and they will ask you what you consumed and then you pay for your own portion. Please note that not all places offer this service, so don't be offended if they don't.

Japan has a 'coin tray' etiquette, where you should place money on the tray at the cash register and your change is likely to be returned the same way.

ADDRESSES

Japanese addresses can be a little tricky to read, especially if you're used to using street names. Street names are reserved for larger main roads here in Japan, but other addresses usually follow a grid format.

The easiest approach for addresses in Japan is to input the venue name into Google Maps or a map app. It is even useful for using public transport, as the maps will show stations and sometimes even the best exit to get you to your venue.

When addresses are written in Japanese they follow this format:

- Postcode
- Prefecture name (for example, Tokyo)
- City or Ward, known as 'ku' (for example, Setagaya-ku)
- Suburb (for example, Kitazawa)
- Suburb numbers or 'chome', divided by hyphens (for example 1-2-3). This would be suburb/area 1, block 2 and building 3.
- Building name, floor number and room number.

In English, the addresses are often written in reverse. The addresses in this book follow this format:

- Building name, floor number and room number (where relevant).
- Suburb and suburb numbers or 'chome', divided by hyphens (for example 1-2-3). This would be suburb/area 1, block 2 and building 3.
- City or Ward, known as 'ku' (for example, Setagaya-ku)
- Prefecture name (for example, Tokyo)
- Postcode

SAFETY

Japan is an incredibly safe country! Generally speaking, you could leave your laptop or phone on a cafe table and pop away from your table and it would still be exactly where you left it. Umbrellas and bicycles, however, are the exception to this rule so be sure to keep an eye on those.

I've seen YouTube videos of people dropping their wallets and 50 out of 50 times a nearby local ran after the person to return the wallet. I've also been on a train where a person, who might have had too much fun drinking sake at an izakaya (small bar), fell asleep with their belongings falling from their bag out onto the floor. Moments later, a lady picked up all of the person's belongings and neatly packed them into the person's bag. It's so heartwarming.

On a personal note, I took a family from Australia to a gaming parlour and, while the kids were playing the catcher games, the mother accidentally left all of her family's passports next to the game. We had walked about five minutes away from the parlour when she realised, and naturally they were exactly where she left them when we returned.

If you do happen to lose anything while you're in a city, head to the local police box as this is where lost and found items go. Alternatively, if you're on a train, head to the ticket counter and let the station master know, and they will often call the other stations and arrange for your items to be returned to you.

Trains can often be crowded during peak times, so expect to be squashed up against others. If you prefer, many trains have a women's only carriage which operates during peak hours and is marked by a pink graphic on both the platform and carriage.

I've never felt unsafe walking around Japan by myself at all hours. Through dark alleyways and busy streets, I always leave my handbag open, too. Having said that, I would hate you to be the exception so zip your handbag if you're worried.

If you do happen to run into any trouble while you're in Japan, you can call 110 to report an accident or crime to the police. Or call 119 to call an ambulance or report a fire. Touch wood.

LGBTQIA+ TRAVELLERS

LGBTQIA+ travellers should not experience any problems, but because Japan is a very traditional and conservative country, all travellers should refrain from any personal displays of affection in public, even holding hands, as this is frowned upon. Foreign travellers are more likely to be looked at out of curiosity for simply not being Japanese.

Booking a double room or ryokan (traditional Japanese inn) shouldn't be a problem. And I'm always jealous when my gay friends are able to enjoy onsen (hot springs) together as they are usually segregated!

Tokyo and Osaka have energetic gay bar and nightclub scenes. Tokyo has over 300 gay bars, mostly in Shinjuku's ni-chome area. Some of my best nights in Tokyo have been when my best friend David takes me to these bars.

Although marriage equality is not recognised in Japan, some temples in Kyoto are now offering wedding ceremonies. Both Tokyo and Osaka host rainbow pride festivals, which are thankfully gaining momentum. Disappointingly I don't see a lot of all gender bathrooms around Japan, but I am sure this too will gain momentum in time.

ELECTRONICS

It's best to leave your hair dryer and hair straightener at home and use the facilities at your hotel or Airbnb, as the voltage is low in Japan (100v) or you'll find yourself standing in front of the mirror blowing a tiny breeze of cold air at your hair. I learnt this the hard way on my first trip to Japan when I was 18. The Japanese plug and socket are Type A, so make sure to check your laptop or tablet before you leave home to work out the adaptor that you'll need.

WI-FI

Although Japan increased its wi-fi hotspots due to the Olympics (postponed from 2020), wi-fi is notoriously hard to find in this country, so I suggest checking if your Airbnb or hotel has a pocket wi-fi or smartphone that you can use for free during your days wandering the city. Alternatively, you can ask your phone provider in your home country for an international data plan before you leave. Or if your phone is unlocked, you can buy a SIM card or rent a pocket wi-fi upon arrival at the airport in Japan.

DINING OUT

CHOPSTICKS

You should never pass food to another person from one pair of chopsticks to another (it's a funeral ritual where the bones of the deceased are passed using large chopsticks among family members). Be careful also to not wave your chopsticks around when you're talking, or use them to point at another person. Also, don't leave them sticking vertically inside noodles or rice, instead rest them on the chopstick rests or along the plate or bowl.

When using chopsticks to divide any type of food, such as okonomiyaki (Japanese savoury pancake) or croquettes, you should keep both chopsticks in one hand and gently pull the chopsticks apart rather than putting a chopstick in each hand and trying to emulate the knife and fork technique. If this is too tricky, you can always ask for a knife and fork. Be sure not to bring your hand to your mouth like a plate, but, instead, if the dish is small (approximately 15cm/6 inches in diameter) you can pick it up. You should also not stack any empty dishes unless you're at a conveyor belt sushi restaurant.

IZAKAYA

An izakaya is a Japanese informal bar and restaurant. They are sometimes called 'Japanese pubs', but there are so many differences, such as you will often be charged a 'table charge' which includes a small dish per person, and it's common to eat at izakaya, unlike pubs where it's completely acceptable to only order a drink.

Once you're seated you're often passed an oshibori (wet hand towel) to wipe your hands, but definitely not to be used on your face. We aren't on an airplane, people! After you use your oshibori, it's typical to roll it up neatly and leave it on the table for occasional use during your meal. Oshibori are often changed in temperature according to the season, with izakaya offering hot oshibori in winter, and refreshingly cold ones in summer.

KISSATEN

Kissaten (often shortened to kissa) are retro-style coffee houses, inspired by European cafes that peaked in Japan during the '70s. Kissaten serve drip coffee and food, such as simple Japanese sandwiches (often a 'mixed sandwich' like ham and lettuce or egg and mayonnaise), and soda float drinks, which are usually blue or green with a scoop of ice-cream and a maraschino cherry on top. Aside from these basics, you can also find some menu variety, depending on the kissaten, including curries, katsu (cutlet served with rice and shredded cabbage), omuraisu (omelette rice), spaghetti and a range of cakes. Kissaten are usually very cheap and cheerful and you can easily find a lunch or breakfast set with a main dish and a drink for under ¥1,000.

ETIQUETTE

TIPPING

There is absolutely no tipping in Japan. On one of my first trips to Japan in 1998, a shop assistant chased me out of a shop in Harajuku to give me a few yen change. Let me be the only one who gets embarrassed by this mistake, so be sure to take your change.

SHOES

Many izakaya (see p. 314) will require you to remove your shoes before entering. You should do so in the genkan (entrance area) and then step into the shoe-free space. Many izakaya have a shoe locker system where you can leave your shoes, and you will be given a locker key to retrieve them on your way out. Be sure to pop your shoes on in the same area where you took them off (not just outside the lockers).

Shoes should be taken off when entering the home of anyone you might visit on your trip. It's impolite to be barefoot inside restaurants and homes, so if you don't have

socks on it's common to carry a spare pair inside your bag that can be easily slipped on in the genkan before entering.

Another tip is not to step on the edges of tatami mats, but rather step on the main parts of tatami.

VISITING HOMES

If you are invited to a Japanese home, you should take a small gift, either from your home country or something small like tea, boxes of rice crackers or cookies, or fruit. If you are unsure of what to buy, visit the basement level of a department store, where they have entire floors dedicated to these type of box presents. Upon entering a home, be sure to take your shoes off and say 'ojyamashimasu', which translates roughly as 'Excuse me for intruding in your home'. It's common to then ask to wash your hands and, if you can, gargle a handful of water to avoid bringing any outside germs inside the house.

ACCOMMODATION

Japan has a wide range of accommodation options, many of them offering a traditional experience.

HOTELS & HOSTELS

The range is from budget to boutique. Most hotels have beds rather than futons, and some business hotels also have a sento (public bath), in addition to a shower bath in your room, for guests to use.

CAPSULE HOTELS

A tiny sleeping-only cabin just large enough for you to lay down in, with the shower and bathrooms shared in a communal area.

LOVE HOTELS

Say no more. Some are so retro – think a Björk-style swan boat bed, or a rotating mirror bed, which can be rented by the hour.

RESORTS

As you would expect, the most Western option of all. Luxurious and at times comforting if you don't fancy branching out into Japanese culture 24/7.

MINSHUKU

A small, often family-run bed and breakfast usually found in smaller towns. Perfect if you want to really engage in Japanese culture.

RYOKAN

A traditional Japanese inn that usually feature beautiful tatami floors, futons and sento (public baths). It's common for ryokan to offer yukata (traditional Japanese robe) that you can wear to breakfast and dinner. Some ryokans offer dinner in your room – a feast of sashimi, pickles, salad, fish, meat, rice, miso and nabe (hot pot).

SEASONS

SPRING

If you like your days to be a little chilly, but pleasantly chilly, and the possibility of seeing sakura (cherry blossoms), then this is the season for you. Enjoy some hanami (cherry blossom viewing) parties on picnic rugs in Japan's numerous beautiful parks. Spring is one of my favourite seasons.

SUMMER

If Hiyashi chuka (cold noodle salad) is your kind of thing, you'll love Japan's summertime. For me, summer is torture and the humidity just unbearable. A 9am ten-minute walk in Tokyo will leave you wiping your face with a wet towel. However, if you don't mind the heat, you can stay cool with cold green tea from vending machines and kakigori (shaved-ice dessert). Shopping centre air conditioning should also keep you cool. The good news is that Japanese beer is rather refreshing, and they also make a frozen beer, so be sure to try it!

AUTUMN

Autumn is amazingly picturesque in Japan. It's incredibly beautiful to watch the leaves turn red and orange, and crunching them under your feet is so much fun. Then there is mulled wine to drink and winter outfits to plan. The start of autumn can also bring the rainy season, but don't worry, as many department stores have a self-dispensing umbrella jacket machine at the entrance, so you don't have to worry about any unwanted drips.

WINTER

If you like wearing super-cute woollen scarves, kairo packs (self-heating stickers that you stick on your clothes to warm you up for the day), coloured tights, woollen mittens and you enjoy getting cosy under a kotatsu (heated coffee table), then you will love winter in Japan. It's the Hello Sandwich favourite season! Warm up by popping into a sento (public bath), enjoy a few glasses of ume-shu (plum wine) and do multiple loops on the Yamanote-sen circle JR train line in Tokyo to keep warm with the heated seats. Not to mention the skiing and snowboarding in Hokkaido!

PUBLIC HOLIDAYS & FESTIVALS

Japan has a long tradition of year-round festivals, so it's well worth checking what's on where before you travel.

With the exception of Japanese New Year and Golden Week, most shops, cafes and galleries are open on public holidays.

Japanese New Year	1 Jan
Coming of Age Day	2nd Mon of Jan
National Foundation Day	11 Feb
Emperor's Birthday	23 Feb
Vernal Equinox Day	20 or 21 Mar
Shōwa Day	29 Apr
Golden Week	29 Apr to 5 May
Constitution Memorial Day	3 May
Greenery Day	4 May
Children's Day	5 May
Marine Day	3rd Mon of July
Health and Sports Day	2nd Mon of Oct
Mountain Day	11 Aug
Respect for the Aged Day	3rd Mon of Sept
Autumnal Equinox Day	Sept
Culture Day	3 Nov
Labor Thanksgiving Day	23 Nov

EARTHQUAKES, TSUNAMI AND NATURAL DISASTERS

Japan is prone to earthquakes and various natural disasters so it doesn't hurt to have a meeting place planned with your travel companions just in case. An open area such as a park is a good idea as there is less risk of things falling on you. If you are indoors during an earthquake it's recommended that you hide under a desk, or away from falling objects. Doors can jam closed in earthquakes so it's suggested that these be opened in case of a large earthquake. It doesn't hurt to keep slippers near your bed or near you when you're inside, as shoes are not allowed inside. This allows you to escape any broken glass or items should you need to evacuate.

You can follow earthquake and tsunami warnings on NHK Television on channel 1. Most new TVs will have a button for English dubbing. Local loudspeakers will also announce if an evacuation is required. You can also check the details of earthquakes on the Japan Meteorological Agency website: jma.go.jp

If you're travelling during typhoon season many convenience stores sell out of essentials as people hunker down until the storm passes, so pick up a few items in case you might not be able to travel to the shops during the typhoon. Be sure to stay away from windows as these can often break during strong typhoons. Many people often tape their windows in crosses, or board them up with cardboard in typhoon season. If you're in a seaside area or island during a typhoon please take extra precautions. Each area has a designated earthquake evacuation area which is often found inside an elementary school.

INDEX

Published in 2021 by Hardie Grant Travel, a division of
Hardie Grant Publishing

Hardie Grant Travel (Melbourne)
Building 1, 658 Church Street
Richmond, Victoria 3121

Hardie Grant Travel (Sydney)
Level 7, 45 Jones Street
Ultimo, NSW 2007

www.hardiegrant.com/au/travel

The maps in this publication incorporate data from
© OpenStreetMap contributors
OpenStreetMap is made available under the Open Data
Commons Open Database License (ODbL) by the
OpenStreetMap Foundation (OSMF):
http://opendatacommons.org/licenses/odbl/1.0/. Any rights
in individual contents of the database are licensed under the
Database Contents License: http://opendatacommons.org/
licenses/dbcl/1.0/
Data extracts via Geofabrik GmbH https://www.geofabrik.de
© National Land Information Division, National Spatial
Planning and Regional Policy Bureau, MILT of Japan

A catalogue record for this
book is available from the
National Library of Australia

NATIONAL
LIBRARY
OF AUSTRALIA

Hardie Grant acknowledges the Traditional Owners of the country
on which we work, the Wurundjeri people of the Kulin nation
and the Gadigal people of the Eora nation, and recognises their
continuing connection to the land, waters and culture. We pay
our respects to their Elders past, present and emerging.

Hello Sandwich Japan
ISBN 9781741176841

10 9 8 7 6 5 4 3 2 1

Publisher: Melissa Kayser   Art direction: Ebony Bizys
Project editor: Megan Cuthbert   Design: Evi O Studio
Editor: Alice Barker   Typesetting: Megan Ellis
Proofreader: Helena Holmgren   Index: Helena Holmgren
Cartographer: Emily Maffei

Colour reproduction by Megan Ellis and
Splitting Image Colour Studio

Printed and bound in China by LEO Paper Products LTD.

Publisher's Disclaimers: The publisher cannot accept
responsibility for any errors or omissions. The representation on
the maps of any road or track is not necessarily evidence of public
right of way. The publisher cannot be held responsible for any
injury, loss or damage incurred during travel. It is vital to research
any proposed trip thoroughly and seek the advice of relevant state
and travel organisations before you leave.

Publisher's Note: Every effort has been made to ensure that
the information in this book is accurate at the time of going to
press. The publisher welcomes information and suggestions for
correction or improvement.

Photo credits

All images © Ebony Bizys with the exception of the following:

p. 10 directphoto.bz / Alamy Stock Photo; p.15 images courtesy
of Bathhaus; p. 17 (top) KungChuyada / Shutterstock.com;
p. 17 (bottom) ranmaru / Shutterstock.com; p. 21 (top) (middle)
Morumotto / Shutterstock.com; p. 23 (bottom), p. 27-29 images
courtesy of Moreru Mignon; p. 24 (bottom) VTT Studio /
Shutterstock.com; p. 34 (left) image courtesy of City Country
City; p. 49 (bottom) image courtesy of My Home in Tokyo;
p. 50 Alamy Stock Photo; p. 53 (left) Sayaka Minemura; p. 55,
p. 69 (bottom), p. 77, p. 163, p. 165, p. 177 (top), p. 178 iStock
Photo; p. 60 (bottom) image courtesy of Hatoya Hotel; p. 64,
p. 72 (left) (top), p. 97 (bottom), p. 101 (middle) Natalie Schön;
p. 83 john mobbs / Shutterstock.com; p. 84 (bottom) Tuul
and Bruno Morandi / Alamy Stock Photo; p. 92 Stéphanie
Crohin; p. 113 (top) Shinya Yanagihara; p. 127 image courtesy
of Hi! Sandwich; p. 142 (top) (bottom) images courtesy of On
Reading; p. 148 (top) Ai Hasunuma; p. 153 images courtesy of
Pecori; p. 157 Elana Pistorio; p. 160 Shutterstock; p. 166 (top)
Korbut Ivetta / Shutterstock.com; p. 166 (bottom) Sean Pavone /
Shutterstock.com; p. 177 (middle) (bottom) Jigokudani Monkey
Park; p. 178 (bottom) image courtesy of Ch. Books; p. 191 image
courtesy of Shiogama Sugimura Jun Museum of Art; p. 210
Carlos Huang / Shutterstock.com; p. 213 (middle), p. 217 (top)
Unsplash; p. 213 (bottom), p. 214 hedgehog111 / Shutterstock.
com; p. 217 (bottom) ChunChang Wu / Shutterstock.com;
p. 264, p. 290 (top), p. 306, p. 307 BOCO.

The Author would like to thank Toni Fan and the team at Japan
National Tourism Organization for their support.